The name of this book is Dogme95

The name of this book is Dogme95

RICHARD KELLY

faber and faber

First published in 2000
by Faber and Faber Limited
3 Queen Square London WC1N 3AU
Published in the United States by Faber and Faber Inc.
an affiliate of Farrar, Straus and Giroux LLC, New York

Typeset by Faber and Faber Ltd
Printed in England by Clays Ltd, St Ives plc

A CIP record for this book
is available from the British Library

ISBN 0–571–20332–9

10 9 8 7 6 5 4 3 2 1

'Among certain people, I'm sometimes considered the father of European cinema. I don't understand that, since I consider myself much younger, especially with Americans . . . even if it's a young boy in America making his first film, I consider him to be a father or a mother, and I try to revolt against him. I'm older than he is, but my cinema is younger just because there are no rules, and he has a lot of rules. For the first time in twenty years, I have a feeling that rules have to be discovered; one should neither obey nor revolt automatically. It's better to discover what can be yours in the system, and accept or change it. But work it, and discover the unknown . . .'

Jean-Luc Godard, quoted in 'Godard: Born-Again Filmmaker'
by Jonathan Cott in Rolling Stone, *27 November 1980*

Contents

Foreword, and Most Valuable Players (MVPs)

This Book is (in part) a diary of a freelance writer's working days. Consequently, it is one of those books that is concerned (in part) with the manner of its own composition. Sorry about that. It was overseen by Walter Donohue. Kevin Macdonald advised that it should be cast in a form other than the norm for film books. Matthew Evans repeatedly goaded the author to stop loitering and get on a plane to Copenhagen.

This Book is also an account of the production of a documentary entitled *The Name of this Film is Dogme95*. That Film was made under the aegis of Caroline Kaplan and Jonathan Sehring of the Independent Film Channel (US), and Nick Jones of FilmFour (UK). It was produced by a team including Adam English, Braden King, Colin MacCabe, Eliza Mellor, Helle Absalonsen, Jack Lothian, Justine Wright, Nicolai Iuul, Paula Jalfon, and Saul Metzstein. The images in *This Book* are captured from digital video material shot by Saul Metzstein and Braden King.

This Book also has a stab at being a bit of instant film history: a dossier, if you will, of a radical movement in European cinema that ran an effective series of sorties against the operation of the US-directed mainstream. Thanks to all those individuals, variously associated with the production and dissemination of Dogme95 films, who consented to be interviewed herein on this topic, and on related topics.

This Book was irremediably influenced by daily conversations with certain friends who are accustomed to setting the author right. Readers will figure out quickly enough who they are. In addition, the author must doff his cap to Damien O'Donnell and to Stuart McCune, each of whom proposed scabrous alternatives for how *This Book* (and That Film) might be composed. In both cases, the author lacked sufficient cojones. As for written sources, respect is due to *Screen International*, *Moving Pictures*, *Variety*, www.dogme.dk, G. K. Hunter's Penguin edition of *King Lear*, the collection *Jean-Luc Godard: Interviews*, edited by David Sterritt for the University Press of Mississippi, and the French edition of Lars von Trier's *The Idiots*, published by Alpha Bleue.

1 The Author's Confession

The late comedian Bill Hicks had an impish routine about the hellish cul-de-sac into which Hollywood movies had been driven by 'special effects'. He cited the example of the big-budget action picture, with its remorseless need to better itself, attain bigger thrills and bigger grosses, however ludicrous the price tag. But how, Hicks wondered aloud, do you best the return on $100 million invested in computer-generated mayhem for a picture like *Terminator 2*? Surely the technology must hit a ceiling? What then? Hicks's modest proposal was that the studios henceforth employ terminally ill people as stunt persons: to be killed for real, on camera, by Chuck Norris or some such brute. While his audience groaned, Hicks would adopt an earnest, wounded mien: 'All I'm saying is that people are dying every day, and movies are getting more and more boring . . .'

Now, you can't say that's not in poor taste; yet I found that I liked what the man said. The point, surely, was not to advocate the taboo-busting delights of the 'snuff' genre, or to suggest that Hollywood executives take a leaf from extant accounts of the Circus Maximus. The point, surely, was that the more expensive the movie, the more wilful its estrangement from real life as lived; and worse, the more dogged its devotion to an ignorance of what actually befalls us as we die. So might not real agony and authentic death throes be preferable to stylized carnage, glamorized thuggery, fountains of CGI blood, and the generally ersatz awfulness of most Hollywood 'product'?

That said, on first hearing the Hicks routine, I was somewhat stung; because somehow I was making a living by watching movies, and writing (or, on occasions, talking) about them. And increasingly this felt like a disreputable occupation, a bad habit left over from my teens, when movies, like much else besides, appeared to promise everything: the transformation of the world, even. Of course, this kind of disillusion is cheaply bought, and was so even before Holden Caulfield's famous complaint, 'The goddamn movies, they can ruin you.' But in my mid-twenties, this dejection began to bite, and I began to favour long evenings in a pub over more drear visits to the movies. Between 1992 and 1997, I managed to miss everything from *Reservoir Dogs* and *Pulp Fiction* to *Shallow Grave* and *Trainspotting*. If I happened to find myself in aforementioned pub among keen film-goers, my small talk was fitful, since, Eeyore-like, I very often had not a clue what my peers were talking about.

Such movies as I did stagger out to see were usually upsetting, none more so than *Michael Collins*, Neil Jordan's biography of the great Republican warlord, and a virtual compendium of the house rules that underpin storytelling and style in commercial Hollywood cinema. *Michael Collins* bore the Golden Lion from the 1996 Venice Film Festival, but it also carried the stamp of Warner Bros. Jordan, a brilliant and original writer-director, had somehow come up with a picture that could have been made in the 1930s with James Cagney as the ebullient 'Big Fella' Collins, and Clifton Webb as sly old Eamon de Valera. Certainly the film was rotten with references to American gangster movies, and weighted with a fat slice of stagy villainy from Alan Rickman. The great DP Chris Menges had over-lit every fancy interior as if in some ruinous imitation of Bertolucci. Elliot Goldenthal's thunderous music score raped the ears. A needless romance was stapled in between key scenes, doubtless to facilitate the casting of Julia Roberts. And clearly the movie had been 'tested' and remodelled to death, as Warners took fright over renewed activities by the Provisional IRA while Jordan was still shooting. Thus, the film was capped with a futile attempt to confer blessing on the peacemakers amid the contemporary impasse in the Six Counties.

Skulking out of the cinema, I allowed myself a few gloomy thoughts around the notion that movies hadn't come very far in a hundred years. Roughly a century after the invention of cinema, the USA had succeeded in colonizing the global market in film. Fat, foolish, ruinously expensive and ideologically hateful, Hollywood movies were the world's dominant cultural product. Even across continental Europe, where cinema had long been cradled as an imaginative art-form with its own heritage of great works, audiences seemed increasingly to disdain movies made in their own language, choosing instead to hang wordlessly on the tentative courtship of Tom Hanks and Meg Ryan.

To a viewer like myself (born in 1970 but hopelessly impressed by the radical culture of the late 1960s, which naturally imparted some of its galvanism to movies), everything pointed to a loss of aesthetic nerve, a lack of political verve, and a pervasive absence of mischief. Cinema had come off the barricades and gone to work for The Man. Where were the likes of a Glauber Rocha, to propose a pan-American resistance to Hollywood? Or a Bertolucci, to revive the tradition of the dialectical epic? There was at least some consolation in the knowledge that Jean-Luc Godard, undisputed heavyweight champion of the *nouvelle vague*, remained undefeated, if perhaps a little depressed. Having reinvented cinema in the 1960s and 1970s, Godard was now crafting dense and brilliant 'film essays' like *JLG/JLG* and *Histoires du Cinéma*, on video. He was still committed to the notion of a motion picture as an exploratory tool, a way of looking and studying and imparting, one that required formal experimentation and narrative complexity. He was still opposed to the offensive simplicity of Hollywood fairy tales. And his ruminations on cinema still had the virtues of being supremely intelligent, deeply provocative, and often (to the chagrin of his detractors) quite funny.

Nevertheless, fan that I am, I had detected something unsettlingly valedictory in an interview Godard gave in 1996 to Gavin Smith of *Film Comment*. He spoke of cinema as a 'fallen medium', and rehearsed the theory of the USA's imperial conquest of European film: one that got afoot after the Great War, when Hollywood flooded France and cherry-picked German talent. 'The Normandy beaches were the second invasion,' Godard contended. 'World War Two was a way to take Europe definitively. And now, as you see in politics the way Europe is incapable of doing anything without the OK of the US Government, now in the movies America has taken control of the whole planet.' Politically, economically, culturally, any way you cared to cut it – this was a bleak diagnosis. Smith asked Godard if he didn't feel that Italian neorealism and the *nouvelle vague* had represented significant aesthetic resistance movements? But Godard looked back on these moments as mere *arrière-garde* operations: 'They were the last uprising,' he declared. Now, at some level, this sort of emphatically cheerless talk was exactly what an Eeyore like me wished to hear. *'The last uprising'*? What stirring defeatism! And maybe it was so. But maybe not.

Dogme95's new school rules

In early 1998 I was invited by Lizzie Francke, vivacious directrix of the Edinburgh Film Festival, to present a retrospective of the English director Alan Clarke, and to pick a few new films for the main body of the Festival. My preference for a late levée disqualifies me from holding down certain jobs, but has proved no bar whatsoever to my pursuing the freelance life, and I gladly accepted. So, for the first time in a few years, I found myself going to the movies pretty regularly, in the company of Lizzie and fellow programmer Ali Kayley; and without having to pay at the door either. On the whole, things hadn't changed much while I was away. One of my first free outings was Peter Weir's *The Truman Show*. In a past life, Weir was standard-bearer for a 'New Australian Cinema', one that vanished like breath off a razor in the early 1980s. Now he had signed his name to one of those Hollywood films that fancied itself a bit clever: yet another critique of the industry's old enemy, network television. Whatever the hell the movie thought it was saying, the score made sure to say it first. Music was ladled over every scene like gravy, just in case we tasted something coarse or tart. Just what were we, the audience, being taken for? Idiots?

Then again, there are worse hardships than being paid to sit on one's arse, and I duly accepted Edinburgh's invite to attend the 1998 Cannes Festival on their ticket. Then came an excited call from Lizzie. She and Ali had viewed a VHS of something called *Dogme#1: Festen*, by a young Danish writer-director called Thomas Vinterberg; and they were both in raptures over it. I dropped my bacon sandwich as Lizzie told me it was a drama hinging upon incestuous rape, shot on digital video but transferred to 35-mm film; and that it had already been accepted into the competition at Cannes, where I'd get to see it. I fumbled for the fag packet as Lizzie patiently explained that *Festen* was the first product of a Danish movement, tied to a published manifesto called Dogme95 and originated by Vinterberg and Lars von Trier. With mounting incredulity, and no little shame, I listened further.

It transpired that for three years past, this 'Dogme95' had been a kind of spectre haunting world cinema: a set of rules for the making of motion pictures which, if pursued with passion and commitment, could perhaps enable film-makers to make more truthful, less boring movies; surely the most audacious and conspicuous attempt to reinvent the cinema since, well, Godard. Coming this late to the party, it behoved me to play catch-up fast. Cannes was around the corner, and my itinerary told me that not only *Dogme#1: Festen* but also *Dogme#2: Idioterne*, written and directed by Trier, would unspool in competition. And as I had first feared, it seemed the title of Trier's film did indeed translate as *The Idiots*, leaving one to ponder at whose expense the ironies in this strange case might accrue.

Trier, it seemed, was the prime mover. I'd been abreast of his activities since his first feature, a wildly precious essay on the detective genre called *The Element of Crime* (1984). But I'd tuned out of the work after *Europa* (1991): an incorrigibly stylish thing about intrigue on the German railways after World War Two, it was (to borrow an unimprovable bit of Geordie) 'all about nowt'. *Breaking the Waves* (1996) had won the Grand Prix at Cannes and proved something of a breakthrough art-house hit. It was made in English, and its lead actress, Emily Watson, was nominated for an Oscar. But I hadn't disturbed my movie boycott to go and see it. I knew it was set on the coast of northern Scotland in the 1970s, and concerned a young woman called Bess, who's made to suffer intolerable indignity simply because of her earnest wish to enjoy sexual passion. But it looked to be hard on Calvinists, people for whom I have strong, irrational regard; and I turned my face away.

What I knew for sure was that Trier had shown himself to be quite The Man for manifestos. In 1991 he had brought one with him to Cannes, where *Europa* competed; and, in the course of accounting for his addiction to *hommage* and high style, he had teased the puerile among us by confessing to be 'a masturbator of cinema'. Roman Polanski's jury duly awarded him two of the lesser Palmes in their gift, the Jury Prize and the Prize for Technical Contribution. The legend had it that Trier, rating these distinctions no more highly than a cup of cold piss, hurled them away in pique. The behaviour of an uncommonly self-assured maestro? Well, another tale (and Trier was a lightning-rod for this stuff) posited that the 'von' between his proper names was conferred upon him by an old film school tutor, who even then had detected traces of a Stroheimian monocled martinet in the boy.

By March 1995, it seemed, Trier had decided that being Europe's most acclaimed young director just wasn't enough. He was tired of making expensive art movies with hundreds of people at his beck and call. He wanted to get back to brass tacks: simpler films, with less equipment, and a set of self-imposed restraints. He summoned Thomas Vinterberg, a gifted twenty-something and fellow graduate of the Danish Film School, and together they conceived of a new set of school rules. ('It was easy,' Vinterberg had confessed of that fateful meeting. 'We asked ourselves what we most hated about film today, and then we drew up a list banning it all. It took half an hour and it was a great laugh.') The resultant Dogme95 Manifesto railed against how crass and cosmetic movies had become; it called for a new 'avant-garde'; and it proposed ten restrictive Rules for bringing this about. These were branded 'The Vow of Chastity' (somewhat mischievously, one couldn't help feeling, in a land so staunchly Lutheran as Denmark). Thereafter Trier and Vinterberg had invited two more Danish cineastes – commercials director Kristian Levring and the veteran Søren Kragh-Jacobsen – to take their vows and join the Dogme 'Brotherhood'.

A set of rules, though. Gosh. Here was an earnest tilt at the radical end of film history. Dziga Vertov and his *Kino-glaz* 'council of three' provided the model for such rigours. Lindsay Anderson had committed the ambitions of the Free Cinema movement to paper. The French *nouvelle vague* generated reams of rhetoric, simply because all its directors were firebrand critics. And not least among the ironies of art-making-by-rule-book were the tendencies of such signatories towards a kind of revolutionary fervour. With this in mind, perhaps, Trier had chosen to declare his principles in the capital of the world's first modern republic. Since 1789, Paris has been considered the best place to kick up a revolution, political, social or artistic; not for nothing did Marx hymn the city as 'the nerve-centre of European history, sending out electric shocks at intervals that galvanized the whole world'. It was at the Odeon Theatre, while attending a conference on the centenary of cinema, that Trier proclaimed his Manifesto and distributed printed leaflets.

Of course, and rather admirably, Trier was asking for trouble; and he immediately provoked some sharp criticism. 'Why should artists set rules for themselves? Isn't art-making a fundamentally free and untrammelled process?' But then, even if it can be, not all artists would wish it so. Even the Surrealists, the original wild and crazy guys of Modernism, were deadly serious about exactly when and how they were wild and crazy. In his glorious memoir *My Last Breath*, Buñuel wrote passionately of the movement as 'an aggressive morality based on the complete rejection of all existing values', built around 'loyalty to a specific set of moral precepts'. Buñuel granted that this morality was continually challenged by 'egotism, vanity, greed, exhibitionism, facileness and just plain forgetfulness'. 'Sometimes,' he confessed, 'I've succumbed to temptations and violated my own rules, but only, I think, in matters of small importance.' In other words, what was crucial was the frame imposed by discipline; and behind it, the firm

6

resolve to tax one's conscience. (My favourite maxim of this sort is Bresson's, stated with customary razor clarity in his *Notes on the Cinematographer*: 'To forge for oneself iron laws, if only in order to obey or disobey them *with difficulty*.')

Maybe, then, all artists set rules for themselves? (Hadn't the scriptwriters of Jerry Seinfeld's sitcom vowed, 'No lessons, no hugs'?) But to publish them is another matter; and as far as I could ascertain, the Manifesto had been subject to prolonged scepticism in the press. For one thing, that 'masturbator' remark was maybe still too fresh in the mind. For another, where were the *films*? Might Dogme95 be just another self-publicizing jack-off? Or some kind of twisted Danish practical joke? Trier's riposte was delivered fast enough. In March 1997 *Breaking the Waves* was feted at the Bodil awards ceremony in Denmark, as adjudicated by local critics. Rather than attending, Trier sent a videotaped address in which (under the pretence of forgiveness, as 'Bess herself would have done') he excoriated a succession of venal producers and snide journalists who had hampered his career. His virulent, soft-spoken wit was much in evidence (not least as he forgave 'Ebbe Iversen, whom I regarded as the gentleman of the industry, for writing something so incredibly stupid that it carries the punishment in itself'.) Trier's last target, 'and most important of all', was 'practically the whole industry, for being so bloody negative about a one hundred per cent idealistic and economically harmless project by the name of Dogme'. Leaving aside, if only for the moment, what this stunt might tell us about Trier's tendency to petulance, these were fighting words.

Le cinéma de Papa Godard?

Naturally, I had private reasons to be excited about Dogme95. Clearly it was just about bloody time somebody started some trouble. But what kind of revolution were these Danes proposing? Through the good offices of Edinburgh, I obtained an inky fax copy of the Manifesto and donned my reading glasses. Here in plain sight was a self-professed 'rescue action', with 'the expressed goal of countering "certain tendencies" in the cinema today'. And there was the cat, scrapping its way out of the bag, via the coded reference to François Truffaut's 'Une certaine tendance du cinéma français', penned for *Cahiers du Cinéma* in 1958. Whatever its good intentions, the *nouvelle vague* hereby came in for some stick, as a revolution betrayed, a piece

7

of 'bourgeois romanticism' underwritten by the *auteur* theory and its romantic conception of film as personal expression. Instead, the Manifesto offered a draught of pure egalitarian utopianism. 'Today a technological storm is raging, the result of which will be the ultimate democratization of the cinema. For the first time, anyone can make movies.' But then, a caveat: 'The more accessible the media becomes, the more important the avant-garde . . . We must put our films into uniform, because the individual film will be decadent by definition!'

Here I had to fight down a mental image of Trier as the Cheshire Cat, and pressed onward. As the prose reached a pitch, there seemed to be an almost Brechtian scorn for 'cosmetics' and 'illusions' wrought by 'trickery'. 'The "supreme" task of the decadent film-makers is to fool the audience,' the Manifesto scoffed, before making the incredible assertion, 'TO DOGME95 THE MOVIE IS NOT ILLUSION!' And how might such an implausible stance be defended? By adherence to 'an indisputable set of rules known as the vow of chastity'. So what was the substance of these ten commandments?

1 *Shooting must be done on location. Props and set must not be brought in (if a particular prop is necessary for the story, a location must be chosen where the prop is to be found).*
(Right. No stage sets, and no city-for-city stand-ins. So the crew must strike out for the very site where the action of the script unfolds. And once you get there, you use what you find. So, clearly, the writer's influence upon the scale of the project is intensified; as is the mandate of the location scout.)

2 *The sound must never be produced apart from the images or vice versa (music must not be used unless it occurs where the scene is being shot).*
(Fiendishly tricky, this one. Presumably, whatever sound is captured while the camera is running is the only sound that may be heard in the finished film. So no post-synching, no wild-track or foley artistry. But no score? No weeping violins, no driving rock, no pulsing techno? No *Céline Dion*? Thankful news, obviously.)

3 *The camera must be hand-held. Any movement or immobility attainable in the hand is permitted (the film must not take place where the camera is standing; shooting must take place where the film takes place).*
(At this point, the spectral finger of film history, in this case of *cinéma-vérité*, beckons us forth. Before the *nouvelle vague*, hand-held

camerawork was widely thought fit only for amateurs and eccentrics. Then, the lightweight 16-mm Aaton set film-makers free to wander. But what was it Lizzie Francke had said about the format of *Festen*? Was it really shot with a digital video camera, not much bigger than a man's fist? What kind of savage liberties might that permit?)

4 *The film must be in colour. Special lighting is not acceptable (if there is too little light for exposure, the scene must be cut or a single lamp attached to the front of the camera).*
(The first bit is horse-sense: after all, colour stock is industry standard, essential to the illusion we call realism. Whereas black-and-white became a style, an indulgence, and an expensive one at that. Thereafter, the DP must make do with available light; and the exposure clause is fabulously stern.)

5 *Optical work and filters are forbidden.*
(So no matting-in of mountain ranges, no blue-screen sabre duels, no slow-sinking CGI ocean liners. And the lens itself is not to be masked by gels and low-contrast filters, a proscription which, on the face of it, would bar most flash-harry directors of commercials and pop promos from the Dogme brethren.)

6 *The film must not contain superficial action (murders, weapons etc. must not occur).*
('All you need to make a movie', Godard once observed, 'is a girl and a gun.' Dogme won't even allow you that much: no succour here, then, for the votaries of John Woo and Quentin Tarantino. The 'merely spectacular' must be kept in proportion.)

7 *Temporal and geographical alienation are forbidden. (That is to say that the film takes place here and now.)*
(At a stroke, Dogme rules out both the 'period piece' and the journey to outer space. A film beginning with the lines 'A long time ago, in a galaxy far away' is a double offender – an absolute no-no. So, for better or worse, whether their makers care to or not, Dogme films are forced to speak for their own times.)

8 *Genre movies are not acceptable.*
(Within five little words, an enormous proscription. After all, the invention and codification of the genres – comedy, Western, horror movie, gangster picture – was vital to the global spread of the seventh

art. Was it really possible for Dogme to say farewell to all that?)

9 *The film format must be Academy 35 mm.*
(Another quaint gesture towards history. Academy ratio is 1:33 to 1, as it was in the early silent cinema. So Dogme requires one to forget the width in order to feel the quality. How this injunction can be squared with the use of digital video is another matter.)

10 *The director must not be credited.*
(A little harsh, this, given the exorbitant number of producers now routinely credited on movies; and given the wide acceptance of the director's status as dominant creative presence on a film – its *auteur*, even. But then Godard himself had called an end to that game as early as 1968: 'When we began in France, directors were not considered authors. They just were considered craftsmen or workers. So we had to say a director is an author just like a painter or a writer. But since now everybody agrees that a director is an author – even any kind of Hollywood director is considered an author – we have to say after all an author is only the first step: we have to go further.' Perhaps that's what Dogme95 intended.)

The Manifesto climaxed with a set of pledges that were in some ways more provocative than the Rules: 'I swear as a director to refrain from personal taste! I am no longer an artist. I swear to refrain from creating a "work", as I regard the instant as more important than the whole. My supreme goal is to force the truth out of my characters and settings. I swear to do so by all the means available and at the cost of any good taste and any aesthetic considerations.'

Now, call it a mental tic, but it seemed to me that if I held this Manifesto up to the light, I would clearly discern the shadow of Godard, smoking a small cigar and chuckling. Lacing between every line was a red thread, linking these Rules to Godard's pronouncements and actions across four decades. Case in point: somebody clever, whose name escapes me, once claimed that all revolutions in art mark a return to realism. In other words, the bravest artists are ceaselessly borne back to a concern for what is truthful. This was the mind-set behind one of Godard's most famous and durable maxims, 'Le "travelling" est un question moral.' 'When style and content are one,' he later explained, 'you can't say artificial things.' Wasn't this self-same spirit embodied in Dogme's daredevil pledge to 'force the truth' by any and all means?

Clearly, Dogme95 was also proposing a certain stripped-down model of production, which reminded me that one of Godard's abiding masters was Brecht, himself a big movie buff who nevertheless had precious few satisfactory encounters with cinema. Brecht hated the cumbersome size of the 'apparatus', the entrenched and rigid system of finance and production, the sheer number of working parts which made it so damnably hard to produce films on one's own terms. In his mercurial early years, Godard minted innumerable strategies to combat this kind of torpor. He favoured direct sound, natural light, the teeming life of real streets, a smaller, more nimble production unit: all ways of helping him to find truth on the spur of the moment. He worked quickly and frugally, he didn't fuss over the fine points of screenplay (which he dismissed as a mere producer's regulatory tool), and he was respectful of the unexpected things he could seize from his actors on the day. For all these reasons and more, he became the most influential director in the world.

Could it be, I wondered, that Trier now fancied such a mantle for himself? Like Godard, he clearly had a facility for the role of brilliant provocateur, even if his cinema to date had looked to be incurably spectacular. But then *The Idiots*, like *Festen*, had been 'originated' on digital video. And, again, Godard had been way ahead of the pack in setting himself this kind of dare; hence his fractious collaboration with the inventor Jean-Pierre Beauviala to come up with a small 35-mm camera that could be used for 'sketching'. But in the meantime, video made its own leaps and bounds, and Godard was quick to embrace the form and find beauty in it. The economy of video held out prospects of its own, as I was reminded by a piece in the April 1998 *Sight & Sound*. Praising a spiky new director called Harmony Korine and his début feature *Gummo*, Geoffrey MacNab cited Francis Coppola's well-known prophecy that the future of cinema might one day rest upon a fat girl in the Midwest, braces on her teeth and camcorder in hand. Though a rather lithe fellow of twenty-three, Korine certainly hailed from Middle America, and seemed to have made a startling use of video in parts of *Gummo*. But then, *pace* Coppola, why should Tennessee make the running? What about Copenhagen? Might not Dogme95 offer a truly radical new form of cinematic realism? These were the kinds of questions preying on my mind as I packed for Cannes; these, plus the easier ones about currency and footwear.

2 An Insider Speaks Out:
Mogens Rukov & Dogme's labour pains

Now then: I beg that the reader permit me a single flash forward in the time-line of my narrative, one that is simultaneously a bit of a flashback in the account given thus far of Dogme95's inception . . .

The Lux Cinema, London N1: Saturday, 4 March 2000

For some weeks now, the capital's most discerning film venues have jointly played host to a season entitled 'Danish Cinema: Past, Present, Future'. Tonight's platform presentation at The Lux is consecrated to the theme of 'Danish Cinema After Dogme'. The guest speaker is Mogens Rukov, renowned instructor at the Danish Film School, and professional script doctor to some of Denmark's leading directors, including the by-now semi-legendary 'Dogme95 Brothers'. The pristine new auditorium is impressively populous; more or less full, save for a few seats at the back. It's a conspicuously young crowd for a Saturday-night lecture on foreign-language cinema. A lot of pens are poised over notepads. After a brief introduction, Rukov mounts the dais: an avuncular man in his fifties, bearded, bespectacled, clad in a good dark suit. For some moments, he fumbles patiently with the clasp of a radio-mike; extracts a cigarette, flares up; then begins to speak. He will address us without notes for a little more than an hour.

He pinches the cigarette from his mouth between fingers and thumb, exhales a blue cloud. His technique, he explains through an engaging grin, is a kind of *hommage* to Jean-Paul Belmondo in Godard's *A Bout de Souffle*. After all, who can deny the 'deep, deep inspiration' of Godard? Certainly not the Dogme Brotherhood. We should know, he confides, that one of Lars von Trier's most prized possessions is a letter he received from Godard, in praise of his achievement in *Dogme#2: Idioterne*. No one else has yet been permitted to see this letter, Rukov chuckles. But Trier is most adamant of its existence.

So, to the matter of the evening. Why Dogme95? Exactly what happened back then? Well (Rukov sighs), as we are all painfully aware, in cinema there is this thing we call The Mainstream. 'And it just keeps streaming and streaming and streaming . . . you can't stop it.' But every now and again, we may discern these 'little dots' appearing round the edges. Like German expressionism. Like neorealism. Like the *nouvelle vague*. These 'waves' do not, indeed they cannot, endure for much more than six or seven years; or amount to more than a fraction of a film-producing nation's output. But they are crucial. And now, says Rukov, we find ourselves once again in a period of cinema that requires manifestos to be written. Firstly, and obviously, because technology enables too vast an array of choices. Film-making customarily permits you to do whatever you want – to walk into a room and change it utterly, paint the walls or knock them down, strip the floors, change the furnishings. Film enables you to enact a version of the impossible counsel offered by Brecht to the East German Government in 1953: that they dismiss the people and elect new ones. But what if one were to purposely *restrict* such choice? Seek the relief of being simple-minded? Put oneself in a chain of causality, where any one decision inevitably begets several more?

So, then, to Lars von Trier: the most eminent of Rukov's former students. 'The main character in Danish cinema,' says Rukov, shaking his head fondly, 'a genius.' And, like all geniuses, a difficult man to sit down and work with; because, in doing so, one must strain to be a little of a genius oneself. A fearful task. But it was Lars von Trier, with some very personal motivation in mind, who invented these Dogme95 Rules. Rules that invite one to look really close and see just how odd reality can be. Rules that issue a simple challenge to film-makers: 'Come down to street level, and tell stories from there.'

Early in 1997, Rukov received a telephone call. At last, two years after the publication of this vexatious manifesto, Trier was himself about to make a 'Dogme film'. The two men met and talked for four hours. Trier's scenario was simple: a group of youngish people live together in a large house, under the leadership of a fellow called 'Stoffer'. They venture out together, into society, and they behave like mentally retarded people. Then, rather like 'seventies people', engaged in some socio-political communal project, they come home and discuss what they've done.

Together, Trier and Rukov discussed the core dramatic problem: why on earth do they do it? Are they theatre students messing about? Might they be a group taking evening classes in psychology, and testing their social theories? Did they answer a newspaper ad placed by this Stoffer? Pah! None of these suppositions felt adequate. 'Each one made us vomit – figuratively speaking.' Finally, Rukov hit on a simple solution, born of experience: as long as you don't show something to be a problem *within the action of the film*, then the audience will not bother to question its validity. They will take the idiots' motivation as a given – whatever its lunacy.

A more pressing problem, Rukov felt, was one of dramatic monotony: there were altogether too many of these self-critical sessions, and not nearly enough day trips. So he and Trier came up with the notion of the idiots visiting a swimming pool. This presented an ideal opportunity to get them naked – good! And then, why not an outing to a café? So they devised a scene where Stoffer leaves his comrade Jeppe among a group of greasy bikers. Unable to blow his cover, Jeppe is forced to 'spass' (pretend to be retarded) and be grudgingly indulged; even to suffer an assisted visit to the urinal, where one biker kindly holds his penis and directs the jet as he pisses. Well and good.

But then, another central problem: that of the main character, Karen; and her 'unusual stature', as such. Karen loves the idiots, supports them, keeps telling them how admiring she is of their project, what a beautiful idea it is. And yet it is perfectly clear to everybody in the audience that it is an absolutely crazy idea. And the deep reason for her approval can only be revealed in the very last moments of the piece: it is one of *those* films. At last, Trier and Rukov figured out a meaningful way to introduce her to the audience. She would stumble upon the group, as an outsider, sitting in a restaurant. She would observe their antics, become a party to them, join them. And why a restaurant? Because that's how Godard would do it. He dislikes the intimacy of private rooms. Godard excels in public places: in cars and bars and cafés, on boulevards, in hotel lobbies, at gas stations.

So, the session was concluded. As they bade one another farewell at the train station, Trier remarked, 'We will never talk of this film again.' Three weeks later, he called back, anxious. He had booked himself into a hotel room and undertaken to start writing. They talked a little more, and there was a good deal of bracing laughter. 'Now', Trier exclaimed, 'I can write!' And the script was written in three and a half days. Rukov never read it. Eventually Trier screened the completed work for him. Afterwards, the exchanges went something like: 'You didn't like it?' 'It's not good enough.' 'Damn. But I made it for you.' 'It's still not good enough.' In the end, though, Rukov came round to it. It is, he thinks, a moving film: a film about a very lovely, very idyllic, very friendly little fascist country. (Rukov's audience laughs, a little nervously.)

So much for Lars. What, then, of Thomas Vinterberg, another prize pupil of the Danish Film School and co-signatory of this Manifesto? Thomas had been told by a friend about a young man who made a confession over the radio airwaves, of how he stood up at a family party and revealed that he had been sexually abused as a child. What a *coup de théâtre*! And what an idea for a movie. Who can fail to imagine the kind of complicated feelings that would arise? After all, notes Rukov, when you attend a large family gathering on a great occasion, you are concerned primarily with what kind of soup you'll be served; and whether you will see the man or woman with whom you customarily flirt on such occasions. Matters of this order. You don't care to be informed of unsettled truths. You don't want to hear about *incest*.

This, then, was the germ of *Festen*; and Vinterberg duly invited Rukov to collaborate with him on the screenplay. The first matter concerning the co-scenarists was how long the story should take. They opted for the classical twenty-four hours – the unities of time and place and action. (In the end, it would be only eighteen.) But in this way we see how crucial is time to the story. We always know what time it is. That is because Vinterberg and Rukov committed themselves to faithfully following every step that such a celebration entails – the arrival of the guests, their unpacking, their dressing, each course of the meal, the speeches, the brandies, the dancing. 'We respected this rhythm.' The structure determined what scenes would be made, and tested the dramatists' wits. Suppose a man is dressing for dinner. What kind of drama is that? You are obliged to galvanize the moment. Perhaps he has mislaid his dress shoes, and must wear loafers. Perhaps he blames his wife for this mishap. Perhaps this is an index of simmering resentment in their marriage.

There were other determining factors. The Rules commanded that shooting be on location. They had considered an opulent country mansion, but also a typical Danish countryside inn: the kind of appallingly 'hearty' place where one can always smell last night's cooking. Scouting was carried out, snapshots taken. Yet Rukov found Vinterberg reluctant to sit down with him and survey this evidence, to make a final choice. Impatience mounted. Finally, Rukov asks, 'Thomas, where do you really want to spend six weeks this summer?'

Obvious. A mansion. The choice of the house where the film would play begat so many things in turn. Thomas found himself especially partial to the mansion's elegant staircase; so they made six or so scenes using the staircase. Then casting begat dialogue. Three actors – Ulrich Thomsen, Thomas Bo Larsen, Paprika Steen – were cast as siblings; none of them resembles one another in the slightest. The structure could spare precious little room for exposition on this score, so the problem would be solved in the opening moments. Larsen's character would refer constantly to 'my brother', 'my sister'.

Festen was written in seven weeks. 'It is a classic Ibsen drama,' says Rukov. 'Thomas doesn't know that. But it's true.' It's also inspired by *The Godfather*, and a little by *Hamlet*. And there is another *hommage* to cinema. As the evening unravels, the party guests dance through the house in a chain. Inspired by – what? Rukov asks the audience. '*Fanny and Alexander*,' is the general murmur. But then, Bergman too was making an *hommage*: to what? asks Rukov, ever the teacher. No takers for this. *Il Gattopardo*, Visconti. But who was Visconti stealing from? Well, Rukov admits, we're not to know.

One momentous decision remains unmade throughout most of the production. How to end the thing? Clearly, the father is unmasked, Christian's story is proven. Perhaps Helge will commit suicide, a broken man. And yet the Rules forbid any 'weapons'. Maybe he could jump in the lake. Or maybe one of his siblings, or his wife, could kill him? And yet the Rules forbid 'superficial action', 'murders'. No, if Helge is to die, the action will have to occur offscreen. Not good enough. At last they're agreed – Helge will make a speech of his own, a speech in which he concedes defeat. 'You won. You fought a good game, son.' He knows he is a bastard, he admits his crime. But he will not slouch away, beaten, saying, 'I'm a beast.' He is a proud man. So they shot the speech; though, Rukov suggests, it was longer, and better, as written.

Festen was shot in six weeks. After post-production, when the key personnel projected the film for the first time, there was a mood of gloom. Thomas was heard to reflect that one can so easily turn 'cold' towards something. 'Nobody will go and see this shit' was the unhappy consensus. Thomas estimated that they might sell maybe seventy thousand tickets, tops. But Rukov is smiling as he recounts this seemingly sorry tale, and the audience appreciates the joke.

3 Ragged glory:
Cannes & Dogme's fiery baptism

Palais des Festivals, Cannes: Monday, 18 May 1998

I haven't visited the Festival since 1991, the year Trier so boldly disdained Polanski's largesse. Rattling down the Croisette in an over-priced cab, passing the perennial billboards, I sensed that little had changed. As Penelope Houston once noted, Cannes is a film festival like Christmas is a religious festival: so it involves films on screens, yet seems scarcely to depend upon them. My problem now is that I'm no longer a critic with a pretty pastel pass, just an industry delegate accredited by the Marché. So I must queue up, mostly with humourless women from Canada, and bargain patiently for 'invitations' to screenings. *The Idiots* is among the hottest tickets, and I wonder if I'll get in, particularly when I find myself fist-fighting to gain admission to the Taiwanese entry, *The Hole*, a sort of musical romance about heavy rainfall. Now, at the turn of the second week, *Festen* takes its bow in competition, and I dutifully troop along with the hordes, into the cathedral-like munificence of the 2,500-seater Salle Lumière. The great blue stage-drapes are slowly drawn apart, then, comically, they creep towards each other again. The penny drops: the projectionist is preparing us for Academy ratio. Then we're off.

Autumnal patriarch Helge (Henning Moritzen) has summoned his extended family for his sixtieth birthday celebration. Guests include son number one, the blond and angular Christian (Ulrich Thomsen); son number two, the dark and disreputable Michael (Thomas Bo Larsen); and daughter Helene (Paprika Steen), who carries the airs of a determinedly capricious ex-debutante. But a second daughter, we're told, died at her own hand some months previously. From the get-go, *Festen*'s evocation of bright, brittle, unhappy families, of barely sufferable bourgeois awfulness, is on the button. What could be more ghastly than the clan gathering, utterly devoid of real fellow-feeling, clearly rotten with fake sentiment and unspoken hostility? The malaise is encapsulated in a moment when Helge draws aside the ill-favoured

Michael and grudgingly offers him an entrée to freemasonry, one that the wretched fellow accepts with gratitude and relief.

Half an hour in, and I feel comfortable with the DV image, and rather tickled to be seeing it on this vast screen. Moreover, Dogme95 and DVC make for some nice rough-hewn visual quirks. As Michael greets arriving guests outside the mansion, the roaming hand-held camera brushes up against his arm and he smacks it away irritably. A little later, as Michael's wife Mette lolls in post-coital languor, the camera flies down from the bedroom ceiling and lands at her eye level. Not a crane-shot, clearly; and, yet, I find myself noting mentally, 'Was that hand-held? Was it *Dogme*?'

Then, amid a stuporous dinner, Christian rises to make the first speech, and smilingly relates how Helge ritually raped both him and his late sister throughout their childhood. It's a moment of comic dread and awful embarrassment. Some of the older guests seem scarcely to have heard, and somehow the party lurches on, but the game is now afoot. Later, ordered by his mother to make a formal apology for fouling the mood, Christian says he's sorry only that she was aware of her husband's foulness, yet never intervened: 'I'm sorry you're so hypocritical and corrupt that I hope you *die*. I'm sorry you're all such *cunts* . . .' At this juncture Christian is dragged from the house by the dutiful Michael and a few cronies, who beat the bejesus out of him and lash him to a tree trunk in the woods that surround the house. Seizing this moment to inherit the paternal mantle, Michael disciplines his brother with empty words about how family bonds must not be violated. Dusk settles, and we get strange, graceful images of Christian, bound and pensive.

By now it's clear that, on paper, *Festen* is a classical piece of Scandinavian chamber theatre. With talent to burn, Vinterberg could doubtless have mounted the piece on 35 mm with the same eerie elegance as Resnais's *Last Year in Marienbad*. But under the Dogme restraints – the available light, the hand-held camera, the limited post-production – the film has acquired the force of a disturbing home-movie. Good. It needs a bit of rough, a bit of dirt, lest it all get too chic. Nevertheless, I still get the sense that certain characters would be more at home on a stage: not least Thomas Bo Larsen's Michael, whose frenetic and not disassociated urges to fuck and fight would be well suited to bedroom farce.

Another facet of Michael's odiousness is his knee-jerk racism towards Helene's black American boyfriend, who shows up unannounced. But this too feels stage-managed, as if Vinterberg wrongly assumed that Michael wasn't enough of a creep. As for Helene, though her mother has derided her as a student *trotskisant* with a profitless passion for anthropology, she still seems like a spoilt rich girl who brings unsuitable boys to parties. Ulrich Thomsen is fine as Christian, tight-laced and gnawing at his own innards. Like Hamlet, he's painfully aware that he must kill The Father, and isn't at all sure if he's up to it. He has better reason than most, but he can't manage it. Instead, he attains heroic stature as a victim, one who summons the nerve to speak out. Of course, it may be a gain for civilization that Vinterberg felt no violence was required in his scenario; and Dogme Rules forbade him 'weapons' and 'murder'. But movies are movies, this one as dramatically contrived as any, and I wonder if Christian wouldn't feel a whole lot better with his dad's evil head jammed on to a spike.

Another discomfiting question suggests itself: why is 'Fathers Who Fuck Their Kids' such a current vogue amongst young white male directors? There's no way around it: this Cannes has several examples, such as Todd Solondz's *Happiness*, an arch account of suburban paedophilia, rotten with hatred for humanity; and Gaspar Noe's *Seul Contre Tous*. In the wings is Tim Roth's film of Alexander Stuart's novel *The War Zone*, a fantasia about a schoolgirl who entices her father into incest, fascinated by her own nascent feminine wiles and his wilting virility. 'Dad's got us,' she tells her appalled younger brother, 'but we're not what he wanted, we're about two per cent of what he thought he was capable of.' The same noxious spirit is invoked in *Festen*. 'Is it my fault I have such talentless offspring?' Helge protests. 'I've just never really understood *why* you did it,' Christian challenges. 'It was all you were good for,' is Helge's unblinking riposte. That's more like it! The moment passes; and yet this disgusting sentiment has told us much about the pathology of an abusive father. The urge within sons to kill their fathers tends to burn off with age; but when do fathers cease wanting to destroy progeny that they consider second-rate?

From this point, *Festen* grows darker yet. The party staggers onward into the morning, with only table-lamps and candles to illuminate these lofty rooms; and the video image starts to crackle at the edges of the frame, as though poised to disintegrate. Christian is visited by the ghost of his sister: a visitation we've feared from the outset. ('I've got a really bad vibe,' Helene has murmured, while poking about in her

19

sister's old boudoir.) It's another Shakespearean device, and one that carries the hoary old baggage of genre. Finally, the next day at breakfast, Helge concedes defeat in front of the gathering, and wanders off to the potting shed, disgraced but unbowed. Vinterberg even has the matchless nerve to reward Christian with the love of a pert and slightly saucy blonde maid. But Christian's lingering disquiet is writ large in a last close-up before credits.

Lights! Applause! It's a hit; and clearly a formidable work. No question, then, why Trier picked Vinterberg as a partner-in-crime. At the same time, being who I am, I'm left wondering if what's most interesting about *Festen* is its shades of conservatism: not only in what it looks to skewer in the material (the racism, the fake bourgeois consensus), but what's embedded in its own construction. I don't stick about for the press conference, but I glimpse the preamble to proceedings on a TV monitor as I leave the Palais. Centre-stage on the dais, shades on head and sweater around his shoulders, Vinterberg is a shockingly beautiful young man. Trier's choice looks more discerning yet.

Palais des Festivals: Wednesday, 20 May 1998

The Idiots are a bunch of middle-class malcontents who decide to provoke the community around them by publicly masquerading as people with mental disabilities; 'spassing', as they call it. Under the leadership of Stoffer (Jens Albinus), they function not unlike the Maoist cell of Godard's *La Chinoise*, making guerrilla sorties from base-camp, retreating in orderly fashion for stern sessions of self-criticism. What sorts of people do they seek to antagonize? Stiff-necked waiters in piss-elegant restaurants; shysters from the local council who offer financial incentives to move these 'retards' on; parvenu home-buyers who feign 'concern' but want no such nonsense in their backyard. Karen (Bodil Jorgenson) is a listless working-class woman who stumbles upon the group and drifts into their number. She refuses to spass, but she observes the others with a growing pride and indulgence. She does ask Stoffer why they do it, but he can't answer very well. 'You can't justify it,' he says; still, he manages a few arch remarks about the value of locating one's 'inner idiot'.

Halfway into Lars von Trier's *Dogme#2*, I'm irresistibly reminded of Joey Deacon, a spastic man who was the subject of a well-liked BBC documentary film in the late 1970s. Inevitably, Joey provided me and my school yard contemporaries with jokes for much of that year. We all learnt how to 'spass' from Joey; and 'Joey' was the gibe you pinned on any kid who gave the impression of being inept, or naïve, or shy. Having been such a little bastard, I now feel that I understand Trier's point, even if I'm somewhat flabbergasted by it. Plus I like the performance of big, straw-headed Jens Albinus as Stoffer, who strikes me as the kind of amusing trust-fund ne'er-do-well one often encounters in life, without liking very much. Eventually, Stoffer implodes, runs naked through the streets, screaming about 'Sollerod fascists'; the gang have to tie him to a mattress in the attic. The next day, they throw a silly party for him, with hats, streamers, cake and pop. It becomes an orgy, and the physical frankness of this 'gang-bang' scene is quite startling. Watching a livid erection slipping in and out of a dilated vagina on the huge Lumière screen, I find myself grinning helplessly at the heart-warming loveliness of it.

But what kind of savagery has Dogme inflicted upon Trier's filmmaking? He certainly hasn't stinted in the non-separation of sound and image. The film is full of jump-cuts and sounds clashing in the cut. And the Trier of old would never have allowed himself such lackadaisical framing. But he seems to be testing himself, changing his spots, shedding the finical habits of his past. At one moment, so brazen that it can only be intentional, we see a DVC cameraman trailing Stoffer and aforementioned parvenu house-buyer (*Festen*'s Paprika Steen). It's a touch of Brechtian *verfremdungseffekt*, as if to say, 'Careful, it's only a movie.' Again, one has to think of Godard, and the flaunting of the slate in *La Chinoise*. And, as if in overt homage, *The Idiots* is structured around retrospective interviews with the group members, shot to-camera, Trier himself acting as question-master from behind the apparatus.

The group begins to unravel, painfully. In a splendid scene, Alex, by day a slack and typically reactionary advertising copywriter, is humiliated at his workplace by the inspired spassing of his erstwhile girlfriend Katrine. Increasingly, Stoffer acts the martinet, demanding that his disciples 'spass' before their friends and families. 'Prove you are into it,' he sneers while slumped in a wheelchair, sounding like an especially disagreeable film director. But the group suffer a predictable and collective loss of nerve, and finally only Karen is able to oblige. She leads Susanne (the durable nursemaid of the group) back to a drab flat, her family home, where her family are quietly appalled to see her. She has not been seen since the tragic death of her son. In the awful silence of the sitting-room, Karen's husband glowers down at his feet, and Karen begins to 'spass'. He strikes her across the face; and Susanne, now understanding everything, leads Karen away.

Lights! Modest applause, scattered boos and hoots. Back out in the sunshine, I go in search of a dry beer and a clear thought. The film has certainly managed to live up to the last paragraph of the Manifesto: it has no 'aesthetics', no 'taste'. It's messy as hell. It has its moments, in exposing just how confused and weak and unhappy youngish people can be today. There is a rather affecting moment where Katrine weeps to camera as she insists, 'I don't think we can find the same fine things that we found there.' The same *what*? But then I sense the film is like a sixties 'happening', or a theatrical workshop where the process was more rewarding than the outcome. The nineties give-away about the whole thing is that, while it superficially recalls *La Chinoise*, it's uninterested in politics. It concerns a bourgeois attempt to *épater les bourgeois*; and even sceptics who would dismiss the revolt of the *soixante-huitards* as so much street theatre would concede that Godard's film captured some of the living, breathing, fighting dialectics of its era.

I examine the Zentropa press-kit, and face again that disconcerting level of irony in Trier's every utterance. He speaks of a 'desire to submit' to rules, born of his 'humanistic, cultural-leftist upbringing'. What is it with this guy and his incessant romance with authority? Still, there's one remark that strikes me as something like genius: 'Some people say it's all very silly, and yes, that is exactly what it is. In some places, disastrously silly: malicious, foolish, and meaningless silliness. But the film contains other facets . . .' Regardless of whether or not it's commendable, how many directors would admit this of their work? One thing is for sure: von Trier is smarter and sharper than most of his critics. 'Is the purpose of both Dogme95 and *The Idiots* to give up control?' asks Peter Ovig Knudsen. 'Yes, you couldn't put it more precisely . . . So we don't need to talk any more?' And this in the friendly pages of the press-kit, no less. I find myself wondering how many more interviewers will take a mincing before Dogme is through, or Trier grows bored.

So I figure this is one press conference worth eavesdropping upon. Sure enough, about a dozen 'idiots' mount the dais; but no Trier. Producer Vibeke Windelov apologises on his behalf. Zentropa's MD Peter Aalbæk Jensen sits impassively behind a big cigar, and issues a few gnomic provocations, concerning the fun to be had in playing with one's own shit, throwing it at the wall. Inevitably, the actors struggle to say anything more penetrative of what they've done. But Jens Albinus is impressively earnest. He contends that their communal mission was to bring more 'fun' and 'pain' into the act of storytelling, and so to broaden the range of Danish cinema. A female reporter says she felt the sex scene looked half-assed. Smart as paint, Albinus replies that it's no bad thing, and cites Brecht: when you listen to a story, be aware you're hearing a professional storyteller. It's instructive, he argues, to put real, unfeigned embarrassment into a movie; so that at the end, audience members will turn nervously to one another and say, 'Well! What did *you* think?' But at Cannes, of course, such exchanges are sadly unavoidable. I don't know what *I* think. And across the dinner table that evening, I sense that the critical reaction is generally luke-warm: a lot of frowns, winces and shrugs. Inevitably there are scattered outbreaks of 'spassing', but the only accomplished piss-taker in this respect is Shane Danielsen, an erudite and superbly coarse-humoured young Australian critic. 'Gangen-bangen!' he groans, in strangulated cod-Scandinavian.

Highbury, London N5: Tuesday, 29 March 1999

As a freelance, you're always looking for a job of work to get you out of the house. Otherwise you occupy a kind of ivory tower, even if it's only a converted flat in north London. But even there, all kinds of bricks rattle against your window-frame. This month I find myself editing interviews with Hollywood film-makers conducted by Mike Figgis for Faber and Faber's *Projections 10*. Mike has shot all his interviews on DV, and his guests are uncommonly thoughtful about the format. Jean-Jacques Beneix, a child of the *nouvelle vague* and 1968, com-pares Hollywood to 1970s Detroit: 'They keep making things that are obsolete . . . But there will be a backlash, some kind of revolution.' This ravishing stylist now claims to disdain the Louma crane and the big trucks full of track. Now he dreams of a Spartan set-up: a tripod, a sim-ple camera, two lens. He compares DV to the Aaton and the Nagra: 'When young kids tell me they want to make movies, I say, "You can, you can do it. We couldn't. But you have *this*."'

If an exemplar were needed, *Festen* is now playing in London cine-mas, and playing uncommonly well, assisted by an elegant poster campaign. It has arrived garlanded with the Jury Prize from Cannes, awarded *ex-aqueo* with Claude Miller's *Le Classe de Neige*. Perhaps more crucially to its fortunes, the film has also secured US distribution from October Films, and bears Best Foreign Film from the New York Critics' Circle, plus a Golden Globe nomination. Browsing the Internet, I see that Vinterberg has given an interview to Dana Thomas of *Newsweek*, in which he speaks with charm, eloquence and assurance, every inch the voice of Young European Cinema. He also sounds a robust clarion call: 'To compete in American terms is impossible. We shouldn't even try . . . The strength of American film-making is that it's an industry. European film-making is trying to become one, but it shouldn't. If you start to make these Euro-pudding things you'll just kill it. To be a success, Europe must maintain the individualism and irrationality of its cinema.'

Hmm. While suggesting an accommodation with the Hollywood imperium, is there not also an implicit challenge in Vinterberg's words? As he points out, *Festen* may seem to the wider world 'a narrow film on videotape about child abuse'; but in Scandinavia 'it's a blockbuster, right next to *Titanic*'. And this for a film funded to the tune of seven million kroner ($1.3 million) by Danish television channels and the state-funded Film Institute. I'm put in mind of famous words from John Maynard Keynes's 1933 lecture at University College, Dublin, entitled 'On National Self-sufficiency', once dismissed as an aberration of a great mind, now widely cited by critics of free trade: 'Ideas, knowledge, art, hospitality, travel – these are things which should of their nature be international. But let goods be homespun whenever it is reasonably and conveniently possible; and above all, let finance be primarily national.'

Meanwhile, *The Idiots* too is poised for UK release, though the heralds are more modest in its case. But its delightful frames of hard-core penetration have been passed uncut by the British censor. And Trier has given an interview to Simon Hattenstone of the *Guardian* from Zentropa's new production base in Copenhagen. He expatiates upon his fascination with Rudolf Steiner's theories about children with Down's Syndrome: 'He said they were angels, not in the sense that they were very good, but in the sense that they were sent from God because they were a different breed. I always thought that was a very beautiful idea.' So it's official: Trier isn't mocking the afflicted – he envies them. Elsewhere, of course, irony persists. Hattenstone notes 'a weird kind of hum' beneath

Trier's conversational tone of voice, and realizes it's a kind of 'muted, self-conscious laughter'. But there's a teasing idealism too, as Trier describes the generously-scaled production set-up he and Zentropa have engineered: 'We have underground film-makers who come here and use our sets to make splatter films. And another group are making porn films. Every month we're going to have a master-class which will be free and go out on the Internet. Wouldn't it be great if this became some kind of socialist co-op? I feel quite touched when I hear myself . . .'

I'm starting to feel there's a nagging and persuasive ubiquity about this whole Dogme thing, and it's confirmed when I call in at my local pub to meet Geoff Macnab, a neighbour and hard-driving freelancer, just back from the Berlin Film Festival. He tells me there was a veritable frenzy of foreign sales for Søren Kragh-Jacobsen's *Dogme#3: Mifune*, produced, like *Festen*, by plucky little Nimbus Film. Finally, it even made off with the Silver Bear. Geoff sketches it briefly for me as a sunny romantic comedy that (*de rigueur* for Dogme?) toys with the notion of the holy fool; he liked it very much, while finding it to be nothing out of the ordinary. But, staring deep into my glass of Newcastle Brown Ale, I sense that when all roads lead to Copenhagen, it's time to buy kroner and go. A few days later I call into Faber and find a commission awaiting me. My task is to make a book about this Dogme95 phenomenon. It seems that film editor Walter Donohue (who thinks *The Idiots* a masterpiece) and chairman Matthew Evans (who was quite tickled by *Festen*) are also laying wagers on the abiding worth of the movement. For Faber, there's also a spot of synergy in it: for it seems that the mercurial Harmony Korine, twenty-five-year-old writer, photographer, street-fighter and all-round *avant-garde* iconoclast, has committed to make the first US Dogme film, *The Julien Chronicles*; Faber are Mr Korine's UK publishers, having issued his first novel, an unclassifiable collage called *Crack-up at the Race Riots*.

So, to business. I look afresh at the Dogme website, www.dogme.dk. I'm amused to see that each Dogme director must make a Confession of his 'sins', and submit to a Reprimand from his Brothers. It's all redolent of a spirit of mischievous piety which really ought to be entered into. So, inevitably, I sit down to compose my own Manifesto for a book about a Manifesto. A 'vow of chastity' is far too Catholic for me; I need something Protestant and exhortative. I pull my notebook towards me and begin, steadily, to write: 'I Promise to Try Harder' . . .

4 Comparing the lies to find the truth:
Dogme's forward march

The Star Cinema, Rue d'Antibes, Cannes: Thursday, 20 May 1999

Edinburgh is tabbing me for another Cannes excursion; and though the Official Selection is Dogme-free, the wave is still crashing. Beneath the legend 'Dogme's Sweet 16', the daily *Moving Pictures* reports that Zentropa has struck a deal to produce (or co-produce) sixteen more films around the $1 million mark. Eight will be shared between Zentropa and Nimbus. The rest are divvied up among four small Zentropa-related producers: Wave in the UK, Pain Unlimited in Germany, Liberator in France, and What Else in the Netherlands. *The House of Klang*, a $1 million comedy about the fashion business, is also mooted, and from Warhol's old accomplice Paul Morrissey, no less. I'm aware of having met Jill Robertson of Wave at the Soho House Club, where she chatted with hilarious candour about her past employment as a showgirl. At the same time, the idea of Dogme UK feels implausible: the English always struggle to attain a total void of 'taste', usually stooping no lower than red-faced vulgarity.

Now I'm squeezed into a seat at the Star to view a buyers' screening of the film touted as *Dogme#5: Lovers*. It's the (uncredited) directorial debut of actor Jean-Marc Barr, who got famous in films like *The Big Blue* and Trier's *Europa*. A brief kerfuffle at the door indicates that the organizers are desirous of expelling the press. Then a camera crew trails the personable M. Barr and his leading lady Elodie Bouchez (last year's Best Actress at Cannes for *La Vie Rêvee des Anges*) up to the dais. Bouchez is wearing a russet-coloured sun-dress that exposes her sun-kissed shoulders. Barr addresses us in French, Elodie surveys us all impassively; then the lights go down, and Elodie and some bloke are on screen, making eyes at each other in a bookshop. But there's no sound. And we the audience are curiously muted. Normally Cannes is exactly the place for audiences to raise their voices; critics even boo movies they dislike, an act of astounding crassness. Finally the projector is snapped off and the screen goes white. 'Typical Dogme, right?'

murmurs the pretty blonde girl beside me. Ah, wit! In a flash, we're back.

So, what's going on? Dragan (Sergei Trifunovic), an unkempt young Yugoslav painter, is intrigued by Jeanne, the girl who serves behind the counter of the Parisian art-bookshop he frequents. Since his manners are, frankly, idiosyncratic, he's fortunate indeed that she takes a shine to him and suggests that they spend an evening together. Sparks are struck, and fast as you please they are passing whole days between the sheets, exploring each other's newly adorable nooks and crannies. Love blooms. She's keen. He's erratic, but touchingly romantic. She worries he'll drop her. 'Oh, baby, worry about that when I'm dead,' he replies. But he's a Balkan male, and worse, an artist. She works regular hours; he takes up his paintbrush whenever the muse descends. Fully capable as a painter, he struggles as a man. 'You'd better learn, my dear,' she warns. At a drinking party, with lachrymose Balkan guitar music, he boozes and behaves boorishly. But when she's sick, he takes care of her. Neighbour Genevieve Page keeps popping in to give her blessing ('Being together is what counts'). Somehow, these two learn to live inside one another; save for one crucial secret Dragan clasps tight: he has no visa. They move into her place, live like mice, and feud over the bills and the washing-up. A child of Tito, he refuses to live like some 'capitalist hermit'. But he learns, too late, to count himself lucky, when the cops come knocking at Jeanne's door.

Of course, as the title betrays, *Lovers* is a genre film. It's an itemized account of the things young lovers do when love in itself seems sufficient to live on – simple as that. Obviously I shouldn't have been thinking about that blonde girl beside me, and obviously I was. What was her romantic history? Did she find the same sweet things in the movie as me? We both emitted a yelp of amused recognition at one point. And yet she left before the last reel. I felt bereft, and naturally wondered if it was something I'd said. During Bouchez's brief moment of graceful nudity, had I involuntarily emitted some regrettable exclamation, like 'Wow'? Paranoia, maybe. Or maybe she just didn't like the movie. If today, as the Dogme Manifesto insists, 'anyone can make movies', then *Lovers* proves it – it's often amateurish. The last shot, one long take of Jeanne forlornly climbing the stairs back to her apartment, is interminable and doesn't work. The determined use of music is poor – there's a terrible bit where everybody bops about awkwardly

27

to Linton Kwesi Johnson's 'More Time'. And Jeanne and Dragan conduct their intimacies in English, which sounds awkward and feels like a commercial sop.

But in its all-for-love ethos and larking-about-in-Paris lightness, I'm fondly reminded not only of the *nouvelle vague* but also of what Trier has dubbed 'Swinging London' movies ('the Beatles films where they ran through London carrying a giant iron bedstead'). That's because it's a film about intimacy, and Dogme surely *means* intimacy, between camera and actors. There's no sex in it, but a lot of kissing, nuzzling, and caressing. Bouchez seems just like a Real Girl, Sergei Trifunovic much like a dozen Balkan men I've met in London since Yugoslavia got dismembered. The freezing flat and the cheap cooking and that whole 'love on the dole' ambience – Dogme has helped Barr to make it real, at least for a few decent moments. Or else I'm going soft.

Upper Montagu Street, London w1: Thursday, 27 July 1999

On a sunny rooftop over Baker Street, I am dancing (albeit with less of my usual élan) for the benefit of a digital video camera. This rooftop is one of the most photogenic in London, dearly beloved of pop-promo directors and producers of cheap television. In-between steps (hip-hop moves, mostly, with a spot of the Black Bottom), I address the aforementioned camera on the phenomenon of Dogme95 ('It's hip, it's happening, it's dangerous, it's Danish'). Yes, that's right: I'm 'pitching' a TV documentary, and consequently, beating my gums like a semi-literate idiot. 'I'm just gonna hit the road to Copenhagen,' I threaten, 'and hunt down these crazy Danes, and ask them face to face what the hell they think they're doing.'

How did I get here? Barely a month ago I had a seemingly innocent drink with Professor Colin MacCabe and Paula Jalfon, friends and former colleagues at the British Film Institute, now partners in the independent production company Minerva Pictures. Mine was strictly a fizzy water, after a crushing weekender in Belfast. As I hung my head, they proposed a little Dogme doc, based on my Faber book. 'Couldn't hurt,' I thought. After all, in two years spent as their researcher at BFI TV, not one of my abstruse ideas had attracted a shred of finance; so it would be nice to try and give something back. A few days later, we had a few glasses of wine at Colin's Islington home, joined by designated director Saul Metzstein, a young Scot I'd met through Edinburgh duties, now squaring up to his first feature. Dogme seems still to be *en vogue*; and Colin and Paula are confident they can attract finance from the Independent Film Channel in the US, and FilmFour in the UK. Colin is fairly certain that the entire movement is little more than Godard *redux*, but then that's no bad thing in his eyes.

So I typed out a 'proposal' for a documentary, phrased, as these things tend to be, as a sequence of imponderable questions in need of straight answers. To wit: 'Is this all an elaborate joke? If so, is it funny? If not, how seriously should sincere lovers of cinema take it? If the cinematic *avant-garde* has at last resurfaced, why now? And why in Denmark? Is it a passing art-house fad? What do young film-makers think of Dogme95? Will they disdain the Dogme95 game? Or will they *all* want to play? Are low-budget DVC opuses about to break out like the Plague?' That last question, I know, has currency. At Cannes, most of the fires got started by Dan Myrick and Eduardo Sanchez's *The Blair Witch Project*, a creepy mock-documentary shot on DVC and 16 mm. A lot of big talk about 'the digital future' ensued, and lip service was paid to last year's wall-breaching exercise by Dogme95. At the same time, to my eye the two most glorious films at the Festival were works of very familiar lineage, both shot on film: the Dardenne brothers' *Rosetta* and Bruno Dumont's *L'Humanité*. And in a startling coup, David Cronenberg's jury divvied up the top prizes between them. These two films make me feel that European cinema is enjoying a magnificent flourish, and has not quite the need of Dogme95 that it so assuredly had four years ago.

But there's a flip side. I've now read the script of *Dogme#4: The King is Alive*, co-authored by Kristian Levring and Anders Thomas Jensen, part-funded by the New York outfit Good Machine. It's hellishly exciting. Written in English, it's the story of a bunch of European and American tourists on a coach trip through the Namibian desert. When the coach runs out of gas in the middle of nowhere, they find themselves in a life-or-death predicament; at which point one of their number, an ageing literary type, suggests that they attempt to raise their spirits by rehearsing a version of *King Lear* that he has transcribed from memory. Of course, that isn't necessarily how you or I would handle the situation. But as Lear himself would say, 'O reason not the need!' It's an insane idea, a black, sorry, comic tale with a wonderful literate sensibility: the appropriation of Shakespeare is magisterial. That it should be backed by US money, and that 'name' actors like

Jennifer Jason Leigh should have signed up for the trek to Namibia, points to the happy conclusion that this Manifesto is getting movie-makers excited about ideas again. Dogme lives!

Edinburgh Film Festival: Saturday, 21 August 1999

'Dogme is dead,' cries Lizzie Francke, slapping a fresh copy of *Screen International* on to a typically slatternly Festival desktop. Sure enough, Louise Tutt's front-page story ('Every Dogme has its day') reports that the Brothers 'are expected to announce drastic changes to their Dogme manifesto by the end of this year', in the wake of having certified Harmony Korine's film. Oh, for fuck's sake . . . By now I'm accustomed to at least one fresh scurrility per week from these guys, but this is different. There again, I was forewarned. A few weeks previously, Walter Donohue had told me of a lively phone chat with Harmony about his trip to Copenhagen, and the Brothers' response to his *Julien Donkey-Boy*, as it's now known. Trier, it seems, held up his hands and said, 'My God, you've made the perfect Dogme film. We're going to have to write new rules. And can you help me with my musical?' Or something like that. Meanwhile, Trier has been stretched on the rumour-rack himself. It's mooted that he has demanded the withdrawal of all extant prints of *The Idiots*, apparently because they were regraded by Zentropa without his knowledge, to make the image a tad less murky. Is this a case of true Puritanism? Or yet more public relations?

I can appreciate, though, that fresh stocks of novelty might be required. On my first night up in Edinburgh, I met my pal Fraser Macdonald, a young director at the National Film School in Beaconsfield, who acts as Technical Manager for the Cameo Cinema during the Festival. A staunch Alan Clarke fan, he groaned to hear of my new project, and told me that the NFTS students have since composed 'Dogme99', a manifesto committed to the maximum in cinematic opulence: every shot has to be on a crane, below-par actors should be sacked mid-take, and so on. Fraser reckons Dogme95 has quite gone the way of Monty Python's dead parrot – it's a Danish Blue, if you please. 'It is deceased,' he roars, 'it is no more. This is an ex-manifesto.'

All in all, and more than ever, I'm sure that I will have to compare the lies to find the truth in this strange case. Thankfully, I have an expert witness at hand. Søren Kragh-Jacobsen is in town, to present a screening of *Mifune* and submit to an audience Q&A, which I'm to compère.

He looks like a great Dane: fiftyish, close sandy curls, a good blue suit, striking eyes and an affable, rascally manner. My notes tell me that he was formerly a recording artist, a singer-songwriter-balladeer of considerable fame in Denmark. At the bar beforehand, we chit-chat about recent events: he's not wild about *Lovers*, and curious about Harmony Korine's endeavours. I'm in the slightly ticklish position of having to watch the film for the first time immediately prior to standing up on stage with Søren and asking him about it. But I'm spared any insincerity, because it's terrific. It *is* another genre film, though: a very simple, romantic, Scandinavian town 'n' country comedy.

Kresten (Anders Berthelsen) is an upwardly mobile bloke-about-Copenhagen who's married the boss's daughter. On his wedding night, he gets a call from his family home in rural Lolland: his father is dead. Having convinced his new family that he has no relatives, he must lie his pants off to sneak away. At his dad's dilapidated farmhouse, he finds his childlike elder brother Rud (Jesper Asholt), alone and quite helpless. Kresten has only a few tricks up his sleeve to pacify Rud; one (fabulously unlikely and funny) is to mimic Toshiro Mifune's irascible, belly-scratching belligerence in *The Seven Samurai*. Not such a bad sort, albeit a tremendous liar, Kresten improvises a way to protect his lifestyle and care for Rud. He advertises for a housekeeper, and gets Liva (Iben Hjelje), a Copenhagen hooker who's fleeing both a rough pimp and an obscene phone caller. The job is less than Liva hoped, and more than she bargained for; but there are consolations, and these are semaphored to the viewer the first time she gets a peek at Kresten's muscled shoulders.

The film (and it *is* film: 16-mm blown-up) fairly clips along. As in *Festen*, there's that good unhinged quality to the acting; but here it's more appropriate to the broad comedic set-pieces. Anders Berthelsen is handsome, likeable, a tremendous physical comedian whether mimicking Mifune or an enormous ostrich. Iben Hjelje is a real charmer, with good humour around her eyes and smoke in her voice. She plays bemusement, desire and hurt with equal aplomb. (Small wonder Stephen Frears has cast her alongside John Cusack in his filming of *High Fidelity*.) Further down the cast, there's Paprika Steen again, as one of Liva's frolicking prostitute-pals. And a dirty vicar is played by Klaus Bondam, who was *Festen's* toastmaster: clearly a specialist in officious idiots. You can see Søren is more of an old-school director. It's in the way he shoots Kresten moodily savouring a cigarette, smoke trailing over his face, as it so often doesn't in real life. There's a lot of music in the movie, clearly a passion of Søren's. In particular, one comic sequence involving a burst of Spanish guitar does the heart a power of good. But we hear non-diegetic music too, and Dogmatically one has to wonder whence that's coming?

Mifune affirms the benefit of real locations. Without the Rules, you suspect Søren might have shot it in a Copenhagen suburb. Instead you feel you're seeing the Danish sticks. But I get to wondering about what kind of real-life town and country divide Denmark is lumbered with. Certainly life in Lolland is made to seem fairly intolerable without booze, classy Copenhagen blondes, and a sack of scratch-card cash. The word 'redneck' is bandied about very freely in the subtitles; not necessarily with malice. But still . . . And there's a fair bit of doggishness about women. It's not a crude film, yet somehow the girls are all defined by their tits and arses. The way Kresten and Liva start to dig each other is nicely played, the way she inclines her head to his shoulder, the first casual kiss. But shortly after, drunkenly, he more or less rapes her. And, in effect, she's not much more than miffed about it. They have a very generic tiff as they whitewash an outer wall, redeemed by the big laughs of her emptying the paint-pot over him. But finally, what makes everything all right is that he takes a beating while saving her from, yes, a gaggle of redneck rapists. She tends his wounds then rewards him with a real shag, which is always the very thing you want after you've taken a kicking. And yet, and yet . . . the ending seems cheerfully and charmingly to admit all such contrivance.

In the Q&A, Søren performs brilliantly. He holds up his hands and admits that his recent films, such as *The Island on Bird Street*, turned out as stodgy Euro-puddings; but *Mifune* put a spring back in his step. He grins as he confesses that he just wanted to spend a summer among beautiful actresses (like Paprika, apparently the mascot of the Dogme movement). He owns up to some code violations: OK, so he pruned some overgrown bushes around the farm to ease the camera's passage, and he borrowed a couple of chickens from a neighbouring farm, as set dressing. But the audience have been roundly entertained, and show no apparent urge to take such a genial fellow to task.

Faber and Faber, London wc1: Friday, 8 October 1999

The Dogme website posts a press release from the Brotherhood, emanating from somewhere called Hornbæk, and confronting the gossip over Harmony's film: 'To the best of our knowledge, *Julien Donkey-Boy* does, indeed, observe the Dogme criteria to a satisfactory extent. Our judgement is based on an actual review of the film as well as an interview with the director.' But then comes the kicker: 'Considering the fact that there are numerous practical problems connected with our review of aspiring Dogme films, we have decided on a change of practice when issuing Dogme certificates. In future the director himself is solemnly to declare his adherence to the Dogme95 Manifesto. As a personal signature on the Dogme certificate would be inconsistent with the rule that directors not be credited, certificates will be issued by us the moment a signed, sworn statement from the director is in our hands. For this purpose a Dogme secretariat will be established.'

As the cause of such deliberation and consternation, Harmony must be tickled. I chat with his friend Oren Moverman, screenwriter and editor-at-large for Faber. He says that Harmony fairly bristles with Dogme gags, not least in relation to the tortuous labelling system. The first UK Dogme film, he feels, should be shot in London and called 'Fogme'. *Lovers* is self-evidently 'Frogme'. And naturally, given his penchant for the more *outré* personages of the rap world, Harmony fancies that *Julien* should henceforth be tagged as 'Snoop Doggy Dogme'.

Meanwhile, our Dogme documentary is a go: the Independent Film Channel and FilmFour have thrown down the needful dollars. So, to the slippery business of scheduling the needful interviews. Jean-Marc Barr calls from Illinois, where he's already on to his next picture, *Too Much Flesh*. He seems truly enthused about his Dogme experience, even if few conspicuous others are. Lars Bredo Rahbek of Nimbus Film is able to vouch for Søren and Thomas. And Lene Neergarb of Zentropa calls to say Trier too is up for it, though he's very busy finishing his new musical: the $15-million *Dancer in the Dark* ('a big film, a musical melodrama colliding with real life', Lars has claimed). It stars Bjørk as Selma, a Czech immigrant, single mother and factory worker in rural America. Her passion is the classic Hollywood musical. Her secret is that she's losing her sight, and her ten-year-old son will suffer likewise unless she can raise money for an operation. So *that* all makes sense. The film has been shooting since May, first on locations in Sweden, now in Zentropa's new studio in Hvidovre. Lene says they're building 'a new Cinecittà' out there; the Nimbus team are moving in

33

too. She also tells me the place is a traffic-free fifteen-minute ride from Copenhagen airport, 'very convenient for foreign journalists'. Like all these Danish women, she has a lovely musical laugh, and I start feeling good about the project.

Not that I was ever down; but everyone needs a kick sometimes, and it can come from anywhere. Case in point: was it only a month ago I sat with my friend Kaleem in Soho's Toucan Bar, watching the England football team fumble about in front of a well-marshalled Polish defence? Result: 0–0, and the seeming collapse of Euro 2000 dreams. We traipsed down to Bar Italia, where the crowd had spilled out on to the street, yet still were glued to a tiny TV set deep within showing Denmark v. Italy. Two robust blond guys stood rocking on their heels, nursing cans of Stella Artois. We asked them the score. They were Danes, and of course their English was pristine. It was 3–2 to Denmark, a rousing fight back from a 2–0 deficit. Obscurely, this cheered me no end: I found myself clapping these blokes on the shoulder, telling them how much I loved their country. At the final whistle, Bar Italia's proprietors shut off the set smartly, and autumn descended upon London's Italian contingent. But the streets seemed suddenly to teem with euphoric Danes. A good omen?

There again, there are less happy portents. The Gate cinema in Notting Hill had invited me to lead a platform discussion after a screening of the newly released *Mifune*. And only a fortnight earlier I had passed the Screen on the Green in Islington, the marquee already promising 'THE NEW DOGMA FILM'. Now, the shooting schedule of the documentary has nixed my date with the Gate, and I call the manager, Lynn, prepared for a ticklish conversation. But she has ticklish news of her own. The Dogme event is cancelled because ticket sales for *Mifune* have been hugely disappointing. For sure, everyone who's seen it has loved it; but the numbers just don't add up. So it's been pulled early, from both the Gate and the Screen on the Green, and Wim Wenders' crowd-pleasing *Buena Vista Social Club* stuffed in its place. In relaying all this, Lynn sounds solicitous, as if she wishes to cushion a blow, and I struggle to disabuse her of the notion. After all, it's only movies. And she perks up immeasurably when I tell her that I'm off to meet M. Jean-Marc Barr.

5 Tools for intimacy:
Jean-Marc Barr & *Lovers*

Strange, the vagaries of film scheduling, that we should commence our investigation of a Danish *avant-garde* by trekking to Illinois to meet some French people. But here we are, me and my crack digital video crew: 'uncredited' director and first camera, Saul; producer Paula, doubling up somewhat tentatively on boom; and our impish guest cameraman, Saul's screenwriting partner, Jack Lothian. We fly into Chicago then promptly head out on the long, lonesome highway in a rented people-carrier, for a three-hour drive to Hoopestown, Illinois: something of a one-horse town, by reputation. Streaking past corn-fields for some hours, our only friend is AM radio; and there's little to spot outside the window, save for the pleasing green of John Deere's famous farming equipment. Finally, pulling into Hoopestown at dusk, I fear all four of us feel some scales fall from our eyes as we finally behold this weathered pocket of small-town Midwest America.

After a couple of days of motel living, I come to appreciate that certain key works by David Lynch and Stephen King are actually rock-bottom documentary realism, rather than the overheated fantasies I'd first taken them for. I also figure out at last what Springsteen's 'Born to Run' is really about. But among the locals, we generate mild perplexity rather than outright hostility. Waitresses and barkeeps offer laconic speculation about just what kind of motion picture is getting made down the road. 'Some kind of sex film' is the sage consensus. I assure them that it's an artwork, and try to forget that the scenario of *Too Much Flesh* concerns a young man (Barr) coming to terms with his possession of an uncommonly large penis, thanks to the not-disinterested solici-tude of two women (Rosanna Arquette and Elodie Bouchez, no less).

Early one morning, we zip down to neighbouring Rankin, and hook up with Barr, his collaborator Pascal Arnold, and their crew, at a makeshift production office. In truth, our crew very nearly outnum-bers theirs. *Too Much Flesh* is not bidding to be a Dogme film, but it's being shot on DV, and Saul is mildly euphoric upon discovering that our Sony PD100AP camera is a newer, more elaborate model than their Sony TRV900P. Up close to Jean-Marc, the reasons for his high standing among female film-goers are readily available to the eye. In tee-shirt and combats, ruddily tanned as if from a summer of rural toil, he's just a deeply handsome man. We head out to the fields with the team, and observe as they shoot a brief dialogue scene. Then they streak off down the dirt track, but not before Jean-Marc pledges to rendezvous with us for lunch. We go to the diner that's serving as crew canteen, and wait a couple of anxious hours. Then a bustle at the door: it's Jean-Marc, Pascal, and Elodie Bouchez. I notice first that the top button of her faded jeans is unbuttoned; then decide that I shouldn't be noticing.

RICHARD KELLY: OK, Jean-Marc: you and Pascal are out here in the Midwest, shooting a film with a video camera. How come?
JEAN-MARC BARR: Well, Rankin is where I spent my summers as a boy. It's changed a lot since, just because the farming industry's changed, and taken away the individual farmer. So this kind of town won't exist in ten, fifteen years . . . But what really brought us here was the experience we had making *Lovers*, shooting with a Sony digital video camera under the principles of Dogme95. It gave us the feeling that we were enjoying the same kind of freedom that somebody like Mack Sennett had, back in the early days of cinema.

RK: Like with the Keystone Cops?
J-MB: Sure. Because those guys just went out and shot it, you know? Simple as that. So Pascal and I had the idea of doing a trilogy of films on the theme of freedom. *Lovers* is about the freedom to love who we want. *Too Much Flesh* is about freedom of sexuality. And after this, we'll finish the trilogy with a film called *Being Light*, about freedom of the spirit.

RK: In the case of *Lovers*, were you invited into the Dogme brotherhood? Did Lars von Trier suggest you make a Dogme film?
J-MB: No, Pascal and I were just inspired by what happened at Cannes in 1998. Suddenly you had two films in competition that were shot on digital video, and *Festen* won the Jury Prize, and all of a sudden it gave the format credibility. It felt like the *nouvelle vague*, when the shoulder-mounted 16-mm cameras came along and put production in the hands of the directors themselves. I think that Lars, by using this digital technology, put himself in that same position. And with *Lovers*, we wanted to try the same: to do what we want, and not just follow the same rules and marketing systems that have defined the cinema for the last twenty or thirty years.

RK: Clearly, you and Lars are close comrades, you've had several adventures with him as an actor: *Europa*, *Breaking the Waves* . . .

J-MB: Right. And I've just played a part in *Dancer in the Dark*. Then there's *Dimension*, which is a film we're shooting for two minutes a year, over the next thirty years. I mean, Lars has always thrown me on my ass. (*Smiles.*)

RK: If you believe the press cuttings, he's this obsessional creature of cinema. And people used to say films like *Europa* were amazing to look at, but cold, impersonal.

J-MB: Well, in many ways it's true that Lars hid himself behind the technology. And in the end I think he learned a lesson, and he made the big skip. First with *The Kingdom*, then with *Breaking the Waves*. And then by going even further with *The Idiots*, destroying the usual conventions, almost destroying the image, you could say. From someone who's made films like *Europa* and *The Element of Crime*, I found that incredibly courageous. I mean, *The Idiots* still has a real 'Lars von Trier' ending to it . . . But he let himself go, he took a risk. Sometimes the shot is out of focus, or you see the boom in full frame. But I think something Lars really wanted to stress in Dogme is that you shouldn't care so much about making mistakes; but try to find yourself in your mistakes. With Dogme you have to deal with a lot of imperfections, but the Rules also allow you to find inspiration in those areas. You're at liberty not to care; to look for what's human instead.

RK: So, clearly, you saw aesthetic freedoms in Dogme. Did you feel there would be budgetary freedoms too, shooting this way?

J-MB: Pascal and I had been collaborating for five years, writing scripts and trying to raise money. If we'd shot *Lovers* on film in the standard way, it would have taken maybe two and a half months and cost about five million dollars. But shooting digital, we found we could reduce the budget to one-fifth, one-sixth of the normal film. That was a big deal. We felt we could work freely in the knowledge that we weren't risking our necks if it didn't work out. Whereas a lot of first-time film-makers today get their five-million-dollar budget, knowing that if it doesn't work out then they've got to go and work at McDonald's. And that pressure puts them in a very stressful, uncreative situation. As it was, Pascal and I had the idea for *Lovers* in July 1998. We wrote it in September–October, and we got it financed in ten days. We shot it 25 November to 22 December, and we finished editing after four or five weeks. So, in all, it took us about seven months. And in all that time, not one studio or television company told us what to write, or how to shoot, which made a real change from what we'd been doing before on bigger projects.

RK: Which doors did you knock on to get _Lovers_ off the ground?

J-MB: We live in Paris, but our whole concept was to do European films in English for a world market, as Lars has done. So we went to the director of Canal Plus, Pierre Lescure, and said we need _this_ amount of money. And we went to TF1 International and saw a woman called Perrine Teze, and told her we need _this_ amount of money. And in both cases we said, 'This is not a big investment for you to make a film you'll be able to sell abroad.'

RK: So there was a degree of commercial calculation in having your lead characters speaking English?

J-MB: Of course. I mean, I'm not really French, I'm a product of World War Two. My parents met in England after the war, he was in the US Air Force, she was a French nurse, and I was born in Germany. I'm Euro-trash basically (_smiles_) because I really am not of one culture. But I can identify myself with the rest of the world. Pascal feels the same. Europe is basically defined in commercial terms these days, but we believe in a Europe that exists as an entity, creatively and culturally. The American presence in Europe has been evident, but it's had some positive effects. For instance, people, especially Elodie's and Sergei's generation, speak English – or 'American', let's say – much better than our generation. And I think European cinema will find itself in shared communication in English because it will also be able to profit by the potential of technicians from Poland, from Copenhagen, from Spain, Italy, France, England, Scotland . . . I think the combined potential of all of those cultures is something that the United States does not have. And in terms of storytelling and acting and technical knowledge, European cinema can offer a real alternative to what's happening here in the States, where cinema is nothing much but an industry.

RK: The dismemberment of Yugoslavia has been all over European movies in recent years. Why is your leading man – Dragan – Yugoslav?

J-MB: Well, you always write from what's close to you, and I have for-tunately been with a Yugoslav woman for the last fifteen, sixteen years. But Dragan's story is a story that's common. He hasn't fought in the Balkan war, but he's a victim of it, and so are the people around him, the other refugees in France. Nine years ago you could go anywhere with a Yugoslav passport. Now you can't leave the country, you're almost a prisoner. And if you get out, you have to hide. There's constantly that feeling of separation in Europe. World War Two's been over for fifty years now, but the aftermath is still lingering. But I think people, especially the younger generations, have had it with the nationalism that has plagued this whole century. If we do find some kind of unity and shared identification it will be through, hopefully, culture. With *Lovers*, we want to say that we believe in, and we have a desire for, Europe; and it is a possibility.

RK: Jeanne puts it very nicely in the film: 'When I fall in love, I don't ask for ID.' But then, Rule Eight of the Vow of Chastity forbids 'genre films'. Your film has a generic title. And it's a 'boy meets girl' story, if you had to write a one-line pitch.
J-MB: Sure. But we would say it's a love story that's so intimate that it hasn't been filmed like that before.

RK: I like the fact that it's a love story in which all the material routines of a relationship are shown, and given their proper importance. We understand that Jeanne and Dragan have figured out the lovemaking thing. But then there's the key question of who's going to vacuum the carpet?
J-MB: Well, you know, for many people, myself included, love is constantly trying to solve problems. And those problems arise daily – hourly, even. And if you come from different cultures or you've been raised differently, they become enormous, just because of misunderstandings.

RK: As when Dragan tells Jeanne that he refuses to live like a 'capitalist hermit'?
J-MB: Exactly. He leaves all the lights on and doesn't think about who'll pay the bills. But the way those problems are resolved is love; because you only resolve them if you really want to.

RK: Directing for the first time, did you take any lessons from your experiences with Lars?
J-MB: Lars works regular hours. So that's what we did for *Lovers*. We never took overtime, we never took ourselves too seriously and we tried to have a good time. Sometimes when you're making seventy-million-dollar pictures about killing a monster, it's so serious and yet so ridiculous that you really can't find the fun any more. As an actor

it's very difficult if you have to wait six hours to do one shot, and then another three hours for the next. But with DV, instead of shooting one sequence a day at the most, we could shoot four or five. So it really is concentrated work. Also you're very mobile; instead of having thirty people on set, you have seven on the crew. At first we hired a camera operator, but two weeks before we actually started shooting, we realized we would be trying to explain to the operator what we could maybe do ourselves. So Pascal told me to hold the camera myself, and I did, just as these gentlemen are holding them now (*gestures to Saul and Jack*). And the camera really becomes your eye. It brings a new dynamic, and, I think, a kind of humanity to what you're doing. I mean, this is a great tool for intimacy.

RK: How did you bear up under the constraints of the Rules?
J-MB: Well – we took Dogme as being a chance to get the film done, OK? When we found the apartment for Jeanne, it didn't exist quite as you see it in the film. We created it; and that's not really Dogme. Then we didn't know how much light this camera could go by, so we put a lot of lamps around the place and tried to make it as clear as possible. When we were shooting exteriors, the streets were very well lit, but when we were on the Pont d'Hasard which crosses the Seine, we used a little portable fluorescent light – we called it the 'Luke Skywalker' – to shine on one scene. So we broke the rules there. And sometimes we linked sounds from one scene to the next. In a pure Dogme film like *The Idiots*, if there's music going on then it jumps between cuts, because the takes don't have the same timing. But sometimes we kind of arranged the timing of our cuts against music.

RK: As in the singing to guitar during the drinking party?
J-MB: Exactly. But then, once we finished the film, the hardest thing to deal with was trying to get by the Dogme police, and see if the film could pass. We had to write a letter of confession, and the four Brothers watched the film and made their criticisms. They allowed us three or four 'sins'. For example, we had done the credits very quickly in post, because we wanted to be ready for Cannes. But anything that's added after the fact isn't Dogme at all, so we had to redo the credit sequence later on.

RK: Do you credit yourself as director?
J-MB: No, just for holding the camera. Pascal and I had thought that

Rule was a little bit bourgeois, not putting the director's credit up there. But Lars wouldn't let us get away with it. I mean, it was a process that we found a little bit fascistic. (*Smiles.*) But Lars is a purist, and I respect that. And he was very happy with the film, he actually liked it.

RK: Were you satisfied with the quality of the final image?
J-MB: I think we got a very good picture. The kinescoping, the transfer from digital to 35 mm, was done by a company called Swiss-Effect, and they're in the middle of their own revolution, which is very exciting. Last year we were told they would take three months to do the job. Now they can do it in three weeks. Every month, things are changing. On laptop computers now, they've got programmes so you can make a *Star Wars* film at home.

RK: Well, the Dogme Manifesto does suggest that there's a revolution going on, a digital revolution.
J-MB: Right now, it's an alternative. Maybe in five or ten years, we'll see that it's been a revolution that's changed the system, like sound changed the movie business in the 1920s, like colour changed it somewhat in the 1950s. Or like the sampler changed things thirty years ago for musicians. It could also be dangerous for the profession, it could take a lot of jobs away: the studios might not be able to afford that big payroll any more. But I don't think DVC will replace the beautiful image you can get with a lit 35-mm film; it just creates the possibility of more production, more communication. And we need change. For so long, the industry defined what the markets were, where profits could be made. Then all of a sudden, *The Blair Witch Project*, this film shot on digital video, made more money than the big studio films.

RK: So now the executives are running to the hills, terrified that they really have no idea what the kids want?
J-MB: Oh, I doubt they're running in terror. What they're going to try and find, and I'm sure they will find, is a way to control that low-budget digital-video market too.

RK: The depiction of penetrative sex has really broken out in European cinema over the last couple of years. But your film is rather chaste, and touchingly so.
J-MB: It was important for Pascal and I that kids in their teens could watch this movie and understand it. I think that for the younger generations, sex now lacks the big romantic qualities we gave it in our

generation. That's partly because of AIDS, but also because they have more access to porno films and MTV, which show you everything, and yet are everything *but*. I love old movies by Lubitsch and Billy Wilder; films like *Ninotchka* that were so sexual, without showing you so much as a kiss. *Lovers* was a little bit inspired by that kind of ethic. *Too Much Flesh* is something else. We're not going to show lovemaking, but it's a film about desire, about someone who hasn't been able to make love and suddenly discovers what those sensations are, the beauty and the fullness of what sexuality is about.

RK: Of course, Dogme95 has acquired a bit of a reputation for scandal. In the movies so far, you've got incestuous rape, you've got people impersonating spastics, prostitutes urinating on parquet floors. Do you worry that people will come to *Lovers* expecting a more explicit film than the one you've made?
J-MB: What we wanted to make was a film that would touch people, and have an emotional intimacy that the previous technology didn't have. We wanted to be able to tell a story where anyone who's fallen in love would be able to identify with what's going on. That's what we did, and we're incredibly proud. I mean, it's been a long time since I've been so content with the work going on in my life.

RK: And if *Lovers* is bashed by critics, those critics can always go and make a Dogme film themselves?
J-MB: Well, the thing about critics . . . I mean, everyone needs a job, you know?

RK: I ask because the Manifesto says that this 'technological storm' will 'democratize' film-making: anyone can make a movie.
J-MB: I don't think everyone can do it. You need a love for cinema, and a sensitivity to it. And you still have to have a real discipline: it's still like preparing a regular film. But certainly for Pascal and myself, it's put us in a situation where no one's telling us what to do.

RK: And now you're carrying those lessons forward?
J-MB: Well, this film is much more difficult. We're not shooting in Paris. We're in a place where people don't necessarily understand cinema in the way we understand cinema. Pascal and I are doing eighteen-, nineteen-hour days, and just yesterday it was almost zero degrees outdoors. But then today, we have this good weather, like summer. So Pascal and Elodie and I have been out in the fields, just the

three of us, shooting things in two hours that otherwise might have taken days.

With that, they're off again. The afternoon light is fading, and Elodie is urgently needed elsewhere. We dawdle back to Hoopestown. That night, we should be curled up in our scary motel rooms, watching Harmony Korine discuss *Julien Donkey-Boy* on *Late Night with David Letterman*; but we all seem to have developed a thirst. There are only two bars to choose from, and we pick the one wherein the clientele look less inclined to haul us from our seats and set us swinging from some tree. We drink tots of bourbon chased by Lite Beer, shoot umpteen games of pool, exhaust the jukebox selection of countrified rock, and manage to make a few friends. Paula is a more impressive model of womanhood than this hostelry has seen in recent years, and Saul mounts an impressive streak on the pool-table. Across the bar, I see Jack striking up what looks to be an affable, back-slapping conversation with some good old boy. Later, he tells me that this guy is called Homer, and that his mild eyes fairly teared up with mirth as he told Jack, 'Y'know, if that woman wasn't with you guys, y'all would be dead by now.' I decide to take this in the jesting spirit that was doubtless intended, whilst retaining an easy grip on a pool cue; and so the night proceeds to get a little more lively.

6 Millennial anxieties:
D-Day, and the view from Kristian Levring's cutting-room

Berwick Street, Soho, London w1: Tuesday, 26 October 1999

Now, what fresh wheeze is this? The Dogme website proclaims that the Brothers have accepted an invitation to direct a joint television project in Copenhagen on New Year's Eve 1999. It will be broadcast simultaneously by the four national channels on 1 January 2000, and so marks the first-ever collaboration by DR-TV, TV2, TV3 and TV Danmark. Nimbus and Zentropa will co-produce, and the Danish Film Institute will also contribute. Each Brother will create a character, and jointly conceive a plot; each of the four actors will be followed by a camera crew, in live contact with their individual director. The Brothers will work from joint headquarters, a common control room; and the films will be shot in 'real time', without editing. The plan is for viewers at home to edit their own unique film by clicking between channels. 'The pressure is now on the directors' shoulders,' says Bo Damgaard, TV2's chief of programming. Bloody right. But Mr Damgaard seems sanguine and proud: 'I believe in this original gamble – a gamble which most likely could only originate in a country like ours.'

Meanwhile, the Minerva team are back out in the field, albeit on home turf, in the fashionable village of Soho: once stomping ground to the author of the most influential Manifesto yet written. Marx passed several years of ceaseless misery in rooms over Dean Street, and would later admit to shivers down the spine whenever he revisited its environs. I know something of how he felt. Now Soho reckons itself as the hub of the British film industry, as may be discerned on the streets by the sheer numbers of cancerous cell-phones, lunatic motorbike messengers, and drones in coffee bars developing scripts over tall *lattes*.

A week earlier, Paula had a lively conversation with Kristian Levring. He's in the editing room, chiselling away on *The King is Alive*, and reckons on another six to eight weeks before he'll have a cut. He 'still doesn't know what he's got'; but the mood is positive. Today we go knocking, and Kristian graciously shows us a tantalizing reel of scenes on the Avid. Shot on DV, the Namibian desert looks magnificent and the cast (including Romane Bohringer, Bruce Davison and the late Brion James) look to have risen to the challenge of the material with great aplomb. We get to work. Kristian looked a little bemused at my choice of headgear: a woollen cap embossed with the legend 'Newcastle: Toon Army'. I explain that, as a crew, we've made a dogmatic vow of our own: to wear amusing hats wherever we shoot. Saul (Arsenal), Paula (West Ham) and Jack (Spurs) nod their heads in a show of purposeful concert. Levring smiles politely, like a man who's heard weirder things among the English.

RICHARD KELLY: OK, Kristian: legend has it that Lars von Trier and Thomas Vinterberg got drunk and angry one night and drew up this Manifesto. Where did you enter the frame?
KRISTIAN LEVRING: Let me remember this right. I was living in Paris. And a call came, 'out of the blue', as you say, from Thomas, asking me to join in.

RK: Was Thomas already a pal of yours?
KL: No, he's a bit younger than the rest of us. But I went to the Danish Film School the year after Lars, and I knew Søren from back when I

started in the business as a runner. Also, you know that originally there was a girl in the Brotherhood, Anne Wivel? 'Brother Anne'? (*Smiles.*) People say Dogme is a man's club, but originally we were five, and she was in there for quite some time. She'd made a lot of documentaries, and I don't think she wanted to do fiction, so at a certain point she left. But she's still a friend of all of us.

RK: This may be the first 'new wave' to have sprung up almost wholly from one film school. Was that schooling formative for you?
KL: For all of us. The teaching is good, the amount of money you're given to do stuff is great. But I think the best students always set themselves against the school – that's how it must be. It's also about a meeting of minds: the school bred strong relationships, the classes were pretty small. It's bigger now, more pupils, and I'm not sure if it's quite as élitist as it was. But it enables you to start a dialogue about film when you're twenty-three, and that dialogue becomes a constant part of your life.

RK: Was there a certain kind of ethos or method being taught?
KL: Mogens Rukov made us watch some great films, and our discussions were very passionate. When I think of Mogens, I think of two directors, who are like opposite poles in cinema: Cassavetes and Visconti. I remember so clearly Mogens' passion for *The Leopard*, and for *The Killing of a Chinese Bookie*, which we saw about ten times. I mean, in Lars's films, there are references, even lines, from *Chinese Bookie*. But then it's great to quote your masters . . .

RK: How about Godard? Was he influential?
KL: Oh, you cannot be a film-maker and not have a big, big respect for Godard. And for me, *A Bout de Souffle, Pierrot Le Fou, Two or Three Things I Know About Her* are wonderful films. Then again, I'm not sure if Godard is more a theoretician than a film-maker. But his influence on other film-makers is enormous. In many ways, he's the Cézanne of film-makers. And of course, when you talk about Dogme, he should be President, you know? (*Laughs.*) I mean, look at *A Bout de Souffle*, made in 1959. I think that's probably the best Dogme film that could be made.

RK: I'm sure M. Godard would be delighted to hear that.
KL: I'm not so sure he would. (*Smiles.*) But I still admire that film. And then look at *Festen* and *The Idiots*, made forty years later. It's like, 'Did

nothing happen in between? How did it take so long?'. Because it's all in there – the hand-held camera, the jump-cuts, the direct sound. It's not exactly similar, of course. But it's amazing to hear people now discussing hand-held camera as some kind of novelty, forty years after Godard.

RK: How did your career develop after the Film School?
KL: Well, after I graduated, I made a film (*A Shot from the Heart*) that wasn't very good – because I compromised. After that, I did commercials for fifteen years, all over the world.

RK: What kind of commercials? Big, glossy numbers?
KL: No, I'm not especially good at that stuff. Mine had characters and situations and dialogue – often quite black in their humour. And I learned so much. So many directors don't spend enough time actually *shooting*, I think. But for fifteen years I spent seventy or eighty days a year with a camera. And in that time you lose your fear of the camera, the awe you might have for it; you learn that the camera is actually your ally.

RK: In those fifteen years, were you keen to make another feature?
KL: Well, I was invited to Hollywood to meet producers, and asked to do action films and so forth. But I was happier to bide my time and wait for the right moment to do something personal. People have asked me, 'Aren't you scared of following the first three Dogme films?' No, because they gave me a wonderful opportunity to do the kind of film I dearly wanted to make even before I went to film school. I was very passionate about all the great films of the 1970s: Italian films, Fellini, Herzog, *The Enigma of Kasper Hauser*. But then I lost a bit of faith over the years. That kind of strength disappeared a bit. In the 1990s it seems very difficult to do films that are actually *about* something. So I felt Dogme was a possible way of doing that.

RK: Presumably Lars and Thomas were aware of this desire in you when they invited you.
KL: They must have been. The way they put it was, 'We want to see you do a *film*.'

RK: Thomas said that he agreed to make a Dogme film, then had to go away and come up with an idea. Are there certain kinds of scripts that suit the Dogme Rules, or do the Dogme Rules beget certain kinds of scripts? What was the genesis of yours?

KL: Oh, there are loads of films you can't do with the Rules, and I started working on a different script that I realized would be too much of a hurdle. But then I have an English friend who lives in the Mojave Desert, outside California, in a small village of two hundred people. And whenever he gets a little homesick, he arranges Shakespeare evenings. He'll get Chuck, the man who runs the gas station, to be Hamlet, and Liz from the diner to be Ophelia, and they'll just sit and read the play. It struck me as very funny, and at first I considered making a documentary about it. But, instead . . .

RK: You made a fiction. And you co-wrote *The King is Alive* with Anders Thomas Jensen, who also co-wrote *Mifune*?
KL: Yes. He's a young, very bright man. He holds something of a record in the Oscars, because he was nominated three times in a row for Best Short Film, when he was twenty-six, twenty-seven, and twenty-eight. After the first one, he joked with me, 'Now I know how to design an Oscar-nominated film.' And after the second, he told me, 'I think I've figured out how to make a winner.' And then he did it. Very impressive. And I think that says as much about the Oscars as it does about Anders Thomas.

RK: How did you two get together?
KL: I invited him. I had written a synopsis, about people stranded in a desert town, but it didn't tell the story so much as the theme. Then I wrote about fifty character sketches, a page of A4 for each, and I said to Anders Thomas, 'These are the people we should work with.' Then we spent a fortnight deciding who we should put on this bus. It became a puzzle. And the story-line wasn't there yet, but we started thinking, 'If we put this character on, then this other one would make an interesting match.' There was a mirror idea going on, for instance between the two Englishmen, Henry and Charles, and the Frenchwoman Catherine. They each set themselves outside the group, at first. And Charles and Catherine end up paying a very great price for that. Henry too is a cynical soul, and initially he keeps a distance, calls the others 'arseholes'. But like Catherine, he has the passion for culture, for literature, the word. Unlike Catherine, that sucks him into the group.

RK: *King Lear* is widely considered the most 'modern' of Shakespeare's great tragedies – in its absurdity, its savagery. Was that why you set it at the heart of this story?

KL: Yeah. Though at the outset I'd considered *Hamlet*. I'm Danish so
... (*Smiles.*) And before that, I'd thought of Beckett's *Endgame*, partly
because it's *Lear* paraphrased. But in the end, *Lear* was right. As you
say, it's probably the first Absurd drama. It's about a man being
stripped of everything, which is parallel to our story. And, really, it's
more Henry's choice than mine. He's at that age. Lear is the role every
actor wants to play. Also, in his sarcastic way, he can see the humour
of staging *Lear* in this place.

RK: I notice there are no Danes on this bus ...
KL: No. I wrote some Danish characters, some Germans too, but they
didn't make the final cut of twelve characters. It was obvious that certain English characters would be needed, because of Shakespeare. And
I wanted some Americans on board because, in my opinion, it's quite
funny when Americans say these words. Then you get an English
actress, Janet McTeer, playing an American reading Shakespeare
badly, which is funnier still ...

**RK: Critics have detected a strong attack on bourgeois manners and
mores in the Dogme films to date. Now you're taking a bunch of
middle-class cultural tourists and sending them to their deaths ...**
KL: Well, these characters are people who haven't ended up where
they dreamed they would in this life. It's a film about what happens to
people when they start acting; when they start thinking about who
they are, and where they are. And – this is pretentious – but in a way,
this ordeal is a form of cure: for some of them, not all. Part of that cure
is that they 'get' *King Lear*, you know? They start to hear these words,
and understand them. Perhaps they can return to their normal lives
and live them slightly differently.

RK: At what point did you make the choice to shoot on DVC?
KL: Quite early. I was just fascinated by the fact that I could shoot so
much, and with three lightweight cameras.

**RK: Presumably *The Idiots* and *Festen* had convinced you that this
format could be visually compelling?**
KL: Specifically *Festen*, I think. It's a very visual film, although it's shot
on hand-held video. It's very well framed: it has images where you feel
that something is there, and something is left out, you know? And
that's the true quality of an image: something's there and something's
left out.

RK: Now, Dogme Rule#1 demands that all shooting be done on location: good for credibility. But on paper, it looks like you made a rod for your own back by choosing Kolmanskop in Namibia. It's considered to be something of a 'ghost town' since the diamond mining industry moved out.

KL: Well, I was looking for a location before I finished the script. I went to Chile, to Mexico. But then I heard of Kolmanskop, and I went there in October 1998 after the first draft. I had to check out what props would be around, because of course the Rules say you can't bring them with you. But I found it was the perfect place for shooting a Dogme film. So many of the things we needed were already there. There are two parts to the town. One part is where the engineers and the architects lived in their wonderful big houses. They had a wonderful theatre, and of course it occurred to me to set the play there, but it was too obvious. Then there's the other side of town, with eighty or ninety houses where the workers lived, and it looks rather more like a concentration camp, or a stage-set out of Beckett – like *Endgame*, you know? You have these plain dwellings, just like houses in Scandinavia or Northern Germany, but just full of sand. Perfect. So we decided to use only that part; that's why we took no real wide shots of the town, because it's much bigger than it's meant to appear, and not nearly so far from civilization. There is a museum there, they get a lot of tourists, so we had to pay rent on the place. After that, we did two more drafts of the script, adjusting it to the location.

RK: When you finished your script, did you show it to the other Brothers?

KL: Sure, and that's one of the fun things about Dogme for the four of us. Usually, as a director, you're on your own. The fact that fellow directors will read your script and look at your edit and really help you – it makes you feel like we're in the same boat.

RK: You assembled quite a remarkable cast for this film. How did Janet McTeer join the company?

KL: Well, five days before we were due to leave for Namibia, I still hadn't managed to cast that part. Then suddenly the casting director said, 'We're sending you a tape of Janet McTeer, she really liked your script.' Being the ignorant Dane that I am, I'd never heard of her. I say, 'OK, fine.' Then I got this incredibly impressive tape.

RK: Then you've got Jennifer Jason Leigh, who's always seemed to have a taste for the dark stuff in her material.

KL: I've always admired her. And the American casting director told me early on, 'Jennifer likes the script and wants to be in your film.' Yet the way Gina was described, it wasn't obvious to cast Jennifer. Gina was younger than Catherine, and I wanted that disparity. But I went to see her in Los Angeles, and very fast we realized we could make changes. So I reversed the ages, which was less obvious, but actually rather more interesting.

RK: So you brought your cast and crew out to this perfect place. How did they deal with it? It looks kind of lonely out there.

KL: Some of the actors were a bit frightened of going there. 'Oh, Africa! Are we going to get diseases?' But I think for everybody it was an adventure. And we lived in a very comfortable hotel about five kilometres from the location. What better can you get, you know?

RK: But given the darkness of the themes in the piece, I wonder if that didn't sometimes spill over into the evenings after shooting?

KL: Well . . . the film grew darker than the script had been. The script has more obvious black jokes. But we shot in sequence, and we realized as we went along, the actors and myself, that as the situation gets increasingly grave for these people, there was a point when it couldn't be 'funny' any more. So certain lines were cut, or said a little bit differently than I'd envisaged.

RK: Presumably shooting in chronology was a realistic device?

KL: We couldn't really do anything else. There's no make-up in Dogme, yet this is about people stranded in the desert. So the actors got more and more tanned, the men grew beards. Many of them lost a lot of weight. They were very impressive.

RK: Certainly in what you showed us, the actors look impressively sun-baked and half-deranged.

KL: Yeah, and what you saw was only about a third of the way into it. They get much worse. (*Laughs.*)

RK: Did you feel guilty asking these brilliant, trained performers to act Shakespeare 'astonishingly badly', as the script says?

KL: No, that was actually very, very amusing. (*Smiles.*) They did complain now and then that I was destroying their careers. But it made us laugh a lot. And over the course of the film, they do get better. They never get, like, fantastic; that wouldn't be very credible. But they do improve, and so you see and hear *Lear* in different ways of acting it.

RK: It imparts a fineness to the characters, too, when you hear this magnificent language coming out of their wretched mouths.
KL: Yeah. We chose lines from the play that somehow reflected the characters.

RK: Were you wary of how the actors would respond to a camera the size of your fist, rather than the traditional apparatus?
KL: I was, but to my big surprise they loved it. One reason why I wanted to shoot three cameras was so that they didn't really know which camera they were on. We made up rules that the camera should never come between them: so they could always see each other. It became more like on a stage; and I honestly think that it adds to the performances. We shot like the way you're shooting now. There's no lighting, so the actual set-up of the scene is very, very fast. That makes it possible to concentrate on the essence of the scene; instead of spending 90 per cent of your time working at peripheral things, so that when you're finally ready to shoot, the energy has disappeared. So we were able to reshoot a lot of scenes, just going on and on until we had it.

Also, as we went along, whenever we had a problem with the definition of a character, we would do improvisations, which I really liked. We didn't use them in the film itself, but we taped them and watched them for guidance.

RK: Of course, shooting digital you doom yourself to a long edit.
KL: Of course. I came home with one hundred and fifty hours of material. You just can't sit down and watch six hours every night, or you won't sleep; and you *have* to sleep. But, on the other hand, shooting is so much cheaper. You win some, you lose some.

RK: Which Rule caused you the biggest headache out there?
KL: You can only use the sound you can get, right? But we were shooting in a windy desert. Every day we'd wake up and think 'Oh, it's calm, we can do an outdoors scene' or 'It's windy. Interiors today.' But the crew were good, resourceful. We made wind-screens out of blankets and so on.

RK: On Dogme's website the directors must confess to the Rules

they violated. Are you contemplating your own statement yet?

KL: Of course I am. (*Smiles.*) I think one of the Rules that I find very, very difficult is that the film must have no 'aesthetics'. If I tell the DP I want a close-up, that's taste. That's how I want to see it. If I frame it like this or like that, that's an aesthetic choice. When you write a script, every line in there is taste. And I think it's a very difficult habit of thought to free oneself of.

RK: Rule eight forbids genre films. But your film, about a group of individuals falling apart under adversity, is also like the classic disaster-movie plot: like *The Poseidon Adventure*, or *The Towering Inferno*. Did you worry that you were telling a familiar story?

KL: Well, I was thinking more of some of Altman's films that I really admire. My film is an ensemble film, as is *Festen*, as is *The Idiots*; and you can say that's a genre. In a way, all the Dogme films are genre films: *Festen* is a family tragedy. Maybe *The Idiots* is the purest Dogme film. But it gets very complicated. I think the Rule is meant to stop you from making a western, or a *film noir*, or a science fiction. Also, you shouldn't make characters so 'stock' that genre takes over the story. It was very important to me also that my Dogme film wasn't like Lars's or Thomas's or Søren's. Otherwise there's a danger that Dogme becomes a genre in itself. That would be the end of it, to me.

RK: Some critics say Dogme is primarily a marketing tactic: a label is stamped on the movies, they go round the world, which is very fortunate for Danish cinema. But cynics do think that the films get made for that reason, that the Dogme stamp legitimizes them. Your script is so bizarre in its conception, do you think it could have got made without the Dogme stamp?

KL: Well, I do also believe that one reason why Dogme has been such a success is because the films are actually good. If they'd been bad, it would just have been this little Danish thing that nobody ever heard about. But I think it was easier to make this film because of Dogme, no doubt about it. And I agree with the critics, I can understand their point of view. I think all four of us agree that Dogme has got too commercial. But Dogme is democratic, it's not some fascist control thing. So people can do with it what they want; it's really out of our hands. I read the trades, I hear stories that worry me: about producers who don't care about Dogme, they just want to write 'Dogme' on the film. And that's very wrong. I feel that the whole thing from the beginning was to get back to the *auteur* thinking. I believe that film is the director's medium. I'm biased of course, but I do believe that the interest of a film is in that fact. I mean, the films I love were made by directors, not by producers.

RK: And producers have their own rules for what films should be.

KL: Right. One thing you realize in making commercials is that, whether you're shooting in Los Angeles or New York or London or Paris or Copenhagen or Moscow, you all shoot the same way. There are also rules of shooting mainstream films. Like 'one page of script is one minute of screen time'. That's a producer-based rule, because it's very easy to make a budget. So everything is made standardized, because what is standard is also very controllable. There are rules for lighting: 'OK, let's have light coming in through the window and perhaps a little bit of smoke.' There are standard ways of storytelling, standard ways of ending a film, standard ways of scoring a film. Every time an emotion is played on screen, you know that, within a matter of seconds, the violins will come in. I'm so glad that Dogme denies you music, because I think a lot of audiences are fed up with being told how to feel, and where to feel it, by the score. Thomas has said that if he'd made *Festen* under normal conditions he'd have put music all over it; and the film would have lost something by that. I mean, manipulation can be wonderful. I love Hitchcock. It's just no one has done it better than he did. So why not try to do it differently?

RK: This New Year's Eve project that's just been announced. Who came up with the idea?

KL: It happened in bits and pieces, really. It first came up over dinner at Lars's house. Thomas was asked to do a film about Denmark, and he came to us and said, 'You have to help me.' But then I think we all drank too much red wine . . .

RK: There seems to be a common link in how Dogme projects get started: too much red wine.

KL: Well, Dogme is very serious, but you must also remember that humour is a big part of it.

RK: Do you hang out together much, as a foursome?

KL: Well, we just spent three days in Denmark in the same house, writing the script for this project. But on this occasion we had to come up with something, which is not so pleasant.

RK: Is there a team leader amongst you, one who cracks the whip? Or one who's especially disruptive and mischievous?

KL: Often it seems to end up with Lars and Søren in each one's camp, and Thomas and me in the middle. But that's just funny, and natural. Of course we are four very different people.

RK: Do you find you hear a lot of rubbish talked about Dogme?

KL: I think it's amusing that so many people bring up the Dogme Rules and then talk as if they've never actually sat down and read them. All four of us get a lot of questions about Rules that don't exist. Just the other day I read an article in which the writer said that *Mifune* was the first Dogme film to have a certificate, his theory being that it wasn't as 'Dogme' as *Festen* and *The Idiots*, so it needed a certificate to prove it. That's just not true.

RK: Well, you see now what you guys have started. But what's the present status of the Rules and the certification process?

KL: There's been a lot of talk about Rules being modified. You cannot change the Ten Commandments. (*Smiles.*) But one thing that has changed is that Dogme has gone from Catholicism to Protestantism. Originally, the way to get the certificate was that the four of us had to view the film. Now, the director just signs a piece of paper saying, 'To my conscience, I did this film following the Dogme rules.' And then he will automatically get the certificate.

RK: Why that change?

KL: Because all these arguments about Rules get very complicated and time-consuming. For instance, you can easily shoot in slow motion without breaking the Rules. But you'll still have people saying, 'Is it Dogme?' Harmony's film looked to me like it had been shot according to the Rules. But if you really want to enforce this, you have to go on the shoot, and then you end up spending half of your life being a Dogme policeman. That's not very interesting, and it's not really what it is about. So we decided to leave it to a director's conscience – not a producer's conscience – to say, 'I stuck to the rules.'

RK: Are you worried you might tarnish the good name of Dogme95 if the certificate becomes a little easier to obtain?

KL: (*Smiles.*) We talked about that. And we agreed that we could easily stop Dogme altogether; but we felt that would be a little bit sad, you know? And also a bit unfair to other people who want to do Dogme films.

RK: You expect to finish the film for spring 2000. Do you hope to take it to Cannes, where *Festen* and *The Idiots* made such a stir?
KL: Sure. That was a very big thing for Dogme. And this kind of film often finds its audience in festivals, and it would be silly to ignore that. But Cannes decides if they want the film.

RK: Do you think you'll make another Dogme film after this?
KL: Oh, I don't think it's interesting to do the same thing more than once. But I will use what I've learned. One thing I think all of us agree on – Lars has talked about it, Thomas has talked about it, Søren has talked about it, and I experienced it: how *joyful* it was to do a film according to these rules. And that's something that I will try to bring along, you know?

After we wrap, I chat about the form of this book with Kristian. He seems mildly disappointed in me when I tell him that I've found myself unable to stick to the rules of composition I first set myself. He enthuses about a little-known work by Stendhal, one that the writer composed sequentially and without revision over a set period of days. 'You could call that a Dogme book,' Kristian smiles. But then what do you call mine? I feel enlightened, but also about two feet tall.

7 Downtime#1:
Reconsidering *The Idiots*, and hunting Harmony

Minerva Pictures, Soho, London W1: Thursday, 28 October 1999

As we wait for confirmation of appointments in Copenhagen, my research continues. Where Dogme's concerned, I've learned not to ignore the usually negligible back pages of the trades. This week, sure as the turning of the earth, *Screen International* reports a spot of turmoil on the bulletin board of the Dogme website. It seems there have been recent exchanges between 'Lars von Trier' and 'Steven Spielberg', suggesting that *Jurassic Park 3* might be made under the Vow of Chastity. This preposterous notion drew a stinging electronic retort from 'Thomas Vinterberg': professing to be sick of von Trier's grandstanding, damning any association with Spielberg, and tendering his resignation from the Brotherhood. Regrets were promptly expressed by 'Trier' and 'Kristian Levring'. Whether or not the press were gulled by such clear-cut fakery, they duly called Zentropa, where Mia Elming expressed dismay at the number of pranksters and mountebanks infesting the Web. However, MD Peter Aalbæk Jensen is more ebullient: 'We encourage anarchy. The Dogme concept is getting out of the Brothers' control. That's what we want.'

Brentford High Street: Saturday, 30 October 1999

I'm hunched over a coffee at the Waterman's Arts Centre, gazing out on to black sheets of rain over west London: and it doesn't get much more westerly. An e-mail from Paula prompted today's adventure ('Saul noticed a special "Dogme Day" at Waterman's this Saturday, from 11 a.m. onwards. I called about filming the Q&A session. Do you want to go along?'). At first I imagined my brief would be to turn up and start a fight. But actually the event is quite sufficiently stimulating. A group of thirty or so local cinephiles sit through *The Idiots*, then programmer Sara Steinke leads a discussion, full of lively exchanges on the film and the Rules. One chap raises a thoughtful point about those flash-forward interviews to camera: *pace* Rule 7, couldn't they be construed as 'temporal alienation'? Sara herself is unconvinced by the proscription of 'optical effects', since digital video cameras offer so many 'special features' that enable in-camera trickery.

But it's not all this kind of jousting. Some people have clearly been touched by the film, not least a lady with an eastern European accent, who says some fine and earnest things. What she admires in the piece is its 'touch of humanity', its implied criticism of society. (This is the kind of movie-talk I like to hear.) 'Karen couldn't be helped within society,' she insists, 'because society was sick. And only that group could offer her help, even if they didn't know they were helping her so much – just because they were really caring.' The spassing, she thinks, is 'a lovely metaphor for people who don't fit into society. It's a sign, a way for them to pass on the message that they're in pain.' Nicely put. I find myself wishing I'd sat through the film again.

Crouch End, London N4: Monday, 1 November 1999

A night in with a VHS of *The Humiliated*, Jesper Jergil's documentary study of the making of *The Idiots*. And I don't think I've seen a more fraught and fascinating portrait of a director at work. Jergil has had privileged access to proceedings, and the piece is somewhat haunted by Trier's voice-over, a daily diary he committed to Dictaphone. But few film-makers would acquit themselves so well under these circumstances. Watching Trier gather his troupe about him and explain the fantastic notions that begat the script, one can feel his desire to denude the film-making process, to challenge himself, to build a company and work through his ideas, in an intimate environment of work and play akin to theatre. 'We'll be as free as in the seventies,' he tells them with a smile. I'm reminded of Francis Coppola's nostalgic hopes for Zoetrope, how he dreamed that film production might attain the infectious team spirit of the theatrical rehearsal room.

We see them set up in their mansion lair, then venture out for a failed stab at a scene wherein the idiots try to call in on Queen Margarethe. The spassing looks weak, and Trier knows it. Perhaps his heart fell into his boots right then. But the next day, as they wrestle with the restaurant scene, he finds the right words. 'You have the same problem as Jens,' he tells Bodil Jorgenson. 'When you're on camera, you think you have to deliver.' But she doesn't, and that's the virtue of the

Dogme game. Of course, Trier is right in the thick of the scrum, operating one of the cameras. Nevertheless, he confesses to being somewhat afraid to participate fully in his own idea. But his cast, a vivacious bunch, seem to ease the passage. 'This is an investigation', he tells them, 'in which we're trying to find the *value* of it.' And together, with wine and cigarettes, they sit and debate long into the night. Trier confesses to being moved by their 'commitment to the idiot cause'.

Inevitably, each day's shooting poses unique problems. There are wrangles over the needful erections for the shower scene and the orgy scene. Trier admits that a consultant in a home for mental patients had advised him to confront the issue of spastic sexuality square-on. An emotional exchange between Karen and Susanne (Anne-Louise Hassing) takes for ever, and Trier finds himself acting as amateur psychoanalyst to Ms Hassing in order to draw tears. But the scene works. Still, the moments of euphoria that Trier is fully entitled to ('Life is wonderful') seem only to make him more anxious. He fears for his talent, fears that 'hubris' will smite him. His fear of testicular cancer clearly mirrors his fear of flying – he doesn't want to die too soon or too dismally, not with so many Lars von Trier films yet unmade. What an artist he is!

In the end, Trier's nemesis emerges under more pedestrian circumstances. He confesses to initial problems – 'wars', even – with actresses. Clearly he's a director unaccustomed to the 'touchy-feely', living-in-each-other's-pockets way of working that flourishes in theatre. Midway through the piece, we see his mood plummet. He's got himself embroiled in some situation with Anne-Louise Hassing. There's a group barbecue, full of bad vibes. It feels like the fag-end of a former intimacy: the actors are drifting towards their next jobs. Trier looks like thunder. The morning after, he seems to pronounce a plague on the whole project, informing them that they may all return to lives of 'calculated hell'. 'It's all about being loved and about having power,' Trier advises his tape-recorder, in what sounds alarmingly to my ears like a paraphrase of the young Nero in Racine's *Britannicus*. He derides his former faith in 'power-hungry young actors', laments that only he believes in the film, and, rather irascibly, sets about finishing it. Clearly there'll be no more of the touchy-feely stuff; and henceforth 'Susanne' has a fairly tough time at his hands.

Onward, Saul and I, to a press show for Harmony Korine's *Julien Donkey-Boy*, prior to its formal outings in the London Film Festival. Rattling into Waterloo by Underground train, I gaze up idly at an advertisement that promises 'Copenhagen for Christmas Magic' and invites us to sample the 'world-famous hospitality' of the Danes. Hold on, we're coming! In the meantime we had hoped that Harmony Korine himself would do our documentary an incalculable financial favour by popping over to London for the Festival. But no dice: it seems he's ensconced in New York gouging out a new script. At ease, gentlemen.

Korine's ascent was something else I missed during my mid-1990s sojourn from movie-going. So I sat down last night with tapes of *Gummo* and *Kids*. The former is a joy, a ragged scrapbook-essay about two rangy kids, Solomon and Tummler, who ride bikes and shoot cats somewhere in Tennessee. It's hit-and-miss, partly because of Korine's clearly incorrigible need to goof off. Sometimes cleverness strains: Linda Manz, last seen in Dennis Hopper's *Out of the Blue*, turns up as Solomon's mom; and it's great to see her. But her scenes with the boy are laboured, because she seems to be improvising furiously alongside a non-professional who only has one card to play. Still, *Gummo* is hilarious and exhilarating, and there is considerable poetry in it. In voice-over, Tummler speaks flatly in praise of all the unlikely beauty that's in the world: a truth of which I'm always ready to be told. And here, it seems to me, Harmony has prefigured – not to say pissed all over – the character of 'Ricky Fitts' in *American Beauty*, a slick suburban comedy of mid-life crisis, already touted as 1999's 'Film of the Year', blah-blah. Ricky is a glassy-eyed teenage poet, liable to wax rhapsodic at the sight of a paper-bag flitting in the wind. Had producer Steven Spielberg only seen fit to hire Harmony rather than the Englishman Sam Mendes, what sport we might have seen!

Kids, though, is deeply dispiriting. I can see why Korine, having moved onward to direction, has been so vocal in disdaining 'plot', because *Kids* is lumbered with a real cracker: a sort of *La Ronde* yarn, predicated on the indiscriminate spread of the HIV virus among promiscuous teens. The film is juicy and vicarious to its core, and falls some way short of the pathos Warhol and Paul Morrissey managed to pull out, twenty-five years ago, in movies like *Flesh* and *Trash*. But the hip-hop argot and sexual badinage of the young cast is all very snappy; and Chloe Sevigny, Korine's Anna Karina, is a terrifically unforced and affecting presence. So I can see why Korine (by all accounts, unwittingly) became an instant poster-boy for all the youth-oriented style mags (*I-D, Dazed and Confused, Sky*), several of which offer their vacant endorsements ('A masterpiece') on the video box.

What, though, has the Vow of Chastity done to his film-making? Straight away, the look of *Julien* is brilliantly distinctive: digital video transferred to 16-mm-reversal, and blown up to 35 mm. Julien himself (Ewen Bremner) is a young schizophrenic man, hardly able to manage himself: he lurches around Brooklyn, talking to himself in gibbering incantations. He goes to confession, and the priest gives him numbers for psychiatric counselling: a seemingly hopeless intervention, as we then see Julien conducting an imaginary dialogue with Hitler. His pregnant sister Pearl (Sevigny) dances in a tutu, and he watches her from the staircase, with big eyes. They have playful phone conversations, where she acts fondly as his absent mother. But when Pearl gets an obstetric check-up, she won't say who the father is, and the audience has to fear the worst. Family life is scarily disturbed. Julien's Dad (Werner Herzog) is a loon, riddled with private obsessions, such as moulding son Chris into a champion wrestler. 'Don't shiver. Be a man,' he drones at the poor half-naked boy, while soaking him with a water-hose on a freezing afternoon. Worse, we later catch him offering the kid ten bucks to wear his mother's dresses.

Very quickly one can see that *Julien* falls squarely within Dogme's vague thematic frame, owing to its interest in 'damaged' people. In *Gummo*, Korine revealed a ready identification with the afflicted. Here, Julien works voluntarily with blind children, who might ordinarily consider this a dubious benefit. But he washes a little girl's feet, and they chat about death. 'I died before,' offers Julien. Another of his charges is a young guy who busts out with a stupendous rap ('I'm a black albino, straight from Alabama'). And Herzog has a scene with an armless man who is a fantastic drummer and card-sharp: these skills, he declares, are his payback in the grand design. Such moments are exhilarating, but the mood of the piece is mournful. The family visit a Pentecostal church, and amid exuberant preaching and singing, Julien claps his hands; but tears spring to his eyes. Dad grows increasingly violent towards his offspring: attacking Pearl's harp, ordering Julien to slap his own face. On a visit to a skating-rink, Pearl falls to the ice and miscarries. At the hospital, Julien retrieves the stillborn baby from a nurse, claiming that it's 'his'; and then legs it. He rides a bus, cradling his unhappy bundle, and other patrons are quietly appalled. Back at home, he crawls into bed with the infant corpse, and we watch him under the covers, caught on infra-red camera like the proverbial faun before headlights.

Afterwards, Ewen Bremner and producer Cary Woods mount the dais for a Q&A. Bremner (dapper in a suit, and looking relieved to be shorn of Julien's frightful inky-black perm) says that the pages Harmony sent him formed a kind of 'impressionistic poem': a long list of scenes, without dialogue, and somehow inspired by Harmony's Uncle Eddie, a psychiatric patient at a hospital in Queens. Woods testifies to Bremner's absolute commitment to the character, which entailed several months of research in New York before shooting. Curiously, Woods won't answer a query about the budget, and sounds testy as he indicates it's the kind of question people only ask at lesser festivals. He will concede that twenty different cameras were used, and the desired look (that of a 'found film' that might have been shot 'anywhere over the last thirty or forty years') was achieved in a Swiss lab. A questioner wonders how much Werner Herzog brought to the film. Woods explains that Herzog brought whatever the hell he wanted, and Korine was beside himself with excitement. Woods also fields a question about the dead baby: in fact, a doll loaned from another movie. But (I mentally reckon in my role as amateur Dogme sleuth) that's still a brought-in prop: code violation, Rule#1.

Afterwards, Saul and I confer in the foyer. He had twisted in his seat some, but he found plenty to like in the film. His main beef is that the Rules seem to be so loosely interpreted that the Dogme certificate is nearly nugatory. We agree that Korine's aesthetic fixation on finding a certain beauty in shabby, unlovely things is very un-Dogme. (There's even a more conventionally lovely moment as Chloe Sevigny wanders through a sunlit cornfield, singing to herself about the lamb of God, her frizzy perm a fiery nimbus.) Certainly *Julien* exemplifies the Manifesto's scorn for 'dramaturgy' and 'works'. It's no well-made three-act opus; it treats the 'instant as more important than the whole'. And like *The Idiots*, it upholds a certain inspired 'mistakeism'. But then, I wonder: is Korine aware how ungainly his inevitable calculations then appear within this context? (The thumping great close-up on Julien's tears in church; the tiresome wait for Pearl to stop tottering and fall over on the ice.)

More problematically for me, I find the film's 'family' plain unconvincing, and as with Linda Manz in *Gummo*, the trouble seems to originate in Korine's iconic approach to casting. It also seems to these eyes that he lacks experience in leading actors through improvisation. It's as if they all showed up on the day and rolled. Korine's hero Alan Clarke had a formidable facility for getting to the bones of unhappy, impoverished characters in hopeless everyday quandaries; but this skill was honed through years spent in dingy rehearsal rooms, and shooting two or three films a year, often on videotape, for the BBC. And this is where Korine, still in his mid-twenties and with two films to his name, makes life hard for himself in interviews: repeatedly declaring his love of Bresson, Dreyer, Clarke and other such rigorous masters.

Baker Street, London w1: Thursday, 11 November 1999

The die is cast: we're all off to Denmark this Saturday. The only real niggle has concerned Trier's schedule. He's still grafting on *Dancer in the Dark*, and initially he didn't want his interview to be on camera. I can appreciate his jaundice. But it seems he's come around. Tonight, over pizza with some friends and some strangers, I get to talking with an expatriate Danish lady. I'm keen to express my admiration for what I take to be the exemplary egalitarian socialism of Danish society: the robust public sector, the superior public transport, the commitment to free and lifelong education, the free nurseries and generous maternity leave, the 50 per cent income tax and considerate unemployment benefit.

My new acquaintance is strangely reluctant to accept the compliment; maybe this is why she's been in England so long. 'Danes are such snobs,' she says, smiling. 'They're so secure and comfortable.' She feels there's altogether too much settled, self-congratulatory middle-class hypocrisy and cant going about. She summons up a term of abuse that she fears will not translate: 'We have always had a lot of what we call "saloon communists" in Denmark, especially in their sixties and seventies.' I assure her that the English have just such an epithet, 'champagne socialist', and that I too have not ''scaped whipping'.

As for the Danish New Wave: she enjoyed *Festen* and *Mifune*, sure, but she wasn't wildly impressed. The Dogme Rules strike her as nothing very radical. What she liked about *Festen* also made her suspicious of it: the very precise evocation of the stifling bourgeois family, and –

something she insists is special to Denmark – of boorish decennial anniversary bashes, the sixtieth being the most ostentatious and insufferable, larded with speeches and songs. I protest that the English (not to mention the Scottish, the Irish and even the Welsh, for all I know) are equally capable of throwing awful parties full of fake sentiment. But what my friend is unable to believe is that directors such as Vinterberg and Trier are truly able to see outside of their own Danish insularity, however they might aspire to puncture and tear it. 'You should ask them whether they feel this,' she insists. She's fairly swingeing. I suppose I'll have to.

8 'Cool Denmark!'

As Paula and I board the SAS jet, Saul and Jack are already seated. They made the error of trekking out to the airport early, to watch the crucial England–Scotland Euro 2000 play-off, but couldn't find a telly. I confirm the result (2–0), but take small pleasure in it, as both England goals were scored by the disagreeable Paul Scholes, rather than my idol, the taciturn and talismanic Alan Shearer. Still, all the Danes are in hog heaven, having trounced Israel 5–0 in their own play-off in Tel Aviv. Copenhagen Airport is hyper-modern and majestic, fit for a shoot-out in a Michael Mann movie. Our guide and boom-swinger, Nicolai Iuul, meets us in the wagon, and we steam into the city. The hotel is clean, functional, and smack in the midst of the red-light district. Over the road is The Exciting Sex Shop, its awning boasting of the delights depicted within ('Anal Sex!'). As if to confirm national stereotypes, my wardrobe contains a magazine entitled *Teenage Girls*, generously discarded by the previous occupant. I flip through it and smile at the antics of several women who, however lively, will not see their teens again. We reconvene in the street, to set out for a night on the lash. I mention that surprise in my wardrobe to Nicolai. 'Better than a Gideon Bible,' he remarks, very reasonably.

As Nicolai steers us through the residential neighbourhood of Norrebro, he points out the boarded shop fronts and street debris that bear witness to a riot. Last Sunday, a group of fifty or so second-generation immigrants ran through the streets, shattering windows, looting, fire-starting, and shouting, 'Stop the deportation!' This was in reference to a controversial judicial decision made that Friday, whereby the Danish Supreme Court had voted unanimously to deport twenty-three-year-old Ercan Cicek, 'for ever, without any option to enter Denmark again'. Early in 1999, Cicek had been served a three-year prison sentence for a series of especially violent assaults on pensioners, but the prosecution then appealed for something sterner. The Supreme Court has usually made it hard to deport a person with family in Denmark. Cicek, though a Turkish citizen, was born in Denmark and has family here: a wife and a baby daughter. The 'immigrant question' seems to dog this otherwise settled Danish society. In 1993, Poul Schluter's discreetly xenophobic Conservative-Liberal Government collapsed in disgrace, after a Supreme Court judge exposed the efforts of the ex-Justice Minister to limit numbers of political refugees from Sri Lanka by illegal means. Mr Cicek's case is clearly a different matter, yet it touches the same nerve.

Naturally, we don't permit any of this to interfere with our pursuit of a pleasant evening, and so Nicolai leads us on a trawl of various happening venues. Much like London, the clothes are Diesel and New Dull shades. The music is garage, even (yikes!) salsa. But the pulchritude is startling; even the girls who dance around their handbags are ludicrously gorgeous.

Sunday, 14 November 1999

Our first appointment is with young scholar Carsten Jensen, who had graciously accepted my request for a briefing on current cultural and socio-political conditions within the state of Denmark. A Ph.D. and author, Carsten has taught at the Institute of Political Studies of the University of Copenhagen. He lives with his wife Birthe, also an academic, and fourteen-year-old son David. Carsten is unabashedly addicted to classic rock of the late 1960s and early 1970s: he professes to be one of the most dedicated Who fans in western Copenhagen, and I'm also pleased to see a robust showing by Springsteen within his outstanding collection of vinyl. Unsurprisingly, then, we get to chatting about Søren Kragh-Jacobsen's erstwhile career as a rock legend. I tell Carsten we've been dying to get hold of one tune called 'Mona' – the hit of 1975, by all accounts. Carsten slips out of the room, and reappears with a CD that he pops into his deck. A lively little folk-pop number bursts from the speakers, sung in Danish over strummed guitar.

RICHARD KELLY: Wow. Is that Søren on vocals?
CARSTEN JENSEN: Yes, and he wrote the music and lyrics. It's called 'Kender du det?', which translates to English as 'Do You Know It?' But everybody really knows it as 'Mona'. You'll understand why when you hear the chorus; it's all about a teenage boy who's in love with this girl, and the problems he has getting close to her. (*Sure enough, the girl's name is repeated three times in entreaty – 'Oh, Mona, Mona, Mona . . .'*) But after he's finally seduced her, he loses interest, and moves on to the next girl.

RK: To Helle or Ghita or whoever. So it's the typical story of a young man's romantic development?

CJ: Exactly. Of course, Søren made some very popular films about young people in the late 1970s. There weren't many big Danish hits at that time, but these were cult films, I guess. Everybody of my age and background saw them and liked them, because we could relate to them, they were about 'us'. But since we're talking music, you should know there are two very significant Danish songs used in the Dogme films. One is in *Mifune*, by Kim Larsen, who's undoubtedly the most popular Danish singer of the last thirty years. It's in the scene where Rud is sitting in the car listening to the tape-deck. The lyrics are all about a guy who's hitchhiking, a long way from home, lost and lonely. He's missing his mum and dad – just like Rud.

RK: What's the other significant song?
CJ: It's in *Festen*: in the scene where Christian is sitting in the forest, tied to a tree. For me, that's the best scene in the whole film – it's just so tragic and funny. But to a Danish audience, what makes it even more so is the song that's being sung in the background by the grand-mother at the feast. It's a very popular old Danish folk-tune; in English it would be called 'In the Deep, Quiet Forest'. It's a very idyllic song, a song to put people in a good mood. And of course, in this film you hear it sung as this guy is being beaten bloody by his brother and his friends . . .

RK: So we may assume it's being used for ironic effect?
CJ: Indeed. But that scene is very aggressive towards something very specific in Danish culture, which is the desire to make things cosy, and not talk about problems. The song is about the quiet life of the coun-try, where everything's nice and easy. But in order for this family to be able to sing it together, they have to have Christian beaten up and thrown out. (*Laughs.*)

RK: *Festen* has been hailed around the world, so, clearly, the story strikes a chord. But I met a Dane who told me she felt it's very specif-ically Danish in its depiction of that suffocating bourgeois familial climate. Is that fair?
CJ: I think so. But then stories about the disturbed bourgeois family form their own tradition in Danish film, and in TV drama especially. It dates back to the 1960s, at least. A Danish writer called Leif Panduro wrote ten or more TV plays on the same theme: families whose inner lives are covered with lies. He wrote a radio play called *Cannibals in the*

Cellar, and the title was a metaphor for the feelings family members have for one another. Up in the house, they live together as 'nice people'. But down in the cellar, where the subconscious feelings are, they want to eat each other. (*Laughs.*) And I think that's revealed in *Festen*, but also in *Mifune*. And even in *The Idiots*, to some extent – especially in the scene where the father comes to take one of the girls away from the group, back to 'real' society.

RK: When we first talked, you told me you had found *Festen* 'surprisingly great'. Why the surprise?

CJ: Because a lot of Danish movies get great reviews from the critics, but then have very little impact on the ordinary public – myself included. I tend to find Danish movies a little slow and repetitive – you're told the main idea again and again. But *Festen* is so aggressive. And it races along, with so many quick changes of situation and so many good one-liners; it's so funny, it has this 'gallows humour' all the way through. But the drama is so strong, and there's tragedy in it. Like in the character of the younger brother who can't articulate his feelings – all he can do is fight. So after his brother's accusations have been proven, he beats his father half to death. That's his liberation, his way of dealing with it. (*Laughs.*) And to me the best thing about *Festen* is that it's not regressive, not backward-looking like the other Dogme films. It's looking forward, all the way.

RK: Forward to what, though?

CJ: I'm not sure. (*Smiles.*) To a new way of family life, for one. At least it gets rid of the old order. It's a rebellion against the classic father figure. Christian has made his mind up, he has planned to make his speech and act as he does, and that's important. Because the characters in *The Idiots* and *Mifune* have no plans – they just muddle along.

RK: Whereas Christian takes arms against a sea of troubles …

CJ: Yes. It's a classic theme in Danish literature, this, that Danes never do what they want – instead they sacrifice their dreams for something else. So it's good to have a widely liked Danish movie about someone who just says, 'Right, I'm going to get rid of this old fart.' (*Laughs.*)

RK: Is *Mifune* a 'regressive' story by comparison?

CJ: I think the story – a guy who leaves the city and heads back to the place of his childhood years – takes up themes that were common in Danish films of the 1950s. Kresten comes back to claim what is rightfully his – his family home. He assumes control and remakes it in his own image. It's almost a Greek theme, if you like. But I think a lot of the imagery of the film – the wheat fields and sunsets and blonde Danish women, and this little brave guy who saves the big dumb guy – I think these are regressive themes, formally speaking. And it's basically a happy-ending story – they even find some money, a hundred thousand kroner, just by a stroke of luck. But of course the little minisociety that Kresten creates with those four people – I wouldn't call that regressive. It points forward, to a society composed of people as they are, or accepted as they are, not as character masks.

RK: In *Mifune*, the southern Danish countryside we see is pretty rundown. Is that a true-to-life picture?

CJ: Only in the sense that the real place, Lolland, does have a lot of unemployment. You could compare it to northern England – big shipbuilding sites left desolate, de-industrialization and so on. That much is true. But I'm not sure that the real population of Lolland would think that they are fairly represented in the film.

RK: And probably it wouldn't be so easy to lure a pretty blonde housekeeper down to that neck of the woods?

CJ: No, certainly not given the way Kresten is behaving when she first shows up. Maybe you would have done back in the 1950s, when Søren Kragh-Jacobsen was a child himself. But the whole film is like a journey back in time.

RK: To a fondly remembered past. Do you think *The Idiots* too is backward-looking, compared to *Festen*?

CJ: Yes, but the era it's looking back to is the 1970s, and the ideals of certain groups of young people at that time. When I saw the film, I felt sure that Trier must have lived in a commune at some point in his life – in a big house, with a big group of people, sharing everything. This apartment we're standing in (*gestures around his elegant habitat*) – fifteen or twenty years ago, it was full of young people. *The Idiots* seemed to be based on those kinds of experiments. It's a wild guess on my part, but I suspect Mr von Trier felt these ideas deserved another thought – that they should be transposed to another time and discussed again.

RK: Albeit in a very bizarre way.

CJ: Bizarre, yes. But the common theme of all these Dogme movies is that they are concerned with people living in the same space, and within certain limits. It's a microcosm of sorts. People come in from outside, but it's really about small groups, tribes almost. And this is very much akin to ideas going around Denmark in the 1970s – firstly that the Danes themselves are a tribe, in relation to the rest of the world; and also this idea of young people trying to live closer together, communally.

RK: Of course, there were films of the 1960s and 1970s that tried to capture the spirit of communal projects; but they were usually underwritten by leftist ideology of some kind. Whereas the creed of _The Idiots_ is fairly fanciful – I mean, it could only have come from the imagination of Lars von Trier. Doesn't the film suggest that real politics have rather drifted out of people's lives since the 1970s? I mean, the idiots' only real objective seems to be to irritate people – the 'straights' in the straight world.

CJ: Well, in a way, that's what Lars von Trier himself is doing, and there are other artists in Denmark who have the same idea. You could say that the Dogme95 movement is there to irritate and provoke people. (_Sighs._) And in a way, you're right. Because you could also say that politics is dead in Denmark. It's not engaging people in the way it used to; they're not on the barricades as they once were. Only two or three weeks ago, a book appeared, written by former leftists, about the need to rethink the left project in Denmark. It's maybe a little similar to Blairism, I think. The idea being to say to people, 'You don't need to invest all of yourself in the political project; just use what you like of it. And don't be ashamed that you're not a manual labourer. Accept that you are middle-class.' And, of course, it may be a reflection of this 'hollowing-out' of the left-wing project, and politics as a whole.

RK: Also of the incessant march of neo-liberalism?
CJ: Oh, but neo-liberalism didn't get such a foothold here. While you had Thatcher, we had a Liberal-Conservative coalition government. Poul Schluter was prime minister, and they declared themselves as a 'Bourgeois Government': they were conservatives who were proud to be bourgeois and they wanted to reclaim the word in a positive sense. Then while you had Major, we had a socialist-democratic shift: a coalition led by the Social Democratic Party, with Poul Nyrup Rasmussen as Prime Minister.

RK: But when Mogen Glistrup's Progressive Party popped up in the

early 1970s, didn't they come out with some fairly white-hot anti-tax rhetoric?

CJ: Well, the interesting thing about Denmark politically is that it's very often a little ahead of most of Europe. In that sense, it's true, we had this 'New Right' movement very early in the 1970s. And then the rest of Europe seemed to get it in the late 1970s, or early 1980s. And then we were very quick to get rid of the 'Bourgeois Government' and see a new type of social-democratic reaction to that. So maybe we'll be the first to see the next right-wing revival. (*Smiles.*) Quicker than the rest of Europe, and certainly quicker than Britain, I'm sure. It's very difficult to imagine that we won't have a new 'Bourgeois Government' within two or three years.

RK: But the attachment of most Danes to the welfare state has been too strong to permit neo-liberalism having its evil way?

CJ: Sure. Very many Danes are dependent on the state in one way or another, and many are also committed to the project. If you took a simple survey of Danish people, asked, 'Do you want to pay your taxes, even though they're among the highest in Europe?', on average, Danes will say, 'Yes.' Because they're satisfied by what they get in return. Now that's a hard one for a new government to attack, because it would be attacking our ports, so to speak – attacking the expressed will of most people. So this year and last, the opposition has backed off and said, 'Look, we're not going to destroy the welfare state, we're just going to restructure it – adjust a little here and there, but basically retain a "welfare society". It'll be safe in our hands.'

RK: I believe you're of a mind that Dogme95 represents a form of cultural reaction to American globalization?

CJ: Yes. Danish film-making over the last ten years has definitely been a success story, compared to the rest of this century. Bille August and Gabriel Axel have had international success, August has gone on to make Hollywood movies; and of course that's one way for Danish film-makers to respond to the challenge of Hollywood – to say, 'We can do it just as well as they can. We can take a classic, Nobel-Prize-winning Danish story like *Pelle the Conqueror*, and sell it as well as Hollywood sells its stories.' I mean, that film is slightly Scandinavian, but basically it's a Hollywood movie – big scenes, epic scale. The same is true of his *Smilla's Sense of Snow*. But there's another way to meet the Hollywood challenge, which is to accept that in the long run we just can't compete like that:

there's just not enough money in the Danish industry to sustain that kind of defence. What we can do, though, is change the battlefield, say, 'We don't want to enter your competition. We'll set our own rules for film-making.' So Dogme defines a new way of making films; or takes up an old one. But it says, 'This is different. This is Danish. Not American.'

RK: There is a view that Dogme95 is as much a marketing stunt as it is an aesthetic experiment; and a challenge to the American imperium. And in London we've seen about as many Danish films this year as we have over the previous decade. Now, if that were true, is it good or bad? Is it an acceptable ruse?

CJ: I think it's perfectly acceptable. (*Chuckles.*) I mean, I like American movies, some of them are among my all-time favourites. But, yes, I'm sure Dogme is a commercial strategy. Zentropa is an ambitious company, its manager, Peter Aalbæk Jensen, is a very entrepreneurial individual, he likes to act the big capitalist with a cigar and shades. And he's a common kind of figure nowadays – the young, self-made 'cultural capitalist', somebody who produces meaning, rather than things. Zentropa is capitalism, but it's backed by state money, of which they get a lot. So it's not the classic capitalist notion of the company; it's a company that reacts to political ideas and sees a role for itself within a new political project. And that is also the new thing: the idea of partnership between business and the public sector.

RK: Sure. 'Public-private partnership' has been a mantra of our Prime Minister Blair and his drones.

CJ: I don't doubt it. It's one of the 'big ideas' of our time; as opposed to during the 1980s, where it was all about the war of business against the state and public authorities. It's worth pointing out, though, that while we speak of 'public' and 'private', within Denmark these sectors are surrounded by civil society, and voluntary work. So much of the cultural production here is done by young people either working voluntarily or being paid a pretty lousy wage. They'll form little theatre groups and make no money, but do it just for experience, so that maybe in time they'll be picked up by some more established employer.

RK: And, finally, they'll get paid ...

CJ: Yes, if they're very lucky. But even after *Festen* had its success, Thomas Vinterberg was still living on the dole. He complained about it in a television interview. 'You might think I'm this internationally famous movie director, but I'm on the fucking dole. Please, please give me some money.' Though I imagine he has it now . . .

RK: Of course, to have a successful domestic cinema, you need local stars. Are the actors in Dogme films familiar faces to Danes?
CJ: Anders Berthelsen, the main guy in *Mifune*, has a lead role in the TV show *Taxa*, and the young actresses who play the hookers have all worked together at the same theatres in Copenhagen. There has been a revival in Danish theatre across the 1990s – at venues like Oescre Gasvaerk, a great dome that used to be owned by a gas company; and Dr Dante, which is an experimental theatre. Many of the Dogme actors have been part of this renewal, so I'm sure it's brought some fresh ideas to the films. The films show a kind of Young Copenhagen, 'Cool Denmark', if there is such a thing. The characters feel as if they're modelled on everyday people. I mean, the little boy in *Mifune* is fantastically real; our boy David talks in just the same way.

RK: Have the films been real box-office hits here?
CJ: Sure. *The Idiots* maybe a little less so. But *Festen* and *Mifune* were hits. They were well liked, much discussed. But right now there does seem to be a trend among Danish viewers to see more Danish films. In this past year there have been some very big Danish hits – *The One and Only*, *The Olsengang's Last Trick*, *Love at First Hiccough*.

RK: So *The Idiots* was less successful. But Trier retains quite a high public profile in Denmark, doesn't he?
CJ: Sure, everybody knows him. But probably for his TV series, *The Kingdom*, more than anything else. And I thought that was 'surprisingly good' too. You just didn't expect to see such well-known actors behaving so outrageously onscreen. I think *The Kingdom* really established Trier with a wider audience here, beyond the cultural élite.

RK: So, when he proceeds to make a movie that contains hard-core sex, and people imitating spastics, is there a general sense of, 'Oh well, there goes Lars, the sacred monster . . .'?
CJ: It's . . . just not so readily accepted. Not yet.

RK: Well, apparently they're not ready for it in Ireland either. The video of *The Idiots* has just been banned over there.
CJ: (*Chuckles.*) Oh, I'm sure Trier was very proud of that.

9 Inside Film City:
Lars Bredo Rahbek & Nimbus Film

Hvidovre: Monday, 15 November 1999

We head for the wooded outskirts of Copenhagen, and 'Film City', the compound where Nimbus and Zentropa have made their common bases; and where, as Lene Neergarb teasingly told me, 'a new Cinecittà' is being constructed. As we breach the outer walls, the place looks to me like some chillingly prestigious public school; or the site of covert 'defence science' skulduggery. Nicolai eases our way past the security hut, and sweet-talks us into a table at the hangar-like staff canteen, where we dine rather well. Then we roll up to a group of buildings at the outer perimeter, and unload the gear. Lars von Trier putters through the car park in what looks like a souped-up golf buggy, painted murky camouflage colours. Lost for words, I tip him a wink, and he amiably (or confusedly) raises a hand. We'll meet, oh yes . . .

Then the youthful Nimbus producer, Lars Bredo Rahbek, guides us through their elegant two-storey open-plan habitat, and we fetch up in his bright, dinky office. Framed lobby cards for Dreyer pictures adorn the shelves. *Screen International* lies atop the in-tray, boasting of several nominations for *Mifune* in the European Film Awards. Lars takes a call from Søren Kragh-Jacobsen, who's bound for Italy and the film's première there. As we set up, Saul mentions that he was watching telly in the hotel room late last night, and for one hallucinatory moment thought he glimpsed Peter Aalbæk Jensen acting in some soap opera. 'Oh yes, that was Peter. *Taxa*, right? Peter is transgressing borders right now. He's on game shows, he's becoming a celebrity. Zentropa is a lot about provocation and image. But Peter is one person in public and another in private . . .'

RICHARD KELLY: Lars, there is the feel of a military operation about this Film City. What drew you out here in the first place?
LARS BREDO RAHBEK: Well, Film City was formerly an army base – these offices we're in used to be a munitions barrack – but they closed it down because of *détente*, and the municipality put it up for grabs. Lars von Trier and Peter Aalbæk thought it might make a good base, so they moved Zentropa out here six months ago. And then we followed, about six weeks ago.

RK: So it's a military installation converted for entertainment purposes. Was the idea behind the joint move to consolidate your power base? So that you could be side by side, planning world domination?
LBR: (*Smiles.*) Oh, we don't have such ambitions. And we're not a subsidiary of Zentropa: we're independent. But we can see that there's a certain synergy in being close. And Nimbus has thrived on Zentropa being out there in the international market before us. We've been able to go to them for advice. Thomas Vinterberg has talked a lot with Lars von Trier about how to do international films. Birgitte Hald, who produced *Festen* and *Mifune*, has talked to Peter Aalbæk. So we play with open cards, we consult each other. And now we've had some success ourselves, they'll drop over and ask our advice now and again.

RK: So there's no superiority in the relationship?
LBR: Well, you'll see that Zentropa employs about forty-five people, and we are a very tiny company of eight, so our philosophies are totally different. Zentropa are very into vertical integration, and right now they're trying their hand at everything from equipment rental to

post-production facilities. Whereas we concentrate on one thing that we think we're good at, which is development. We have five producers here, each of us developing shorts and feature film ideas; and that's quite unique in Denmark, to have so many producers within one company. Then we have offices for some eight to ten teams of directors and writers, who have projects at various stages.

RK: What proportion of your activity is concerned with Dogme95?
LBR: If you weigh it project for project, it's not that much, actually. Of course, of our productions to date, we can't deny that *Festen* and *Mifune* are the ones that did major business. But right now we have fifteen feature projects with money attached at various levels, and only two of these are Dogme films.

RK: What can you tell us about them?
LBR: Four new Dogme films have been financed, and right now it looks like two of these will be produced by Nimbus and two by Zentropa. The unique thing about Dogme films is that they have been financed before you know what they're going to be about. But the international response to Dogme was so immense that both Danish television and the Danish Film Institute basically feel comfortable fronting the money. And the films are still low-budget, around one million dollars apiece. After that, it's about selecting the directors. We've pinpointed some candidates, and definitely one of them will be one of 'our' directors, a guy called Henrik Ruben-Genz, with whom we've worked closely. Henrik was at Berlin this year where we also had *Mifune* in competition, and he also won a prize for Nimbus, the Crystal Bear for Best Short, with his film *Teis and Nico*. Another is Ole Christian Madsen who directed his first feature for Nimbus, *Pizza King*. It was released this year, and did very well for a first feature. It deals with the problems faced by young immigrant boys living in Copenhagen city centre. So it was a political statement, as well.

RK: It's extraordinary, though, to acquire finance without script approval. Enviable, too. In the UK, development is now this inexact science whereby producers want to decree what the script is before it's written, and what the movie is before it's shot.
LBR: Well, Scandinavia has always been something of a haven for subsidy. In Norway, Sweden, Denmark, we have very good subsidizing Film Institutes. So we are used to being a bit pampered, not being

subject to the same cruel market mechanisms as our British colleagues. Also we have a philosophy at Nimbus that we prefer to work with *auteur* directors. Directors come to us with their own ideas – they might not write the script, but quite often they're involved in the writing. And we are there to enhance their ideas, and try to heighten the likelihood of the films catching on commercially. But we are not there to drag down a kind of commercial frame upon the project. We have no ambition to imitate the American model, whereby the producer retains final cut and basically dominates the show. We're now engaged in financing Thomas Vinterberg's new international feature film, and the most important job for the producers there is to ensure one hundred per cent creative control for Thomas.

RK: Well, he's surely earned it. Did the whole Nimbus team accompany *Festen* to Cannes?
LBR: Yes, all the Nimbus producers went down, and we had the red carpet experience. Very exciting, I must admit. Because, then as now, we were a small, young company. At the time *Festen* was finished, there were maybe only four people on the payroll. Then, after the screening in the Lumière, I remember the standing ovation, ten minutes of applause, everybody getting gooseflesh . . .

RK: Then Søren Kragh-Jacobsen went to Berlin and gave Nimbus another hit. But then he's had plenty of hits, hasn't he?
LBR: Oh, yes, we all grew up with Søren. (*Laughs.*) He's the Bob Dylan of Denmark. I never thought I'd work with him.

RK: How have you coped here, given the sudden success?
LBR: For the first year, when we were dealing with *Festen*, we almost couldn't handle the attention. Every day there would be forty or fifty faxes or calls from all over the world, from producers and directors and journalists. Then one day, out of the blue, we got a package in the mail from a young director at film school in New York. He had made 'Dogme2000'. And in the package was a tee-shirt with his own ten rules printed on it: 'The film must be one minute long. It must star the director. It must contain violence', and so forth. And he'd also enclosed a cassette, which we sat down to watch, and it was hilarious. For one minute, there was just this guy running across a bare stage in slow motion, shooting at everything. It was extremely violent, and at last he was killed in a big splatter of blood. Then he called up, asking

us, rather nervously, to please show the film to Thomas. He said he didn't want to offend. But when Thomas saw it, he said, 'Ah! This is one of the few guys who has understood what Dogme is really about.' Dogme is not about following the Brothers' Rules: it's simply about setting some rules and some limitations, and these can be any. The idea is simply to gain creativity through self-imposition. It's often written about as if the Brothers had demanded the attention of the world and claimed to have found the philosopher's stone. But it was never meant like that.

RK: About that guy in New York, though – I especially like the Rule that proscribes 'superficial action', 'weapons', 'murders'. It's meant that Dogme films have been free of balletic gunplay and squib hits. Plus I liked Søren's comment that 'Films don't have to be all wham, bam, and dead babies.'

LBR: Well, at the Danish Film Institute, where we apply for subsidies, there is a system of consultants who are like commissioning editors for projects. And I remember, a couple of years ago, one of these consultants saying that he was fed up with all the scripts he was receiving from young men, full of gunplay and needless violence. I'm sure this is the same the world over. And you know that, if you asked these young guys, 'Have you ever fired a gun in your life?', most of them would have to say, 'No.' In that sense, they are creating fiction that is very remote from their reality. And, certainly in this country, which is one of the least violent in the world, it's rather unreal, and also maybe dishonest, to create films that are hyper-violent.

RK: For better or worse, Dogme is now associated with the production of features on digital video. Are you happy about that?

LBR: Well, we're not unhappy about it, but there is some misconception. We do get a lot of interview requests for Thomas – and Lars gets the same on the other side of the street – where the subject is the digitalization of the film process. And we get a lot of invitations to participate with our films in digital video festivals and suchlike. But Søren's film was shot on ordinary film stock, and none of the Rules are to do with video. But Zentropa have a much clearer philosophy about this, which we share to some degree, but not necessarily in full. They have a 'Power to the People' attitude – a much more communist philosophy. You should ask Peter Aalbæk Jensen about this.

RK: Is he a closet communist as well as a movie mogul?
LBR: Well, I'd say that most people in this part of the world are very good socialists, or have socially minded sympathies. So does Søren, so does Thomas. Lars might be more of a *provocateur*. But those two guys have been out there with political messages. I know they supported the grass-roots movements campaigning against greater integration into the European Union. You can ask them about that too . . .

RK: Clearly, a by-product of Dogme's success has been the slow grinding of a remarkable rumour-mill.
LBR: God, yes. (*Smiles.*) Rumours are spreading as we speak.

RK: Recently there's been some controversy about impostors on the Dogme website?
LBR: Yes. We created the website because Nimbus was clearly too small to handle the attention. I mean, what we really want to be doing is getting on with making new feature films. And we're not a major corporation. On the contrary, it was really only the other day that we realized maybe we would have to found a Dogme secretariat, because we have to contain certain issues and keep our website updated. But we're so small we can't spare it much attention. I mean, we barely have enough money to hire a web master for the home page. We did want to offer a platform by way of a message board, so that instead of calling us with questions, people could get advice from each other. But it does seem that on the Internet there are a lot of pranksters . . .

RK: Oh, yes . . .
LBR: So there have been false Thomas Vinterbergs and false Lars von Triers popping up. And then there have been some naïve journalists who have conducted interviews on yahoo.com with people they believe to be Thomas, without verifying if it's the man himself. So it's been necessary for us to consult entertainment lawyers in the United States to find out how we can rid ourselves of false interviews with Thomas Vinterberg. But we decided not to close down the site, because it's free communication, and that's the philosophy here. So everybody should be able to say what they want. We'll just see to it that there's not too much confusion.

10 'It's a political movement':
Peter Aalbæk Jensen & Zentropa

Back again, then, to Dogme HQ; and a few short steps across the car park from Nimbus Film to the slightly more distressed premises of Zentropa. Lots of youthful Danes are hard at graft, and all signs point to a thriving cottage industry. Nevertheless, the place still resembles a Boy Scout hut with nicer carpets. Peter Aalbæk Jensen greets us in his trophy-lined office, and pauses only to peruse a few urgent pieces of paper. Meanwhile, I have a plan. Contra-Dogme, I've brought a prop with me, a Cuban cigar, to flare up at any point where I suspect that a wind-up might be needed to get the jokes flowing. A waste of time, as it goes.

RICHARD KELLY: Peter, you're the Managing Director of Zentropa. What does your job entail? And what responsibilities do you discharge on behalf of the Dogme95 Brotherhood?
PETER AALBÆK JENSEN: Well, first, my job is to entertain my employees, and the poor talent that we have out here. So, actually, I have nothing to do except be here. Regarding the Dogme Brothers, they're an autonomous unit. I have nothing to say about them, and I have no direct contact with them, because they don't want to be associated with any form of capitalism or commercialism or business activity.

RK: Right. So you handle the filthy capitalist stuff they don't wish to sully their hands with. But you're also something of a public figure on their behalf. You're on the podium at press conferences in Cannes, you appear on TV shows . . .
PAJ: You should understand that Zentropa is owned 50 per cent by me, and 50 per cent by Lars von Trier. And he's a sissy-boy, he doesn't want to show up for any kind of promotional activity. So I *have* to do it – it's as simple as that.

RK: But are you comfortable in that role?
PAJ: Well, at least I find it entertaining. (*Smiles.*) If I can upset anybody with my presence, or my behaviour, or what I say, especially – then, yes, I'm quite happy about that. For example, it really pleases me to know that whenever our competitors open up a Sunday newspaper, they have to look at my ugly face.

RK: In a lot of the wall-mounted photographs that decorate your office, you're smoking a fat cigar. And obviously that has a certain

resonance in cinema history: it conjures up the image of the Hollywood mogul. Is it a deliberate act of homage?

PAJ: Yes, it is. Just as my partner has an artificial 'von' between his first name and his family name, which is totally fake and a part of movie tradition, I have adopted the cigar, which is also traditional, as you say.

RK: So, by adding the 'von', Lars was paying tribute to grand old directors like von Stroheim and von Sternberg?

PAJ: Yes, none of whom were noble at all . . . But I think it's nice that we more or less fake it with our personae, just as we do with the films we make. Because, of course, every film is a trick.

RK: How did you and Lars first hook up?

PAJ: It was in 1988. My first company had just gone bankrupt and so I had to get myself employed, which was pretty disgusting for me. (*Chuckles.*) And you could say that Lars was artistically bankrupt at that time, because nobody wanted to invest in his movies, everybody thought he was too much of a rascal to work with. So we ended up doing a television commercial together. And we had never met before, but one hour later we agreed to start working together. So maybe it was a case of two flops uniting, in desperate need for each other (*chuckles*), I don't know. But we've worked together ever since, yeah.

RK: Presumably there was a strong personal bond between you? Or was it just a case of opposites attracting?

PAJ: Indeed – we couldn't be any more different. People round here call us 'Laurel and Hardy', because there's one fat, stupid guy, and a tiny little guy who's stupid in his own way . . . But it's very seldom we have any kind of conflicts, even though we are so different. According to a test I took when I was going up for military service, I have an IQ of around eighty-two, and that's a bit close to 'imbecile'. I have no intellectual skills, I don't read books, I don't see movies. Lars takes care of the art, I take care of the company. It's a pretty strict split of responsibilities. But we're best friends. I mean, we talk on the phone three or four times a day, about absolutely nothing. Never about work.

RK: Like lovers do . . .

PAJ: Yeah, or girlfriends. We never see each other privately, and that's very important for us: that the friendship excludes any kind of privacy.

RK: Right. So you wouldn't go out for a drink together?

PAJ: Nope. That sounds pretty disgusting for both of us. (*The room breaks up in laughter.*) To be together in our spare time? Jesus Christ, that's horrible . . . We've each made one official visit to each other's home, and that was enough.

RK: Are you building a Cinecittà-style empire here at Zentropa?
PAJ: Yeah, but what we're really trying to copy, more or less, is a 'free town' here in Denmark called Christiania, where all the hippies run a kind of free society – nobody pays taxes, or pays for gas or electricity or water. They just smoke or sell hashish, all day long. So we're trying to make the movie equivalent of that out here – not that we're drug addicts. That is, not officially. (*Chuckles.*) But we wanted to make a place with some kind of, you could say, anarchistic energy. And both Lars and I are old left-wingers, which we're pretty proud of. So we wanted to try to use some of the very precious skills that we learned in our communist youth, about how to organize things.

RK: Just how communistic was your youth?
PAJ: Both of us were members of the Communist Party, so we were spending all of our weekends demonstrating: a pretty tough job, you know, because nobody was interested. So we'd be standing there in the town square every Saturday morning, waving these newspapers with the communist message. And nobody wanted to buy them or read them, they would just yell, 'Go home, creep!' But that was OK, you know? At least it was something to believe in. Then it was a pretty tough time for us after the decline of the Soviet empire – there was something missing after that. So we started Zentropa . . .

RK: Still, it's hard to produce movies on a communistic basis. The medium tends to mean a division of labour and differential wages that can look rather unfair from the outside. How do you address that, comrade?
PAJ: We believe here that the people should possess the tools of production. So we have facilities within the organization to handle everything, from the first receipt of the script to the shooting with equipment to the sound studios to the post-production to the lab. All of that, we own ourselves. Also we have organized our company in forty-three 'cells'. And it's very important that these cells operate totally independently; so that if the CIA infiltrate the Zentropa operation, maybe two or three cells will be damaged but no single cell knows

anything else about the rest of the activities here. So damage can be limited in that way.

RK: Do you suppose the CIA are interested in infiltrating Zentropa? Do you pose that kind of threat to the global order?
PAJ: Well, there are at least some people here in Denmark who think we are a threat, I can promise you . . .

RK: What do you think Dogme means to 'the average Dane'?
PAJ: Everybody here thought we were lunatics in launching it. And now, of course, since the first three films have been pretty successful, everybody now thinks Dogme is something the Danes invented a long time ago. People here are pretty quick to adapt to the idea that if something is successful then it's been a natural element of the Danish mentality for a long time. But if it had been a flop, as was predicted, then that would just have been down to Trier and those other jerks who blew it.

RK: So they don't give you the credit you deserve?
PAJ: No, but then we don't need it. And it's part of the Danish mentality. Whenever you stick your head up a little too high out of the bush then somebody comes along with a baseball bat and beats you back down again. You're not allowed to stick out of the great mass. But we are pretty public. I guess we are the single Danish company that is most often in the media, all across Scandinavia, because there are always good stories around us. Any journalist who's in a panic just has to give us a ring and there's a story here for him. Sometimes true, sometimes a lie. (*Chuckles.*) But then they know that's how we are.

RK: Of course. Is that a deliberate publicity strategy, a way of keeping Dogme95 in the news, for instance?
PAJ: Yeah, yeah. Not a strategy that we thought out, as in, 'I think we should do this or that.' But we think it's fun to encourage people in rumour-making. We use the press, of course. They also use us. But it's some kind of mutual agreement, you know – they need to sell their stupid newspapers, so we deliver crazy stories to that end.

RK: The story doing the rounds last summer was that Lars had demanded the withdrawal of all extant prints of *The Idiots*, because scenes had been regraded without his knowledge. True or false?
PAJ: That's true. He was pretty pissed at me. But I said, 'I did it for the

money.' And 50 per cent of the money is Lars's, you know? In order to maintain the relationship, I sent out an excuse that has been published now. But I've said that I will do it again, you know?

RK: Does Lars accept that?
PAJ: Yeah. We are still partners. It's not a nice thing to do, but I do not-nice things four hundred times each day, that's my job. So who cares in the end? It's a marriage, and now and then in a marriage, there are arguments. But then you always fuck better after an argument, so that's good . . .

RK: At the press conference in Cannes, after the première of _The Idiots_, you said a couple of terrific things. The first was that you felt Lars was deliberately 'kicking the audience in the face', after the acclaim given to _Breaking the Waves_. Do you stand by that?
PAJ: Yes, and I'm pretty proud of Lars because, after _Breaking the Waves_, it would have been so easy for him to make a little more of a slick film, a little more Hollywood-like. And everybody would have sat there clapping their greasy hands and saying, 'Now he's become an adult.' And then, he makes a film that practically everybody hates. (_Chuckles._) There are very few lovers of that movie. And that's power, yeah?

RK: Well, it's found a few more lovers since Cannes.
PAJ: You?

RK: Sure. I was a bit confused by it on first viewing. But about six months later I saw it again. And, yeah, I loved it then.
PAJ: Well, okay. (_Chuckles._) But I hope you respond a little quicker in your other love affairs . . .

RK: Not really, I'm afraid to say. But with _The Idiots_, I think you put your finger on it at Cannes, when you said that every now and again, people like to throw some shit against a wall . . .
PAJ: Yeah. That's a nice activity, and it's a little bit necessary now and again. Otherwise we have to behave so nicely, so professionally. You know, I never understood the film either, but I was proud of Lars for doing it.

RK: Did it cause you a lot of headaches getting around the world because of the 'gang-bang' scene?
PAJ: No, in fact _The Idiots_ has broken down a lot of walls in terms of

censorship. In the UK, in Norway, and in South Korea – all three very strict territories, in terms of censorship – it was passed uncut, which we never expected. Then we heard that in Ireland it was totally forbidden. Not because of the sex scene, as far as I was told, but because it would 'corrupt and demoralize' the population. But we were really proud of that . . .

RK: Well, you join a long and dignified list of film-makers who've managed to offend the Irish. Congratulations.
PAJ: Thank you. And thank you, Ireland.

RK: Zentropa is co-producing Kristian Levring's *The King is Alive*. Are you hopeful it'll carry on the proud Dogme tradition?
PAJ: Well, it's a big pressure on poor Kristian, I would say. I wouldn't like to be in his shoes. But let's see . . .

RK: You and Nimbus have four more Dogme projects in development at the moment?
PAJ: Yes, they'll start in the New Year. And then Dogme is spreading around, too. There's a Dogme film in production in Korea right now. And I know in Spain there's been what you could call an 'interpretation' of the movement, where a group of directors have joined forces, inspired by Dogme. In fact, I would say that's the best kind of inspiration. It's OK that a lot of film-makers are still planning to do films by the Dogme Rules, but I think the most fun would be if some other countries made their own movements and their own interpretations of the Rules, or made totally different rules: 'You're only allowed to shoot on a crane, and you have to set it back in history, and use lots of guns.' I mean, there's nothing new to this fucking Dogme movement – nothing at all, if you look into film history. But now and then, every business needs a movement that tries something new, or at least tries to call it something new. And now we're looking for someone to rebel against us.

RK: The change in the certification process, meaning the Brothers won't watch the films any more, surely injects an anarchic strain? Because now anyone can do it, and then it'll proliferate . . .
PAJ: Ah, you know, it's only because they are lazy boys, and they don't want to see all these stupid movies. They've already given a certificate to at least one film that doesn't fulfil the Rules, only *because* (*chuckles*) they didn't want to see the movie. So now they've found an easier way to deliver the certificate, and I'm sure it will work better.

RK: It's not a worry that the quality of the films might wane?

PAJ: Oh, no. It's not a Walt Disney label; it's a political movement, you can't copyright that. Anyone can do a Dogme movie, and we haven't copyrighted the Dogme name, so it's free for anybody to use or misuse.

RK: If it is a political movement, then what's the objective?

PAJ: It's just to kick some ass in a sloppy business. It's nice to give a bit of energy, to fight for something.

RK: One of your new projects that's been reported in the trades is a film with a female director, Lone Scherfig?

PAJ: Yes, it starts shooting in December.

RK: There is this perception of Dogme as a boys' club – it calls itself a Brotherhood and so on . . .

PAJ: Well, Anne Wivel left for that same reason. She was called a 'Brother' also, and maybe that was too much male chauvinism for her, so she left the society.

RK: Did she part on good terms?

PAJ: (*Smiles.*) Not at all. I think her attitude was 'Stupid boys!' or 'Stupid games!' or something. And of course, women are more serious, you know. She wanted to focus on something else. But Lone Scherfig is a wonderful girl, with a big sense of humour, and she has a very relaxed approach to this Dogme thing. You should talk to her. Are you talking to Lars also?

RK: We're coming back here to see him on Thursday.

PAJ: Oh, right. So he surrendered?

RK: Guess so. We did our best to convince him we were straight people. Where next for Lars, do you think? If Dogme becomes a huge wave, with hundreds of films over the next few years, will he have to reinvent himself again, and turn his back on Dogme?

PAJ: The interesting thing about Lars is that he's so programmed in what he wants to do. When he was twenty-five, he said that he wanted to do three films starting with an 'E', and they were *Element of Crime, Epidemic,* and *Europa*; and after these three films, he wanted to change style completely. I mean, all this he decided at twenty-five, not having made a single movie. But he did it. After *Europa* and those very beautiful, very slick, very controlled movies, he went in the opposite direction and made hand-held, actor-oriented movies, like *Breaking the Waves* and *The Kingdom*. Now, with this upcoming musical, he's finished what he calls 'The Golden Heart Trilogy': three films about women who sacrifice everything for, for . . . for some reason, you know? So now he wants to change completely again. And when I heard what he wanted to change to, my hair stood on end, you know? (*Laughs.*)

We wrap; but Saul cannily asks Peter if he'll now take a spin around the compound on his motorbike, for the benefit of our cameras. He's perfectly agreeable. As we pack up the cases, he gestures at a framed front page from *Politiken* newspaper. The headline is 'Pengkaos hos filmgigant', and the accompanying photo sees Peter in this selfsame office, cigar in mouth, flipping the finger to the lens. 'We're very proud of this article,' he says fondly. 'It's from when we betrayed our investors and the state, for billions. That's why I give the finger.'

'You do look like something of a crook there,' I suggest.

'Oh, I was,' he chuckles.

Then, at the door, he's collared by a fretful employee, and they have a brisk, huddled conversation. Naturally, it's all Danish to me, but Nicolai can't help overhearing, and he duly reports back. The guy had asked what charge should be levied on the new Dogme certificates, as applications are already rolling in. Aalbæk shrugged. 'A thousand dollars? No, make it twenty-five thousand. And you know what? We can put it all in some kind of foundation, and do something really cool with it.' Who says communism is dead? Finally ('C'mon, boys') Aalbæk dons a biker jacket, leads us out to the car park, and revs up his gleaming hog . . .

11 'Money for sandwiches', and more:
Mikael Olsen & the Danish Film Institute

Danish Film Institute: Tuesday, 16 November 1999

Our next engagement is with Mikael Olsen, currently one of the DFI's tenured script consultants, albeit poised himself to make a return to professional writing. First, though, he's assisting his friend Lone Scherfig with *Dogme#5*. The Institute's new building is very fetching: all lightness and whiteness, wooden floors, long windows, a nice café with a cinema attached. The bookshop is full of rare and out-of-print treasures. I make a self-consciously forlorn search for my book *Alan Clarke*, and am pathetically grateful to find it, under a copy of Franco Solinas's script for *State of Siege*, which I purchase. In the midst of the Institute is a large and strangely vacant gallery space. This is where we meet Mikael, set down a pair of metal chairs, and start talking.

RICHARD KELLY: Mikael, what's the Institute's remit in terms of film production?

MIKAEL OLSEN: The Institute is the Government's way of support-
ing Danish films, with money from the Ministry of Culture. And we
have a scheme for funding films, whereby the Institute can provide up
to 60 per cent of the total budget, and the production company has to
find the rest. For feature projects, there is a team of consultants, of
which I'm one.

RK: And what does your job entail?
MO: I work partly as script editor, and partly as a judge of what should
go into production, and what kind of money the Institute should commit. So it's reading a lot of scripts, handing out development money,
trying to improve the script, helping to point the producer in the right
direction for finance, and trying to help the director keep up good
spirits around the project. Because, as you know, it's a long run to get
a film up on the screen.

RK: And presumably your resources are greatly over-subscribed?
MO: Yeah, each consultant deals with around 250 applications a year;
whereas we actually produce about ten features per year, with varying
levels of finance.

RK: What was your first impression of the Dogme95 Manifesto?
MO: Well, having worked in the industry, I'd heard it was in the
pipeline. And at first it seemed like a laugh, like just another of Trier's
crazy ideas. That was a common response. 'What is this "Brotherhood"? And where are the sisters?' But there was a lot of curiosity
about the initiative.

RK: Is it fair to say Danish film was a bit staid back in 1995?
MO: Yeah. Not wishing to offend other Danish directors, but Dogme
injected some energy, and some competition, and a fresh way of looking at things.

RK: At what point did the 'Brothers' ask the Institute for backing?
MO: Initially, Lars von Trier approached the Danish Minister of Culture, who was positive, and interested. But because his role involves
giving money to the Institute, it put us in a difficult position. The system is such that the Institute can't accept the idea of just giving money
to a group of directors, not without its consultants having a say in the
films themselves. Dogme's proposal would have been a radical way of
erasing that system. So the Institute had to say no, without necessarily

wanting to, and the project went to Danmarks Radio Television, which undertook to raise the money. So they deserve the credit for the first four films, as I see it. And the Institute has learned from that.

RK: When did Dogme first land on your desk, so to speak?
MO: It was the point when *Festen* and *The Idiots* were in post-production. Of course, sometimes film-makers come knocking on our door because they're finished, but they just need money to support the marketing and so forth. In this case, they said, 'We're hoping to get *Festen* into competition at Cannes, and we need some money to make a 35-mm Dolby version.' The Institute was keen to show support for Dogme95, so I suggested to the Board of Directors that we should contribute a certain amount, and the Board talked it over with the television financiers. They figured out a nice solution, partly artistic, partly political. On top of that, Nimbus Film had *Mifune* about to go into production, and they wanted additional money for sandwiches.

RK: Was that literally the wording of the application? 'Please can we have some money for sandwiches?'
MO: Yeah, that was a nice investment. Søren Kragh-Jacobsen called and said there was a hole in the catering budget. And we couldn't have the actors and crew go hungry, so we chipped in three hundred thousand kroner.

RK: And now you're chipping in a little more for the next set of four Dogme films.
MO: Sure. We have more money, and we have good artistic reasons to do so. It was suggested by Nimbus Film, and it was nothing to be afraid of.

RK: Right. After Dogme's triumphs at Cannes and Berlin, the investment was seen to be a sound one?
MO: Oh, sure. After a film is successful, everybody runs into the limelight and says, 'I was there.' But that's not quite the story here. They had an idea and they tried it out, and it was a success. If Dogme95 had been a failure, there would have been a lot of people around the kitchen sink trying to wash their hands.

RK: Do you take a view on why Dogme arose in the first place?
MO: I think there are two perspectives on Dogme. The first is purely local, which is that Dogme was partly a reaction by artists against what

I happen to represent right now: the Institute, the gatekeepers, telling them what to do. But how do you make that protest if you're not working on a commercial basis? You say, 'Give us our artistic freedom, so we can show exactly what we want to tell.'

RK: Right. And what's the second perspective?
MO: From a global point of view, you can see that cinematic story-telling is completely dominated by American films. And English, French, German, Danish directors, all try to replicate the American way. In Denmark, since World War Two, we seem to know much more of American society than we do of our own. So, by making rules that compel you to tell stories in the here and now, it forces writers and directors to consider the reality of which they're a part. We've seen it before, with the *nouvelle vague*, with neorealism. It's never new. It's always just a question of where it'll pop up next. It's not that I think the American way of telling stories is so bad; of course we want to be entertained by those more anonymous films. But you should make films that look at your own life, your own way of seeing. Dogme can do that.

RK: I'm wondering which aspects of the Dogme films are particularly novel or startling to a Danish audience?
MO: Well, take *The Idiots*. It depicts an experiment; but the film itself is an experiment. And to me it shows a generation of people who are spoilt, who believe they can act out any role they care to. And some would say that's the role of artists, playing the idiot or pulling stunts to get attention. I find some scenes in the film very touching and sincere, full of life and energy. But it offends a lot of people: they close off, they don't want to see it.

RK: They find it distasteful.
MO: Yeah. And not just because of the explicit sex.

RK: But for what they perceive to be the mocking of the afflicted.
MO: But then a lot of so-called 'well-made', 'tasteful' films do nothing but mock reality constantly, you know? Killing people, and then having a good laugh about it.

RK: Yes. A film like *Armageddon* does sort of scoff in the face of humanity from start to finish, really.
MO: Sure. So who are the real idiots here? (*Smiles.*) I don't know . . .

RK: Some Danes have told me that *Festen* shows a side of Danish

life they find very suffocating; so that watching the film was rather liberating.

MO: Yes, I've heard stories of people fainting during screenings. Danish films have customarily found it difficult to describe our national rituals in an interesting way. We think it's much more exciting to look at an Italian wedding or whatever. But that's part of *Festen*'s success. Every culture has a way of organizing family gatherings; and in every family there are secrets. *Mifune* too is about secrets, and it's set in a part of Denmark that we don't often see in films. It's also about this old Danish idea of a romantic peasant country that's long gone, though it still pops up in children's films. But it's given a fresher description in *Mifune*.

RK: What's your view of the New Year's Eve project?

MO: It's useful in that it will prove whether or not they really are a Brotherhood. It's one thing to say it, but when they work separately, they're inevitably in competition. Now they must work together, and it'll be good sport to see if they can inspire each other. In Denmark, directors are always seeing each other's pictures, or reading each other's scripts, and commenting on them. So there's a friendly competition. 'You show me yours, I'll show you mine,' a little like in kindergarten.

RK: With the change in the certification and the globalization of Dogme95, will its specifically Danish character be diluted?

MO: Sure. And it has to be that way. Dogme has done its work, it has made certain waves. And now there will be a new provocation. Just yesterday I was reading about Truffaut when he was at Cannes with *Les Quatre Cents Coups*. And he said to a friend, 'We've won!' There is that feeling in the Brotherhood. But after winning one battle, you move on to the next.

RK: Lars von Trier and Peter Aalbæk Jensen seem to make a formidable public relations team in the reporting of Danish film outside Denmark. But do they get tiresome?

MO: Oh, you don't get tired of seeing Laurel and Hardy, do you? They're very entertaining, those two, and they've given Danish film great energy. The only trouble is that sometimes their more ironic gestures and comments are taken a little too seriously. But, again, it may be a Danish trait – sometimes you can hate people and call them all kinds of names. Then they go and show you what they can do, and you almost want to worship them.

RK: So the films make up for the needless gossip and mischief?

MO: Well, sometimes the hype is necessary. The idea that Danish films are doing well has political consequences, too. It gives Danish audiences new reasons to go to the cinema, or to go back to the cinema. And this year Danish films account for almost 30 per cent of the home market, which is the highest it's been for years.

RK: That presents quite a challenge to the US imperium.

MO: (*Laughs.*) Oh, I think they'll just see it as another fly.

RK: To be swatted away like all the rest?

MO: Well, if you were also to see a rebirth of Italian film, French film, German film – then you would have a serious competition with America. Entertainment is the world's second largest export. The GATT negotiations proved that it's something the USA takes very, very seriously. And Danish directors get a lot of offers to go to the States.

RK: But that's Hollywood's trick: if they can't swat the fly, they'll swallow it. Can you see that happening to Thomas Vinterberg, for example?

MO: Of course directors will be attracted. But I think it's a question of artistic freedom at stake. And a few directors have tried it and not had the success they hoped for . . .

RK: Do you regret the script decisions being taken out of the consultants' hands by the arrangement with Dogme?

MO: Sure, as a consultant I'm digging my own grave. (*Smiles.*) But the artists know best. If they're able to make a film, they know what they want to do. Often, as a consultant, the better part of the job is not getting in the way of the right projects, instead of blocking the wrong ones: get out of the way, and let them make the film. Of course, I can easily say this, because I'm leaving office in two months. (*Chuckles.*) But I'm not too happy about the slow rise of producer power in Denmark: this idea of 'We must have an industry.'

RK: Kristian Levring said he feared that film was becoming a producer's medium and Dogme just another branding tool.

MO: Oh, to me Dogme95 is already gone. But many directors and writers still want to do these films. Now it's just a question of giving people opportunities to work within a set of rules and make a low-budget film. And if the films are any good, they will still be known as 'Dogme films'. And if they're no good, they'll just slip into oblivion . . .

Afterwards, I hold our clapperboard over Mikael's face and explain that, since we're not permitting ourselves any onscreen captions in the film, we must get a shot of his name beneath his face, for identification purposes. Trying to put the subject at ease, I mention that Peter Aalbæk had jokingly put his nose betwixt board and clapstick, *à la* Kilroy. 'You want me to put my dick in it?' Mikael fires back, straight-faced. He also confirms that Peter Aalbæk is no 'saloon communist'. He was indeed a Party member, and so is unable to enter the United States. But then, whose loss is greater? In any case, the average American would have a tough time comprehending the actions of people so deficient in venality that they fail to copyright even their most lucrative invention.

12 'You're talking serious decomposition here':
Anthony Dod Mantle & shooting Dogme-style

NASA, Copenhagen: Tuesday, 16 November 1999

Back to the spanking white-on-white interior of NASA, a swank three-tiered club where Jack and I had commanded the floor on our first night in town. Nicolai, evidently a made guy in this town, has secured us a private hire for the afternoon; and so, amid a more tranquil ambience, we meet the gifted cinematographer Anthony Dod Mantle. Having lensed *Festen*, *Mifune*, and *Julien Donkey-Boy*, he's become to Dogme95 roughly what Raoul Coutard was to the *nouvelle vague*. His dance-card is now topped by assignments with Gus van Sant and Gaspar Noe. As we fumble behind the bar for soft drinks, we explain our division of labour, and Saul identifies himself as the uncredited director. 'Oh, come on,' laughs Anthony. 'I don't think *that* holds. Everyone knew who Lars was, which is why he could write that Rule. They probably didn't know Thomas then. But they do now. I remember chasing him all over Europe after Cannes. "I thought you weren't supposed to be credited . . ."'

RICHARD KELLY: Anthony, you've been behind the camera on three of the first six certified Dogme films. So, are you afraid of being typecast as the Dogme Cameraman?

ANTHONY DOD MANTLE: Oh, it's already happened. I'm 'Mr Dogme', 'Anthony Dogme Mantle'. You don't have to do much in this business to get labelled, do you? And I have been, for sure: also in respect of digital video, which really has nothing to do with Dogme, ironically enough. But after *Festen* came out, I started being dragged around to various panel discussions, which made me very aware that I was becoming a symbol of something . . .

RK: A prophet of the digital revolution, perhaps?
ADM: I don't know about 'prophet'. There are other ways of spelling it: 'profit', maybe. (*Chuckles.*) But I am worried about acquiring that identity. I mean, every story has its look . . .

RK: And for *Festen*, DV happened to suit the material?
ADM: I think so. Now it's done, and it's gone round the world, and it's opened up the game for some film-makers to get their stories made. Because the mainstream has started to consider that maybe you can make films with electronics, and a certain look can be achieved.

RK: So how did it start? How did you get the job on *Festen*?
ADM: I'd known Thomas for about ten years prior, and I shot his first feature, a road movie called *The Greatest Heroes*. Then he came to me and said, 'We're going to do this film. It's not a normal film, it's Dogme. And it means a strange status for the camera.' But I was interested – especially after I read the story.

RK: And how did you feel when you first read the Rules? Did you foresee trouble ahead?
ADM: Well, the old arthritis started to play up immediately . . .

RK: Because of the hand-held clause?
ADM: Yes, I could feel the old war wound itching . . . To be quite honest, I looked a bit (*looks askance*) at them at first. But I knew Lars well enough to know that if he makes rules, it's for a reason, and you pay severely if you don't abide by them. Then as pre-production started, we came across the pitfalls posed by each Rule, one by one. But Thomas and I were determined to treat it as a form of entertainment, rather than a six-week sentence in Dogme Camp, you know? It was

fun, and if you don't play it like that, it's just a pain in the arse and you shouldn't do it.

RK: Was DVC presented to you as a *fait accompli*? Or were you and Thomas hoping to shoot film?

ADM: Yes, we were both keen on film. And I think, originally, when those Rules were written, on a lavatory seat or wherever, they were imagining those big Second World War-style 35-mm cameras, available light, everything hand-held, 'Let's go for it, boys! Charge!' That kind of attitude. And that's what I fancied. I've shot documentaries like that – the big negative in a low-light situation, grabbing what you can, moving fast. To introduce that legitimately into fiction is a joy for film-makers. So we wanted to make a go of it. But the budget was tight – I mean, where have I heard that before? So we started testing formats, and I tested more on *Festen* than on anything previously. We started on 35 mm, and I had all sorts of sponsored deals going with companies, I was fishing out the old stock, whatever I could get. Then we moved to 16 mm, which looked a real mess to me, 'falling between two chairs', as we say in Denmark. Then I looked at Super-8, but by now the production was saying, 'We think it's video', and pushing the more conventional large cameras up to me. For a while I thought maybe we could shoot the exteriors in Super-8 and the interiors on video; but that was even more expensive than 35 mm. So I thought, 'If it's video then we've got to do something dynamic here.' And we decided to go with these small cameras.

RK: Which model of camera did you settle upon?

ADM: Well, there were Panasonics and Canons around, but for me the only camera that really sat in my hand and made me feel 'This is a weapon' was the Sony PC7-E, a first-generation consumer camera, single-chip, about twice the size of this glass. (*Gestures to a tumbler on the table.*) You can fit one in each hand. So I tested it, transferred it to film, and we liked the look. Now it's often the case that when you make a compromise in shooting, you can still do a lot in post-production. I wasn't allowed that. But what I gained was agility, mobility, accessibility – what I call the 'emotional movement' of these small cameras, as opposed to the more premeditated movement you have to do when you have a heavy film camera on the shoulder. Coming from documentary, I've learned that if you're involved in the situation you're shooting – as a DoP should be – then very often you have to move before your brain really registers what you're doing. I realized I could make those moves with this camera. And Thomas's story felt very appropriate for it – this mad family sitting down to dinner, where it's almost as if the camera is being operated by some family member who doesn't really grasp what's going on.

RK: How many cameras did you run on an average scene?
ADM: I would say about 80 to 85 per cent of the thing was shot on one camera. When we shot Christian's big speeches, we wanted to get reactions first time, because the extras didn't know what they were about to hear. But we couldn't break the sound-to-image Rule, so there we used two or three cameras – I just gave the cameras to whoever I felt was competent, placed them, told them to stay there and behave themselves as best they could. And then I prayed to the gods . . .

RK: Even the actors took a turn as operators, right?
ADM: Yes, there's a nice little moment late on with Gbatokai Dakinah and Paprika Steen. I asked them to hold the camera while they waltzed together.

RK: How did you feel big-name actors like Henning Moritzen coped with playing to this little camera?
ADM: Well, Henning's a great actor, thirty years of experience, and of course all great actors have a certain degree of vanity that's necessary to the job. Birthe Neumann, who plays the mother, was the same. Almost subconsciously, they're used to presenting their best side to the camera; so they wanted to know roughly where I was going to be. But I told them I would never be in the same place twice unless it was absolutely essential, so they should stop thinking about where the camera was altogether. But, of course, they learned to sense when I was about to go off.

RK: Let's talk about the aesthetics of the video image. Did you end up having to push the film?
ADM: Bloody right, John. (*Chuckles.*) 'Push' is not the word. You're talking serious decomposition here. You're talking words like 'disintegration' and 'destruction'. But all those metaphors were appropriate for that disgraceful family. I just wanted to find a cinematic language that could convey that pretty catastrophic, pitiful – also amusing – situation these people were in. In the end, I converted the video to a very high-speed, pushed film stock. That way, the digital noise starts to

speak to the film grain. And I wanted this square, Academy, organic mass to bubble up there on the screen, you know? I wanted to take a Vermeer and a Rembrandt, and get a big soup spoon and really stir 'em up, like porridge oats. That's what I wanted to marry off, progressively, through the film. It's hard to control, and I can't pretend I had complete control of it throughout. But I love the images late on of the father, as if he's slowly disintegrating: those profile-shots of his face where the light is so low but there's so much gaining.

RK: It's very effective. By the time we get to those dark, 3 a.m. scenes, the image looks to be breaking up at the edges.

ADM: Oh, it is. Initially, we were doing the video-to-film conversion here in Denmark, in order to get it ready in time for Cannes. We had a pretty good lab, one that Zentropa use a lot. At that time I was pushing two stops on a fast film. But it turned out we had a slight problem with one of the cameras, and Cannes was pressing, so I went down to a lab called CINECO in Holland to finish it off. And I was only allowed to push one stop there, which changed the effect somewhat. But it's still there. Then, of course, the film came out, did well, people loved it. And at the end of the day, thank God, some people did accept that there was this recipe of gradual decomposition in there. Actually, I think people in America were more open to it than in Europe. Some of my colleagues were a bit dubious. I heard wonderful things as well, but there were some very long silences in conversations I had about *Festen*. Even my wife thought it was a pretentious pile of rubbish. And if it hadn't done so well at Cannes, I think people would have just slammed it completely.

RK: But the film is often very elegant. I especially like the eerie sequence when Christian is tied up in the woods by Michael. The film is rather noisy, raucous, for the first hour. Then, with this scene, you have stillness and quiet, and a moment of real reflection for Christian.

ADM: Yes, he's out in the cold. Something desperate has happened, these two brothers are suddenly at each other's throats. And you're outside of the house for the first time since this appalling, claustrophobic dinner party started. There is something incredibly sombre and sad about that moment: the leaves and the autumnal light through the trees. It's a bit *Conformist*, a bit Bertolucci. Also in that scene, there are images where the camera is starting to lose control. I had some of the shots on auto-focus, so it was automatically adjusting itself, back and forth. And any working DoP might think, 'That's stupid. Why do it? That's what an assistant's for.' But it was one of those games we played. Just an emotional decision, we went for it, and whether the editor, Valdis Oskarsdottir, used it was up to her.

RK: Speaking of moments that might normally have been excised – there's a shot when the camera bumps into Thomas Bo Larsen.

ADM: Yeah, I smacked him one. Serves him right, he was paid more than me. It's a light-hearted scene, it's early in the film, and it was early in the shoot. I'm not getting too desperately involved there. But already there's a certain tension. I'm making these rather odd movements all over the place. And Thomas had been told not to worry about the camera – 'Hit it if you want.' Then it's a question of whether you clear that stuff up on the editing table, or whether you stick it right in there.

RK: One shot in the film clearly isn't hand-held, right?

ADM: Yes, this is my confession, I suppose. Mette is lying in bed after she and Michael have had sex. The camera had to come down from the ceiling to where she's lying; which is very difficult to do, and that's why you have Louma cranes. I couldn't climb up there and stretch out and bring the camera down smoothly like I wanted to. And I really wanted that shot to be precise. So I borrowed the sound guy's boom-pole, like this one here (*thwacks Nikolai's mike*), and I stuck the camera on to it with gaffer-tape. So it was still 'kind of' hand-held, I was still holding it, only it was on an extension to my hand. I get up to the ceiling and whack it down into the actress's face, back and forth a few times. And I realize I've finally got the take I want. And I was getting sweaty, and the mood was getting irritable, and Thomas was asking, 'Is it there now?' So we did it. And this is one for the film buffs, but if you watch the shot in slow motion, and look across the bedroom at the mirror in the bathroom, you can see the reflection of this idiot desperately trying to steer this camera down on a sound-pole. But I'm pretty sure, with my soul on the table, that it's the only scene that involves some kind of cheating.

RK: So it was the heat of the moment, and you didn't tax yourself too much for that little infringement?

ADM: Sure. It wasn't as if we were using a tripod. I mean, even if I rested the camera down on a table, I still made sure I was holding it in my hands. I don't think that's criminal. I mean, I've always perceived these Dogme films as an introduction to a discussion. It's not biblical, it's not like the Spanish Inquisition. It's more like, 'Do what you can. We'll talk about it afterwards.'

RK: For *Mifune*, you were back with the 16-mm film camera. Was it good to be home again?
ADM: Well, I don't know where home is any more. But, yes, 16 mm was more appropriate to *Mifune*. It was pastoral, you had this broken-down farm, you had landscapes, flat fields in the south of Denmark. It was very much social realism, and that's the tradition Søren comes out of. He's a humorist, he likes it gentle, with just a few characters.

RK: But do you think he relished the challenge of a new method?
ADM: Oh, yeah, he was fascinated. He'd be asking me, 'Can we really shoot in this? I can't see the actors. Can you?' And he was relieved that we could do it. But he was tense going into it, he regularly cursed the whole Dogme thing. It wasn't easy for him to start shooting so soon after Cannes 1998, and the enormous success of *Festen*, in particular. I wouldn't say he cursed the success the Brothers already had. But, let's be honest, when you're riding a wave and it's your turn, there's a creative tension and an artistic nervousness that a director is entitled to. That was evident, and I left it alone. Søren knew that *Mifune* was going to be completely different, and that some people were going to ask, 'Where's the edge?' At the same time, he comes from a long line of 'Euro-puddings': well-made, beautifully shot, technically precise films. From that to this small crew and available light? Of course he enjoyed it.

RK: Was there any debate over what format *Mifune* would be?
ADM: Again, we tried to shoot it 35 mm, but we ended up on 16 mm. Then I had to find a film speed that was aesthetically appropriate. With *Mifune*, I wanted the grain just to break down a bit. I could foresee the kind of problem you get when you try to photograph a disgusting environment, like a tenement building in the 1920s. If you bring a sophisticated large-format camera in there and take a picture, the whole place looks beautiful – like you want to stick your tongue out and lick the dust off the image, you know? I wanted more grain and texture, to avoid that potential for a romantic mess. And I had two stocks, so I pushed 'em both – so that they matched in the grain structure. And I pushed two stops, so we were working around about 1,000 to 1,200 ASA. Working with the fast speed gave me kick-lights from things like TV screens, or the reflections that you get off table-tops and walls. At

that speed, they start to expose like highlights. That gives contrast and life and mood to a film. A lack of contrast is depressing to me, and I don't think it inspires an audience. It's like walking into this place here in the day (*gestures around the club*), when the light level is so even.

RK: How was the operating chore? The frame is more stable than *Festen*, where Thomas said you were 'crawling around like a dog'.
ADM: Oh, yes, he loves that line, doesn't he? He enjoyed watching that. And, sure, I'd resolved to put myself in places where it was difficult to shoot, so I was crawling around with my head up various people's knickers. But actually *Mifune* was physically much harder than *Festen* – not just because it was a bigger camera, but because you're trying to hold the camera very still, because you know it'll be more annoying to see any unnecessary movement up on the screen. There were lots of exterior wide-shots, and you don't want the horizon to be tipping up. It would have been even harder on 35 mm. Personally, I feel that even in a fantastic film like *Breaking the Waves*, for all its splendour, it wouldn't have bothered me if there had been a little more gentility and organic camera movement there. But I felt very pressured on *Mifune*, because obviously Søren was pleased to be shooting 16 mm, so we were sitting there for long, long takes. Your breathing is important. And after a ten-hour day, I was pretty damn exhausted, pretty whacked out.

RK: There are some very lovely 'conventional' images in *Mifune*, like a scene where Iben is hanging out some washing and it looks very much like 'the magic hour' before sunset . . .
ADM: Yes, the light's just going, it's seconds before . . .

RK: Did you think, 'I'm going to allow myself to be a little bit aesthetic here'?
ADM: Yes, I loved it. But it's funny, I do get a lot of flak about *Mifune*. Colleagues have said to me, 'Oh, it's clearly lit, isn't it? It's timed and everything.' And I've heard of critics in London saying, 'Oh it's not really a Dogme film.' Well, it wasn't lit at all. I had what I had. I've got a still somewhere of Søren wearing a white bathrobe, trying to add some soft light to a shot from just out of frame, asking me where he should stand.

RK: Maybe what critics were saying was that they had different expectations of Dogme, after *Festen* and *The Idiots*, where the content was more aggressive. Maybe *Mifune* was just too sweet for some tastes?
ADM: Well, it *is* sweet; maybe a little too much. I have my own personal

feelings about the ending. Whatever. It's a gentle, emotional story, and Søren's very good at that. And he's pleased with the film and that's the important thing. On *Mifune* it would have been totally absurd for me to be running around with one camera on my head and one in my breast pocket. The film is about people sitting there quietly, trying to reach each other, and slowly falling in love or falling out of love. I mean, there are scenes where people are fighting and there's a reason for movement, so the camera moves. But I think I operated the camera according to my own personal law of being present in the moment and involved in the story. And I think the style was appropriate.

RK: Right. So how did you get involved with 'Harmless' Korine?
ADM: (*Chuckles.*) 'Harmful', more like. Certainly not harmless. How did I meet him? *Festen* set a lot of things off in America, and Harmony met Thomas briefly. I think he'd been dabbling with this 'Julien Chronicles' thing for about six or seven years. Now of course Harmony's on the edge of film-making in American terms. A lot of people don't know him, so it wasn't such a difficult move for him to make; unlike Søren who comes from that background of immense machinery, or Lars, who's tried for the ultimate in contriving images, as in *Europa*. But Harmony found me because of *Festen*. And actually, from my first conversation with him, I daresay, I felt very related to him – almost spiritually (*smiles*), if you can say that about 'Harmful'. But there's something there . . . Harmony talks a lot about magic, poetry, lyricism. About breaking ground – he's a *provocateur* as well. But he knows his sources. The boy is well-read. Not to be underestimated.

RK: How did he entice you to *Julien*?
ADM: I was on Grenada, in the Caribbean, as I always try to be every year, just sitting and staring at the waves. And he started e-mailing and faxing me 'The Julien Chronicles', deliberately in the wrong order, so that no one could read it. And without any ending – as is often the way with scripts these days. It's getting to be a trend, and I think it has to stop. (*Laughs.*) People should try writing an ending without a start . . . But anyway, I had a couple of telephone conferences with him while I was still on Grenada – me sitting there in my shorts with a beer, a couple of producers on the line, one in New York and one in LA. And then it was kind of kamikaze. I left Grenada for Europe, five days shooting on a feature I was finishing, and then it was straight to New York and working with Harmony.

RK: Back in the summer, Harmony was quoted as saying that his ambition was to push the Rules further than they had been pushed before.

ADM: I think, to some extent, *Julien* bears a similarity to what Lars was trying to do with *The Idiots*. For me, one of the very interesting things about that film is this sudden experience of not quite knowing what you're witness to: whether it's real or unreal. I think Harmony was looking for those kinds of moments. Whereas *Festen* is a more classical narrative: it's very well written, very precise, there aren't many balls thrown up that aren't caught. I think Harmony was looking for something less foreseeable. I mean, I knew the vague destiny of Julien, his plot, his curve; but how we got there, and the order and the juxtaposition of scenes, was unknown. That was the case throughout shooting. So there was none of that 'Continuity? What are we cutting from, please? And what are we cutting to?' I didn't know.

RK: We've heard the look of *Julien* likened to a 'found film', something that could have been made any time in the past thirty or forty years. Is that what you were after?

ADM: Again, it was about decomposing the image: breaking down the official, conventional sharpness we're so used to, losing some detail but finding a texture. Initially, the kind of look Harmony and I discussed was 'archival', something-found-in-a-puddle; like the 1980s Xerox machines, where you didn't get a real black. And we found that via this amazing lab in Zurich.

RK: You were shooting with cameras all over the place, right? Concealed cameras, cameras in hats, cameras in watches?

ADM: Yeah, head-held, hand-held, breast-held – all sorts of strange cameras, even infra-red. For me, *Julien* was about lonely souls floating about in this incredibly intense urban environment; and about the potential voyeurism in being close to people without touching their lives or really feeling anything for them; just walking by them and knowing that maybe they'll be dead tomorrow – you wouldn't know. For some reason, I related that in my head to electronics, certainly to multiple cameras and coverage. I had a slight crisis in the beginning about shooting three-chip and single-chip, and NTSC and PAL. I was thinking, 'How am I going to marry this?' But I found a process, and I didn't think it would work as well as it did.

RK: Did you or Harmony have any visual models in mind?

ADM: We were inspired by the TV show *Taxi-Cab Confessions*, amongst other things. I was inspired by one of my own unforgettable cinematic experiences, by Gunter Walraff, a wonderful German journalist who tends to go underground and create a new identity for himself and then re-emerge with a film-essay. About fourteen years ago, he made an amazing piece about foreign workers coming to Germany and working illegally: all the corruption, all the high-level magnates involved. He shot with a hidden camera, very primitively but with such energy – you felt you were right there in the suitcase where the camera was placed. Some scenes were petrifying, and morally shattering – you didn't feel you were entitled to be there. *The Blair Witch Project* is probably about this same kind of thing . . .

RK: Is it true that Ewen Bremner was on this heavy Method kick, never out of character on the set?

ADM: I arrived in New York in January, and I worked with him every day for nine or ten weeks, and then I finally met Ewen Bremner at the wrap party in March, the evening before we were both leaving. He came in with his hair cut, talking broad Scottish. I could hardly recognize him. Before then, he was just gibbering his way through this schizophrenic ordeal, with his gold teeth and what-have-you. He was reluctant to talk to me outside shooting, because he was worried that he would be affected by my accent. But he was totally involved; he really put his soul on the line for the film, and deserves every possible credit. We had to cover one-off situations, sending a highly competent, improvising actor into a potentially volatile – who knows? – situation on the streets of Harlem. On some scenes I had four or five DoPs – a real mixture of characters, used to shooting American commercials on celluloid. And here they were, sitting with little cameras hidden about their person or in rings or on their heads or in a Bible. I mean, they wondered what the hell was going on beforehand, but afterwards they sensed it was an event. And, I must say, without being creepy: credit to the producers, Cary Woods, and Scott Macaulay and Robin O'Hara. They gave Harmony space, and not a lot of people would do that for him, not at this point. I mean, OK, once he really makes the tickets sell, which he hasn't done yet, they'll all be there, because Harmony's marketable. But not many would have taken the chance here. And they did.

RK: Of course, _Julien_'s very status as a Dogme film has been questioned, critics detecting some flagrant violations of the Rules, wondering why it even has a Dogme certificate in front of it.

ADM: Because you couldn't get it on the back of it.

RK: So you don't feel unchaste?

ADM: But I don't know where this comes from. I mean, Valdis Oskarsdottir, the editor, is vicious about these things: the last thing she wants to do is cheat. There's music in _Julien_, but it was recorded as the scenes were being shot, just like in _Mifune_, where we had a man playing a harmonica in a field at four in the morning. Same thing with the opera music in _Julien_. So I can't really comment, even if I'd like to. Flagrant? I think the only thing you can debate is the fact that we were forced – because of certain post-production situations, and money, and deadlines for Venice – to run a hard-matte 1:1.85 copy. In America, they can't show Academy; and if we wanted the film shown in America, we had to do one of those copies. And that ended up being shown at Venice.

RK: So presumably you caught some flak for that?

ADM: People reacted, because it's quite obvious that Academy ratio is one of the major Rules. Personally, I adore the Academy image up there in a cinema, especially for Harmony's film, which is like a monument. And _Festen_ looked just abstract-gorgeous in Cannes, bubbling away up there. I would have loved to see the same for _Julien_ in Venice, and I think it would have helped it. But I can't say more than that – I think we did our best. Like Baden-Powell: 'Dib-dib, dob-dob. Akela, we will do our best.' At the same time, I'm aware that Harmony's the kind of director who always goes his own way. But he's got a deep respect for Lars and Thomas: he considers them his friends and colleagues, and he loves their films. And he doesn't love many things.

RK: I believe you've been very taken by the way Dogme has distilled the relationship between the DoP and the director?

ADM: I think there's far too little understanding among critics and journalists of that relationship. But these three Dogme films have really highlighted for me the social mechanics of making films, which are about trust and respect. I mean, if you've got the right crew, it doesn't matter if it takes three hours to light a scene: they'll do it perfectly for what the job is. And if I'm working with available light, it's still just as difficult for me to figure out how I'm going to get this actor

from here to there so that you can see him. But in my experiences with Thomas and Søren and Harmony, sometimes they were so amazed or confused by the fact that we could actually shoot in certain places, that suddenly there was no more of that situation where the director thinks, 'Well, the DoP knows exactly what he's doing with his lights and his tools, so I don't have to think about how or why they're getting into that corner.' With Dogme you move in there like gangsters, with the camera on your shoulder and your sound guy, and you've got to try and improvise. The day before, you don't know exactly how it's going to go. So I daresay the directors become hyper-aware and respectful of what can be achieved, and of the fundamentals of what my work as a DoP is. And, for me, that was bloody gratifying. No self-punishment there whatsoever. I'm sure it's good for the directors too.

RK: Are you finished with Dogme for the moment?
ADM: I think I've extracted, or put in, all the energy I can – for the moment. But it's a brilliant experience for any film-maker to be a part of. A lot of industry people feel threatened by Dogme; lighting gaffers are saying, 'Where's my work?' And you hear people saying, 'Oh it'll never become a serious way of making films.' But it's there now; and instead of just cynically condemning it, people should try it, just to find out what their job's really about. And the way it's going, they'll probably get a chance . . .

13 'A spit in the eye of Danish tradition':
Thomas Vinterberg & *Festen*

Nine p.m., a pitch-dark night in the countryside, and Lars Bredo Rahbek guides us down the back-roads of the Film City compound towards 'The Bunker', a chalet where Vinterberg keeps office. In recent weeks, the trades have reported that he's working with Alliance Atlantis Pictures on an English-language follow-up to *Festen*. Entitled *The Third Lie*, it's said to be based on a trilogy of novels by Agota Kristof, tracing the story of a pair of identical twins through the years; and supposedly Thomas will direct from a script by himself and Mogens Rukov. Tonight, the man himself is off-duty, casual in jeans and tee-shirt. Nevertheless, the PC on his work-desk is glowing, and it's flanked by piles of papers and scripts, some bearing the stamp of ICM. Sweetly, he makes instant coffee for us. Rattling a spoon around each mug, he tells us that his wife, a theatre director, is expecting another child in February 2000. (Conception occurred in May at the Noga Hilton in Cannes, during his stint on the jury of the Short Film competition.) 'You can have *Festen* chocolate too,' he says, proffering a gift-box. Each of the sweets in the tray bears a *Festen*-related image on the wrapper: stills from the movie, the Dogme logo, a fetching portrait of Thomas. 'I think it was done as a gimmick,' he says. Yes, me too.

RICHARD KELLY: Have you been surprised – or appalled – by the response to this thing you started back in 1995?
THOMAS VINTERBERG: People don't seem to have picked up the idea in the way I hoped. I was hoping it would create a polemical atmosphere and provoke people to do something of consequence, maybe even contrary to Dogme – to make huge films, say, just to show you can do them another way too. But that doesn't seem to have happened here. In fact, Dogme has become almost a convention in itself, within Danish culture: now they talk about 'Dogme architecture', 'Dogme commercials'. In the commercials industry, you get this very expensive bad lighting, 'to look like Dogme'. I mean, that's not the point. The point is to get angry and do something different. The point is to reflect the movie business as it is – not to just give it another colour. But in some people's minds, Dogme just means 'hand-held films', you know?

RK: Or 'digital video films' . . .
TV: Yeah – which was *definitely* not the point. But in the beginning, it

reated a lot of anger, it provoked a lot of people. And I preferred that, because then people reacted against it. They started saying, 'Well, we'll show you what you can do with a lamp.' I mean, that's the idea, right? To shed some light . . .

RK: So have you grown weary of talking about Dogme95?
TV: I've had a break of about three months now, since I was in Japan. So I'm fresh again. But sometimes in these conversations you get to understand things that you hadn't necessarily thought about yourself. And anyway – as a missionary for the Dogme church, this is my job, right?

RK: How often do you four priests see each other?
TV: Lars I see every day, he lives next door. But all four of us together? That's kind of rare – partly because this shit has become world-famous now, and everybody is travelling around and has lost their roots. But then, really, we don't work that well together, you know? Four huge egos from different generations – it just takes too long to decide anything. Sure, we have a nice time, we drink a lot and yell at each other. But the decisions seem to get made when we're two. Or three. Or one.

RK: Still, you'll all be spending New Year's Eve together . . .
TV: Well, when we invented Dogme, we sat down for forty-five minutes and made some Rules; and it was the same with this New Year's project. We sat down for an hour or so, and again it became a set of rules for a frame, containing nothing – which it still doesn't! So we'll see if something comes up on the night. The nice thing about having four egos behind it is that you can create conflicts on camera, through the actors. And as Lars said, 'If it doesn't work, we'll just have to wait another thousand years to get a second go at it.'

RK: Meanwhile, will *The Third Lie* be your next feature?
TV: That's one possibility. I have two projects at the moment. I'm also writing an original script called *It's All About Love*, and it's set in the future.

RK: A literary adaptation and a futuristic film. So neither of these will be Dogme films?
TV: Definitely not. I mean, that's the whole point.

RK: Do you see yourself coming back round to another Dogme film, or do you feel like you've done your bit on that front?
TV: Doing *Festen* was by far the most uplifting thing I've tried, so far,

in this industry. Not just because of the result, and all the tickets sold
But you were part of a game; and I know this is a big word, but it wa
'cleansing', in a way. We took away all the shit, and I just did what
was interested in. I can't do that again. In order to avoid repetition, I
have to do something contrary the next time. But, yes, I'm looking
forward to that day when I can go back to the Dogme church and do
another film.

RK: After you've made your 70-mm full-costume epic full of swoop-ing crane shots . . .
TV: Something like that. (*Smiles.*) Which people will no doubt hate.

RK: You've used a lovely expression, that the Rules are about 'undressing' the film. And you wondered aloud to a reporter about what a director like James Cameron would look like 'naked'.
TV: I did say that, didn't I? How smart of me . . .

RK: A lot of grand American directors – Scorsese and Coppola and so forth – were invited to take part. But none of them have taken the bait. Can you imagine any of them ever will?
TV: If I were them, I wouldn't; because it's been done now, you know? And everybody wants to be the first. So whether they're going to catch the ball, I don't know. It has been reported, and it's true, that I asked Mr Spielberg if he'd like to do one. And he was very enthusiastic. I don't think he's *going* to do one, but he certainly played along with me about it.

RK: I've been wondering whether the Rules inspire certain types of script, or whether certain types of script lend themselves well to the Rules. It's no accident, is it, that all four Danish Dogme films are concerned with one tight-knit group of people in one location?
TV: Sure, they all seem to be group portraits. They're all very melo-dramatic, in a way; the emotional life is very explosive. And I think that's because you have nothing to tell the story with other than the actors; nothing else to use when you want to express feelings. You don't have music, for instance, to provide a crescendo. But you still have to keep the audience awake for a hundred minutes. The story really has to engage them, because if it doesn't, then nothing else will. And you just have your actors, so you have to make them faint, or puke, or fight – something, to express what it is that you want to get out. I also think that these films, ironically, have become the most

personal films that I've seen from each one of us for a while – which was not the idea, as far as I can tell from this Manifesto I've been reading. (*Laughs.*) But you do remove all the layers between what you're expressing and the audience. We were 'undressed'. That, combined with our concern for the purity of the whole Dogme project, encouraged all of us to dig a bit more into ourselves for these films. Not that I ever slept with my father, of course . . .

RK: But the story of *Festen* wasn't just plucked out of the air.

TV: No, I plucked it off the radio. A friend of mine heard this young guy telling his story, and he told me about it, then I sat down and wrote it. So I got the plot from that, the idea of the birthday party, and the speech. But all the details and the bases for the characters just came out of talking to people, and hearing about their sick lives. (*Laughs.*) Or their beautiful lives, whatever.

RK: Did you notice that the theme of parental rape rather broke out in European films, even some independent American films, around the same time as *Festen* appeared?

TV: Yes. It's a trend. I always seem to be the last one to burst on to the scene of these trends. It's happened before – I made a children's film about a father and a son, and then half a dozen films on the exact same theme were released in Denmark at the same time. I guess it's just that the world is becoming a smaller place – I mean, we all watch the same MTV and eat the same hamburgers, and we hear the same stories every day. So, if there's one big Hollywood movie about a maniac bomber, then you know there'll be four more along very soon after. That's the rational explanation. But maybe it's really something metaphysical . . .

RK: Well, there's certainly a kind of awful energy released when taboos are breached onscreen. I'm thinking especially of the climactic moment when Christian says to Helge, 'I just never understood why you did it,' and Helge replies, 'It was all you were good for.' I mean, that's what I call dramatic conflict.

TV: Well, you have to create a war between your characters, and that war arises from irrational moments. I mean, the rationality of characters is not so interesting. But when they have these small holes in their mind, where you can look in and explore their inner lives, *that's* where it gets interesting. So, to me, it was very natural at that point, when the father has to give in anyway, that he should do the very last thing he

115

can think of to try to kill his son. That scene shows his honesty, which is also brutality. In a way, he's very honest. And my feeling was that at that moment, he might as well be.

RK: You've said there's a kind of *hommage* to *The Godfather* in respect of the brothers. And I must say that Michael reminded me both of Michael Corleone and Fredo Corleone – rather weak, neurotic guys who suddenly decide they want to be cold, hard men and defend the honour of their rotten family.

TV: Well, I'm sure those parallels are there, because I've seen *The Godfather* many times. But what I specifically stole was a kind of framework for the character of Christian. I felt that he should be full of secrets; silent, mature, repressing a lot of things inside himself – like Al Pacino in *The Godfather*. And it's a nice thing to be able to say to an actor – 'Do it like Al Pacino.' They say, 'Oh, yeah!' – they like that. And for Thomas Bo Larsen, playing Michael, it was obvious that Sonny [James Caan] was going to be his part. Thomas and I discussed one thing very early – that Michael always wants to touch people and somehow be in physical contact: in order to feel secure, to feel that he's part of the family. Because he's always been rejected. So he's on top of Christian all the time, grabbing him and jumping on him. Just the way James Caan does in *The Godfather*. So, yeah, we carried on that way – stealing freely from *The Godfather*. (*Laughs.*)

RK: Thomas Bo Larsen's performance is generally very vigorous and energetic, and it does look as if the actors felt they were free to roam. Did you encourage improvisation?

TV: By the time I did *Festen* I was a bit tired of improvisations, because I'd done a lot of them before, and because of that I've heard a lot of nonsense in the cinema, you know? (*Flips his lips in imitation of baby-talk.*) A lot of words that weren't important. So for me it was a challenge to work with actors who respected the written word, like Henning Moritzen. My system was to follow the actor and find out what they were really good at, and then combine them. Thomas Bo Larsen is a brilliant improviser, as is Paprika, so that's what they did. The other actors had their lines, so they would just agree: 'I know you're improvising, but where are you landing? What's your last word?' And they took their cues from that.

RK: Did some of them react better than others to the camera being

this little thing in a man's fist, rather than the usual big apparatus?
TV: Henning Moritzen was shocked by the size of the camera. But he was very loyal to the project, and he adapted very quickly. And suddenly something happened – they started reacting to each other, rather than the camera. And it's a cliché, I know, but the camera became like the fly on the wall. Anthony literally was climbing over the furniture, or hiding away. And they kind of forgot it. They only had each other. And the fact we couldn't add any sound was very important. It meant that if we had an image of one extra, all fifty other extras have to be there too, to create the right sound. So they were on-stage all the time, like in the theatre.

RK: It makes for some lovely, strange moments. When Christian makes his first terrible revelatory speech to all the guests at dinner, there are reaction shots where it looks as if they haven't heard him. The older ones are still fussing over their food . . .
TV: Well, we didn't tell the extras that the film was about child abuse, or that Christian was going to make that kind of speech. That was an attempt to make it more Dogme-like. Plus I knew it would make a good story afterwards. (*Smiles.*) So they were all there at the location for fourteen days, becoming a family. All huge fans of the father, Henning Moritzen, who's done forty films in Denmark as the good guy. Suddenly this guy Christian stands up and reveals all. And it was interesting, because nothing really happened! Quite a 'true' moment, actually. People couldn't really deal with it – so they just kept . . . talking. We had three cameras in the room for the scene, and at that moment all three of them started to rush around like hell, to capture everything – all the reactions, right? And of course none of it was usable . . . (*Chuckles.*)

RK: Were you concerned that you might be incorporating genre elements into the piece: the 'ghost story', for example?
TV: Maybe I'm naïve, but to me, no, it wasn't a genre piece at that moment. I thought a lot about this genre Rule. And I found it a bad Rule, actually. Because it's very difficult to avoid genre. And somehow it's not very creative, because it's unspecific. Creatively, I found that the best Rules were the most specific ones: 'You have to hold the camera in your hand'; 'You cannot bring props with you.' But not being able to make a genre, or not being allowed to have 'taste' is, in a way, impossible.

RK: Right. So much is ruled out of court that you can't get started.

TV: Exactly. And then you can't say, 'Action!' because, if you say it in a certain way, then it's a matter of taste . . .

RK: Anthony has confessed to his one violation of the 'hand-held' embargo, the camera taped to the boom-stick. But did you see that as a venial sin rather than a mortal one?

TV: Well, I'm proud to say that I was the one who invented the Confessions, and actually I did that to emphasise how rigid I was; to make it clear that we really observed the Rules. That was the idea, but then people kind of misunderstood it and pulled me up and said, 'You broke the Rules, it's not a Dogme film.'

RK: You told another interviewer, 'There is nothing in this film that is pinpointing our time or our society.' And yet I've heard it said that _Festen_ is the most Danish of films, especially in the way that it skewers bourgeois family life.

TV: Well, I understand that. But what I was trying to say in that interview is that the film is not a reflection on our time, on the youth of Denmark right now – 'Generation X', all that. I don't feel so modern myself; I wouldn't be the right person to do that. This is a story that could have taken place a hundred years ago. I have understood that it has really touched something Danish, and that people have felt very provoked by a film coming that close to something they know. But that has nothing to do with our time, I think. It's concerned with a very old family topic. The oppression of truth is a story that has always been there, I think. Or at least as long as the culture, the civilization has existed.

RK: I expect that's what Freud would say.

TV: Oh, would he? (_Winks, makes a thumbs-up._) Good work.

RK: One thing that does feel very timely is the racism in Michael's baiting of Helene's boyfriend. I understand that character was created because you wanted to cast the actor, Gbatokai Dakinah?

TV: Yes, he's my best friend. He's Danish but he lives in New York. And I missed him, but I couldn't afford to fly him home; and he's a bass player, so he can't afford anything. So I gave him a part. But then casting him brought up a theme that had something in common with the main theme of the film; because the oppression of the truth is very closely related to being afraid of anything foreign. And I felt that just for a minute I maybe touched on some of the reasons for this growing

118

fascism in Europe. I mean, perhaps it comes from something that is closer than just politics.

RK: What would that be?
TV: If people have to close themselves off in order to oppress their own story, they're not able to be very open to other people. They're very vulnerable, in that sense. And Denmark is a very vulnerable place. That's why we get disturbed by other people, other colours, other ways of thinking – people who could reveal what's going on here. Is that understandable?

RK: Absolutely. Is that why immigration is such a recurrent political issue in Denmark? As with the riots the other week?
TV: This is a place that does not have room for injustice. It's also a place that does not have room for too many foreign people – I mean, that is the *mentality*. And that combination makes for some violent nights, yes. But when you see that in the newspaper, it's also a sign that there aren't that many things happening in this country. So if people burn a couple of cars in the middle of town, it's going to make the front page.

RK: Is there an insularity about Denmark? I mean, one thing the British think they know about Denmark is that Danes were even more opposed to the Maastricht Treaty than certain Brits.
TV: Yeah, we have a small brotherhood going on there, us and the Brits . . .

RK: So is that the sign of a society that's happiest going it alone? Suspicious of outside influence?
TV: Yeah. Which, in this case, is very nice, I think. I'm against the European Union myself: I'm on posters about it. As you say, it is a very self-satisfied country – and yet, at the same time, it's very humble. It won't allow anyone to tell it what to do; but I wouldn't call it a country of nationalists. It's just a nation of very proud and very stubborn people. But that's combined with a kind of vulnerability – because Denmark is so small, and we know it. That's the whole complex of this place. Everyone here is longing for something bigger; and when it's finally offered, we say no. (*Laughs.*)

RK: Are Danes proud at least to have provided the birthplace for the latest European avant-garde sweeping the globe?
TV: Well, it's the same thing as a guy with a small penis who wants a

huge motorbike. I think part of the arrogance behind Dogme95 represents a very small country with very small penises. (*Laughs.*) So it has to be very rigid and arrogant.

RK: Interesting. We met Peter Aalbæk today, and he was very proud of the big hog he was riding, and very disparaging of Trier's golf cart.
TV: Yeah, yeah, they have all these games. And Aalbæk is the living example – shouting all the time, right? I think the reason for hitting the table so hard is that when you're a small country, you have to yell to get heard.

RK: Back to the Rules for a moment: the scene in the woods in *Festen* is a kind of grace note, visually very interesting. But also rather tasteful, wouldn't you say?
TV: Yeah, I guess I became aesthetic for a moment. But the way Anthony and I worked was that we didn't prepare. We just went there and talked about where to put the camera, so it sort of happened in the moment. And of course they became 'aesthetic choices', but they were instant, and improvised. So I thought that was OK.

RK: You used a key piece of music in that scene, right?
TV: Oh, yeah, the grandmother is singing about the woods. It's a Danish hymn. I really like that moment. We wanted it to have that ironic effect. And in the editing it became even more so. It is of course a spit in the eye of Danish tradition.

RK: Which you're happy to do?
TV: Which every artist is happy to do. I mean, that's part of our job, isn't it? That's what you should expect from us. At the same time, I love to be here. Because of *Festen*, I've been invited to many other parts of the world, but actually it tends to bring home to me how much I like being here right now. Being a part of the Danish film industry is a proud thing – at the moment! In a couple of years it'll be time to leave, I guess. (*Laughs.*)

RK: Tempting, I suppose; especially now you've made a pop promo for Blur. Was that fun?
TV: Yeah. They were nice guys, very generous. And brave, too. I said to them, 'Well, I would like to see you sleep.' And immediately they said, 'Right! Let's do it.' And then the record company said, 'Shouldn't you make it a little more smooth, a little more commercial?' And I was the weak one. I said, 'Well, OK, maybe we should superimpose some slow-

motion images of you guys singing.' But they killed that immediately. They said, 'No, stick to your idea.' I liked that.

RK: They had a properly Dogmatic attitude?
TV: Definitely.

RK: How do you feel about the new certification process?
TV: Well, the old way was a kind of policing process, which we've now practised on each other. And of course we're now getting tired of it.

RK: Yet you've only had to play the role twice, with *Lovers* and *Julien Donkey-Boy*. Were the arguments that strenuous?
TV: With Jean-Marc there were some mistakes. I think somebody in the production, not Jean-Marc himself, had credited him, like, seven times or something. Just a misunderstanding, you know. It was corrected quickly, and then there were no more discussions. I've heard a lot of gossip about Harmony's film. And I was a very thorough policeman on this, I even interviewed him. But I truly couldn't find any specific mistakes. For example, the nun that you see was like a 'Nun-a-gram': they just rented a stripping nun. That's fine, that's allowed. So, you see, Harmony was quite innovative in using the Rules. And, really, I don't find these arguments so interesting any more. What I *did* find interesting was that it's a film that is very obsessed with its own aesthetics, which to me is contrary to the whole Dogme concept. But that's just a nice discussion, and it's the way Harmony sees this Movement. He's made his Confession too. And of course, it's true, there's one thing in the film which is a definite violation of the Rules, right?

RK: We're talking about Chloe Sevigny pretending to be with child, though not actually pregnant in real life.
TV: Sure. And Harmony confessed that he tried very hard to impregnate her for the purpose of the film but it just didn't work. Now, to me, that was a very beautiful explanation. So I found it all right.

RK: But when discerning audiences who have boned up on the Vow of Chastity then see a film containing dissolves and voice-over, they're bound to say, 'Surely this can't be Dogme?'
TV: Well, I know the voice-over might sound as if it was added afterwards. But they were actually doing it while they shot the film.

RK: In other words, they were using the button on the Sony camera that allows you to record sound over a still image?

TV: Yes. I mean, using a digital camera is a way of getting around the rule that the film must be Academy 35 mm. Then suddenly you have this camera in your hand and there are a lot of things you can do – stop-motion and so on. So we kind of agreed to that, because it happens in the very moment of shooting. And yet to me it becomes untrue to the basic *idea* of Dogme95. I think a Dogme film should be shot on Academy 35 mm – period. My film, Lars's film, all the films I've seen so far are definitely shot in accordance with Dogme95 as a philosophy, and also as a set of rules – they follow them as closely as possible. I consider them Dogme films at heart. But then, if you apply the Rules strictly, there's a discussion left at the end of the day as to whether there have really been any Dogme films made yet? And my answer would be, 'No.' Not if you're truly rigid about it.

RK: Of course, with the change in certification, it seems to mean that Dogme is about to lose its specifically Danish character. Is that a cause for any sadness on your part?

TV: No, for me it's a rescue, in a way, because I was ready to close this whole Dogme thing down. I mean, we invented this in 1995: we've 'done' Dogme, kind of. But Lars has a very generous mind and he said, 'Well, other people could have a nice experience with this.' To me, that suddenly opened up this Dogme Movement. I realized that people can experience this in Brazil without the tired old faces of the Dogme Danes, right? And I would be very happy if other film-makers could experience the same kind of relief we did a couple of years ago. Also we found it more true to the original concept that it should be up to people themselves. I'm curious to see if people will understand the set of Rules better, now that they have to be their own judges instead of just trying to get a certificate. Because Dogme is a challenge to the conformity of film-making. Cinema is, at the end of the day, the most conservative art-form so far. And this is an obvious way of provoking it, of creating some kind of life. People have a lot of difficulties understanding this. Maybe they'll understand it better if it's their own responsibility.

RK: What do you make of the fear that some people will just use Dogme as a brand name, for marketing purposes?

TV: You know what? That's happening right now, here. I mean, Zentropa has arranged this 'package' of Dogme films, they've signed up for sixteen films. Which is not the idea. Now, all of a sudden, a director comes to a production company and is offered a Dogme film. But

Dogme95 is a set of rules for a director, not for a production company. It's not Coca-Cola we're doing here. And I've said this to Zentropa and to Nimbus Film, but . . . (*Shrugs.*) I mean, the ball is rolling now. And I'm sad about that, because Dogme is not meant to be just another low-budget package. It's meant to awaken some directors, and challenge them. It was not the idea to make cheap films – 'It's a Dogme film, it's cheap, and it'll sell.' (*Grimaces.*) That's nothing. But of course, saying all these angry things . . . Dogme has at least made some people think about what they're doing. I think some people – certainly I include myself – are in better shape to avoid the mediocrity of filmmaking: the auto-pilot aspect of it. You know, whenever you sit down to prepare a film, there's this computer program, Macintosh designed it, and it says you need a Script Girl and a Lighting Engineer, and it tells you who to put in, and where, and how much they get . . .

RK: But if you burn that software, then you're a free man again?
TV: Yeah. You start over, you reinvent it.

Afterwards, Thomas reassures us that he had a good time, as he so often doesn't with 'those North American journalists'. He professes to find the junkets tiring and unhealthy, because 'doing interviews is like celebrating yourself'. He also remembers the offence he caused to the audience when he accepted the Los Angeles Critics' Circle award, and joked that it was an honour to receive a prize for a subtitled movie in a town where people don't read. We part in good spirits, and streak back towards the centre of the city. Saul confesses to having striven somewhat over-zealously for realism by trying to find flaws in the Vinterberg physiognomy. I am confident, however, that Thomas's commonly acknowledged status as The World's Most Attractive Film-maker will be unaffected by the outcome of our rushes.

14 Properly primitivist painting:
Lone Scherfig & Dogme DK5

Morning coffee with Lone Scherfig, the writer-director presently poised to shoot the fifth Danish Dogme film, and thus to take a momentous step as the first practising Dogme Sister. Inevitably, it transpires that she was in the same class as Kristian Levring at the Danish Film School; and she enquires fondly as to how things are looking in Kristian's cutting-room. We couldn't be more effusive.

RICHARD KELLY: Lone, how did the opportunity arise for you to make a Dogme film?

LONE SCHERFIG: I had just done a thirteen-part television series for Zentropa, and then they asked me if I'd like to try this. I've been directing for about fifteen years now, I've made two features and a lot of television: series, commercials. But mostly it's not been very personal material, so Dogme presented an interesting chance for me. Still, I had to think it over for about a month.

RK: What were your reservations?

LS: Well, I didn't want to be the one who made the bad Dogme film. (*Smiles.*) I wanted to be sure that the idea I came up with was fit for the occasion. Otherwise, why do it? But I think I've cracked the nut. I know I wouldn't have made this film were it not for Dogme. And this week, at least, I feel that I'm going to make a very good film; and I've never said that before.

RK: Is there any obvious reason why the Danish Film School has incubated this Dogme Movement?

LS: Actually, Dogme could be understood as a reaction against a kind of schooling that is very classical, very equipment-focused. But there is an inheritance from the Film School. One aspect is the close relations between the students. Another is the licence to make films that you know people won't see. The idea is that the students are locked in a house for four years and allowed to make films, and at the end they don't have to show those films to an audience if they don't want to. They can just shelve them.

RK: So you're taught that the process can be as rewarding as the end result?

LS: That the *failure* itself can be rewarding, I guess. And for me, that's reflected in the fact that you're not supposed to be credited as director on Dogme films. I choose to regard that as an offer to work as freely as I ought to, which is why I consider Dogme a gift, rather than a set of commandments.

RK: So, in some way, Dogme directors are not responsible. But how do you think you'll feel down the line when you're not allowed to sign the film as 'Directed by Lone Scherfig'.

LS: Well, I have written the film, which helps a little. (*Laughs.*) But of course it's no secret who has made these films, nobody has succeeded in keeping it a secret. It's more of a symbolic value. And that's OK with me.

RK: Lars von Trier is credited as the leader of this Movement, and his fame clearly helped it to get known. But is it possible that his fame might also cloud people's perceptions of what Dogme is?

LS: Oh, but this wouldn't have happened without Lars. I'm sure lots of directors around the world talk about starting a movement. There have been many in the past. The difference is that Lars doesn't just talk about it, he actually does the work.

RK: Do you have a favourite among the Dogme films so far?

LS: I prefer *The Idiots*. I was more moved and more shaken, and I laughed more than in the other films. I do like the others, but I suppose I could identify more with the main character of Karen, in that general process of self-projection that goes on when you see a film. She's the spine of the film.

RK: *Festen* and *Mifune* were generally better received.

LS: But *The Idiots* is a much more complicated film, it poses interesting questions. Not about finding one's inner idiot, because I don't have any big problems with that. (*Smiles.*) But the film has the same problem real 'idiots' have: people really don't want them too close. And I find that very moving.

RK: So where will your film fit into the Dogme taxonomy?

LS: Basically it's about four or five characters who run into each other's lives by coincidence. *Festen* and *The Idiots* and *Mifune* are all about people learning to live with their 'shadow' sides: with a childhood trauma, or the inner idiot, or a crazy brother. My film is about people deciding that they have the possibility of becoming very happy, and taking that chance. So it's the anatomy of a happy ending, you could say. But that makes it sound like rather a lightweight ballet of a film – there's deeper material underlying it. At the start these five people are very sad and insecure people.

RK: Nevertheless, so simply put, the film could sound like a romantic comedy, a genre piece, which is *verboten*.
LS: Well, my film will be very light, bubbly, funny – I hope. But I feel I can't place this film. And I'm aware that I don't have the help that a genre can provide – whereby if you don't know where to go next, then the genre leads you, you just follow its conventions. Also, the more I work with Dogme, the more it occurs to me that Dogme itself is a genre. And the more Dogme films that are made, the more you have to fight them, otherwise they become a system too.

RK: Have the Rules shaped your conception of the script?
LS: Well, I think the way the films are financed is very important. You get the money and you go. If it were a slower process of writing a script, having it read and discussed, three or four years of development, you'd lose the bubbles. And the fact that hardly anybody reads what I'm doing while I write means that the jokes don't wear out for me. Usually, few jokes can stand up to being repeated twenty-five times. Now, whenever I think, 'What if this character just said . . .?', I just write it. And they *will* say it. *Then* we'll see if it's funny. (*Laughs.*)

RK: And are you writing for people and places you know?
LS: Sure. I'm writing for actors whose work I know, because as I write the lines, I want to know how they'll sound coming out of those mouths. And I'm writing to a specific town, and putting all the characters in real buildings. We'll be moving into somebody's actual house, and taking their clothes out of the closet, and those will be our costumes. I can choose when I want to shoot, and this will be a winter film. But it so happens that we end up in Venice in the spring. (*Laughs.*)

RK: Do you have a title yet?
LS: I have ideas but I shouldn't say until I'm sure. But then, in a way, the title is 'Dogme 5'. Titles like *Festen* and *Mifune* are subtitles, really. So this is 'Denmark 5', or 'DK 5'.

RK: When Jean-Marc Barr's *Lovers* appeared in the Cannes Market, I think it had 'Dogme 5' on the advertising posters.
LS: Now it's 'France 1', 'F1', I think . . .

RK: What format will you shoot on?

LS: I'm thinking about this every day at the moment. But I think it will be DV. The freedom you get with the actors, and the time you save with the small crew, are too tempting.

RK: Søren has suggested that Lars and Thomas took the soft option in shooting DV. Would that trouble you?

LS: (*Smiles.*) No, I'm not doing this for sport or to compete with anyone. I'm doing it because I really want to see if this film can make anyone cry, or laugh.

RK: Now, whether you like it or not, you're going to be seen as a progressive figure. Dogme has been criticized as a bit of an all-male enclave. Now you're the first Sister. Are you aware of what a giant leap this is for Dogme – even if it's just a small step for you?

LS: But I just concentrate on the work, I can't think about what it means to be a woman in this situation. I have no idea what the alternative is. The material is feminine, in that it has to do with soft values. It's a love story, and two of the five main characters are women. But actually, in order to trust myself to spend so much of other people's money and time, and ask an audience to listen to me for about a hundred minutes, what I need is maybe some of my masculine side.

RK: But you don't think of Dogme as a man's club?

LS: No worse than anywhere else in the film industry. There is a solid tradition for female directors in Denmark, since way back. So I'm not such an exotic creature within this industry as I would be in many other parts of the world. I've worked in this business for so long, I know all the actors and crew. So it's not as if I walk in the door and people go, 'Oh, it's a woman!' It's not an issue for me. (*We pause a moment as I fiddle with my errant lapel-mike. Lone smiles. 'I have to come up with a good answer for this feminist thing, because everybody asks me, and I really don't know what to say.' But it seems unnecessary to pursue the subject.*)

RK: Lars has said that, like 'spassing', the Dogme Rules must be approached with absolute passion. Otherwise it won't work. It's not a set of rules to guarantee a good film. Do you identify with that?

LS: Of course, there are some stories that can't and shouldn't be told within this Dogme regime. There are films you can only make with a big machine behind you, and there are things that you can't say within the language of Dogme. It would be like writing in verbs only, with adjectives forbidden. The criticism of the Dogme – 'Why do they throw away four-fifths of their paintbrushes and make do with the remainder?' – is true. But you just have to make sure that what you do is properly primitivist, that you use those brushes well, and not find yourself longing for the ones you threw away as part of this procedure. Also a primitivist painting should be done quite fast, I'm sure. If you pause for too long, you lose it, you should throw it out and start again. I'm quite aware of the fact that you can make a horrible Dogme film. If the script is poor, you can't hide from that. It's as if you are going to a party and you've not got any money but you want to be dressed fabulously – either you rent some fabulous outfit or you show up nude. It's the only way to make sure people will look at you.

RK: Abroad, people could be forgiven for thinking Dogme is the sum of contemporary Danish cinema, but are there other trends in Danish film now? Are there directors who reject Dogme?
LS: Oh, yes. This is such a small part of Danish production – one or two films out of twenty-five in a year. There's a new wave of socially oriented, realistic films, from young directors who are very inspired by the tradition of Ken Loach and Mike Leigh. Then, of course, there are still the big-budget historical films with women in long dresses. But the mainstream films aren't so successful; usually directors accept a low budget without taking the consequence, and try to shoehorn a big film into a small frame, which is suicidal, every time. It's just compromise, compromise. Whereas Dogme enabled us all to see a way of fighting the usual low budgets – you can turn them into an advantage.

RK: As a former film student, do you feel affinities between Dogme and the previous realist waves in cinema history?
LS: Yes, and I'm sure they will become even clearer over the course of time. The French films of the 1950s, or the Italian films of the 1940s, the English films of the 1970s, are films that are as naïve and clean in their expression as the Dogme films. For me, the prose part of the Manifesto, the fact that you promise to find truth as you work, or at least to look for it, is much more important than whether you have artificial light or props or music.

RK: 'Waves' don't always travel so well, they tend to be strongest in their place of origin. There have been the two non-Danish Dogme

films that have had a curious reception. Is it possible that only Danes really know how to do Dogme films?

LS: Interesting . . . I haven't seen those two films yet, the tapes are still sitting on my desk. So I can't comment. But I wouldn't say it's just for Danes. I mean, prove me wrong! (*Laughs.*) But I think that the kick of working fast with light gear is strongest if you've already made a couple of films with a big crew and heavy equipment.

RK: Right. So it's not to do with, say, being Danish and feeling there's something stifling in the culture that you have to combat?

LS: (*Smiles.*) No. But actually I think there's something in the Danish culture that Dogme can help you get out of. And that's the modesty, and the fear of being over-expressive. That feeling is clear in *Festen* – you have a young director really doing his best to take on very serious, heavy material, and to fight with it. And it's no accident that the antagonist of the film is a man of sixty. The courage to do that is hard to find in a society as Scandinavian as ours. But Dogme forces you to take yourself and the situation seriously, and that's not a very Scandinavian way of thinking.

RK: But what is the Scandinavian way of thinking?

LS: Oh, very ironic, very modest. People will say something and then regret it two minutes later.

RK: Whereas with Dogme, there's no room for regrets?

LS: Well, if you read Lars's diary of making *The Idiots*, you see that he reshot certain scenes. But you shouldn't calculate for that. You have to turn up to shoot the scene and think, 'Today is the day that we will all do our best.' Then again, it is very cheap and uncomplicated to go out and reshoot on video . . .

RK: But ideally you want to be saying, 'Today is the day we tell the truth. No turning back.'

LS: Absolutely. You can't tell your actors, 'Do your best today, OK? But we might end up throwing it out.' In that case, you might as well go home.

15 A night on the tiles, with *Pink Prison* and Porno-Lasse

The evening found us in search of diversion, as the streets teemed with exuberant Danish football fans in horned helmets. So we took up an invitation from Zentropa to the première of the first release from 'Puzzy Power', their spanking new pornographic label. *Pink Prison* was the heart-soaring title of the work under review. Wine and canapés were served beforehand in the busy foyer, and the clientele seemed like hip, youthful, and not obviously perverse, representatives of Cool Denmark; so helping the five of us to fight down the sense of overpowering weirdness in what we were about to do. Then, eagle-eyed Nicolai alerted us to the presence in the crowd of 'Porno-Lasse', the Vancouver-born Adonis who is one of Denmark's premier sexual performers. Though none of us could name any of his credits (you understand), we had learned to recognize him as the star of an advertising campaign adorning the sides of Copenhagen's buses. Nicolai had translated the copy like so: 'Sell us your girlfriend. You'll get twenty-five thousand kroner; she'll get a night with Porno-Lasse.' So it seemed as good a moment as any to get to the bottom of all this.

RICHARD KELLY: Lasse, we've been seeing a lot of your face on the side of buses. What's going on there?
PORNO-LASSE: It's for a radio station here in Denmark. They have some strange ideas, right? They've done things like this in the past. They ran a competition where they would pay for a girl to have her breasts enlarged, or they'd have a couple fucking in the studio while they were on-air. So then they thought, 'We've got to do something wilder.' And they asked me, 'Would you like to do something a little like that movie *Indecent Proposal*?' Basically it has to be a couple, living together, both over twenty years of age – that's very important. And the guy has to agree, 'Yeah, it would be fine with me if my girlfriend had a very pleasant night with Porno-Lasse.' And I thought, 'This is outrageous. I'm in! Let's party!'

RK: Does it worry you at all that the guy in question might feel a little deflated, after his girlfriend's been with you?
P-L: Sure. For me, the worst thing that could happen would be that I have a night with a girl and the next day she cuts loose from her boyfriend, because she never tried anything like that before. We talked

about that at the station, and I told them that the winners have to be a couple with no jealousy between them.

RK: So your conscience is clear. Are you in this movie we're about to see?

P-L: No. They asked me to be in one particular scene, and I said, 'Sure', but the casting director wanted me to shave my hair very close and dye it white. And it took me three years to grow it as long as this, so I told them, 'This is gonna cost you a lot of fucking money, man.' I've seen a few moments from it, and it looks very attractive, very erotic. But it's not my style. I mostly work on real hard-core porno movies.

RK: *Pink Prison* is part of the Zentropa enterprise, who also make Dogme films. Have you seen any of them?

P-L: I was a part of *The Idiots*, in fact, but they cut me out. You know Lars von Trier wanted this big gang-bang scene? And he needed a few close-ups of pussy and dick. He used two couples, and I was in one, but he only used the other couple. I don't know why – maybe I was too limp. But it was a very special situation, funny to be a part of it: you start to fuck, then all the other actors come in and you think, 'What the fuck is going on?' I saw Lars von Trier in a little fight with his actors. He's like (*pointing sharply*), 'You, and you, and you – you're gonna do it like this.' His script wasn't very defined, it looked like they were working it out as they went along, improvising, feeling their way through. But I must admit – I felt like I was just a little on top for a while, working for Lars von Trier.

RK: You were proud to work for Lars von Trier?

P-L: I showed my balls to Lars von Trier! And there he was, hanging over me with his video camera. But he cut me out!

RK: Did you see the movie when it came out?

P-L: Of course. Two or three times. I think it's good, but a lot of Danish people say it's so funny, and I don't agree. In a way, it gets behind certain feelings that people have. But to me, it's too easy. Maybe it's because I'm an old hippie. This idea of pretending to be an idiot in front of people who don't know any better – my opinion is, 'So fucking what?' It's nothing special for me, to do what they did in that movie. But I like this Dogme project. It gives some opportunity to show some honest reactions – not like the typical American movies where everything is so theatrical. In Dogme, the actors just do it and the camera catches that.

RK: Do you think it's possible to make porn in a Dogme style?

P-L: I'd love to. I wanted to make what they call a 'gonzo movie', when you talk to the camera and grab hold of it and tell them what to shoot. 'Hey, cameraman! Get this! Look at her! Oh, it's a he!' But I've seen an English guy do it, a guy called Ben Dover. He doesn't play it like a movie, he makes you very aware that there's a camera there, and a sound engineer over there. And that's kind of a Dogme thing, I think. It's like, 'We're not trying to make a scene here. We're just fucking.'

RK: The camera follows your lead, you don't do it for the camera.

P-L: Yeah, and you can talk to the cameraman and so on. I'd like to do that. And I can do it very kinky, I promise you.

I assure Lasse we'll look forward to it. And we fully intend to make room for him in *our* film, although, clearly, he takes up more space than the average male. Thereafter, and unsurprisingly, *Pink Prison* is a let-down. The premise concerns a female investigative journalist who infiltrates a notorious all-male penitentiary under cover of darkness. You can guess the rest. The word we'd heard is that Puzzy Power is committed to making porn with a female slant, whereby the camera demonstrates an equally lingering interest in the tautness of the male form. Sure enough, the first coupling we're served is an anal encounter between two hot cell-mates, secretly observed by our flushed heroine. Everything afterwards is formulaic, and (perhaps more surprisingly) lacking in conviction. It's meant to be hard-core, but the services of a 'fluffer' were badly needed in the case of certain limp lengths of pipe. Some kind of climax is reached in a 'rude food' sequence set in the prison's uncommonly well-appointed kitchen. Unforgivably, a foaming soda bottle is employed as a visual metaphor. Some moments later, as real semen finally shoots forth in the long-awaited 'money shot', there is an outbreak of heavily ironic applause.

16 'It's all painful...':
Lars von Trier & *The Idiots*

We kick our heels in Lars's crib with yet another charming Zentropa blonde. The agreeably cluttered interior of his office betrays the characteristic preoccupations of a world-famous *cinéaste*: tennis racket and rowing machine on the floor; scripts, CDs and DVDs (*The Blair Witch Project*, no less) stacked on the desk. Finally, the maestro pulls up outside in his customized cart, enters in seeming good cheer, and strips off his parka. As we trade handshakes, he directs our attention to a framed and mounted portrait of Robert Baden-Powell: racist, eugenics enthusiast, and father of the Boy Scout movement. 'Any special reason why you have him here?' I have to ask. 'Well, he's the man behind it all, isn't he?' chuckles Lars. 'Old pervert . . .' Then he casts a professional eye over our cameras. 'If only you had a hundred of them.' I see Saul chafing at this sore point: 'It was hard enough for us to get two. You probably hired all the ones we wanted.'

RICHARD KELLY: So, how's the New Year's Eve project going?
LARS VON TRIER: Well, it's not really a Dogme thing, you know, it just happens to be the four Dogme directors. But it's very difficult – like Dogme in that way, because it's taking something very simple and then putting a lot of difficult rules on top and hoping something will come out of it. But, you know – rules are good. You can ask Baden-Powell about that . . .

RK: You say that, but a lot of British boys have been made rather unhappy by Baden-Powell's rules.
LVT: Oh, I'm sure. But they should learn to suffer with a smile. It's the same with Dogme.

RK: The four of you working together as a brotherhood for the first time: do you expect a clash of egos?
LVT: This is not a 'natural' brotherhood. It's a kind of 'forced' brotherhood. (*Chuckles.*) So of course there'll be problems. But the most interesting thing is how much each of us will be willing to contribute to the whole, and how much we just want to do our own thing with our own characters.

RK: Are you nervous about the idea that the viewer is going to flip over from 'your' channel while you direct?

LVT: You mean, like, 'Don't touch the remote!'? Oh, no, not me. I'm so used to it . . .

SAUL METZSTEIN: What have you thought of the reactions to the Manifesto? Has it been what you expected back in 1995?
LVT: I remember calling Thomas and asking him if he wanted to start a 'new wave' with me. Those were the very words, as I remember. But I haven't really seen this wave yet; just a few ripples. It all got started just after we wrote the Rules – in fact we put them down on paper because I was going to Paris for a meeting, something for the French Cultural Minister or whatever, blah-blah. And in this theatre in Paris, I took these red leaflets and threw them out over the balcony. It was beautiful, you know, like in the old days . . .

RK: Very 1968.
LVT: Then I read the Manifesto, and people started asking me questions. But I said I was allowed by the Brothers to read the Manifesto, but not to discuss it. (*Laughs.*) I thought that was very clever. But then they all said, 'Why do you come here, when you hate film so much?'

RK: Did you bother to answer that?
LVT: No, but I found it very strange. Because I wasn't saying people *have* to do a Dogme film, just that *I* was going to. But I think the provocative thing is this idea of putting limitations on yourself, which, when you think about it, is something that you do all the time. But of course it's particularly provocative to do it in public – to publish it.

SM: Surely all film directors, while they're making something–
LVT: (*cutting in*) –have their own rules. Oh, sure, absolutely.

SM: So you just formalized the process?
LVT: Sure, the one step we went further was just in putting it down on a piece of paper, which (*sotto voce*) we should never have done. Because then I could be taking a nap now, instead of talking to you guys . . .

RK: But now it's possible you'll inspire hordes of young directors to set down their own new manifestos for film-making.
LVT: Or I'll inspire people to throw this Manifesto away. And that makes for a kind of exercise, you know? (*Laughs.*) Good for your muscles.

RK: How did you come to pick Thomas Vinterberg as your co-conspirator in this? What drew him to your attention?

LVT: I must have seen a film he did at Film School. I thought he would be talented, but not too talented. (*Laughs.*) Then later on it turned out that he *was* too talented. But you can't win 'em all, you know.

RK: Are you proud of what he did with the concept?
LVT: Oh, not at all, not at all. He should be grateful, the bastard. (*Chuckles.*)

RK: Thomas has said that the Rules took twenty-five minutes to write, and that it was all a great laugh.
LVT: Well, they may have been a laugh for him . . .

RK: Are there things in the Rules or the preamble to them that are particularly yours, and things that are particularly Thomas's?
LVT: Well, if I had the Rules before me, I probably could say, but . . . no, let that remain a mystery. It was not me and it was not Thomas. It was simply the pen that moved. Both of us had our eyes closed and our hands on top of the glass . . .

SM: You shot *Breaking the Waves* on 35 mm Panavision. So why didn't you shoot *The Idiots* in the same format?
LVT: That's a discussion we had. Of course, the Rules say the film should be Academy 35 mm, but we had to vote about this because some of the Brothers – I'm not saying who – said it was too difficult to operate a 35-mm camera hand-held. Which is nonsense. So we decided that this Rule should apply only to the distribution format, so the idea was that you could shoot on 16 mm and distribute on 35 mm. Again, nonsense, but OK. Then my point was, 'Logically, you can also use video.' And of course it's fun to work with video. This musical, *Dancer in the Dark*, is shot entirely on video; and I get to operate myself, again.

RK: It involves big dance numbers, right?
LVT: All the dance numbers are shot with 100 fixed cameras. The rest is hand-held. You'll get really seasick when you see it. We've made an anamorphic lens to put on the front of all of them because we're doing it in Panavision. It's looking very good.

SM: On *Breaking the Waves*, did you attempt to impose any Dogme-style limitations on yourself?
LVT: Sure, we made up little Dogme rules. The things we built on stage had to be on a one-to-one scale, they couldn't be any larger. We said we weren't allowed to move furniture in order to get in place for a shot and

so forth. For the lighting, we wouldn't use film lamps. Things like that.

RK: When you started on *The Idiots*, did you find it very exhilarating, founding this kind of collective and working so intensely as a group?

LVT: (*Starts to reply, then pauses, amused: Saul is wordlessly clipping a replacement radio-mike to the top of my jersey; the original, having fallen apart at some earlier juncture, now lies uselessly in my lap.*) You need another mike? That's the good thing about Dogme. You can do these little technical things in a very elegant way.

SM: We're just deliberately trying to look non-professional.

LVT: Yes, well – sometimes it works . . . So. What can I say about *The Idiots*? I don't think that we went far enough. I had hoped that it would be much more 'collective', you know. But of course, my purpose was to do this differently than what I had tried before.

RK: In your diary of the film's making, you say you were initially quite moved by the actors' commitment to 'the idiot cause'.

LVT: Yeah, they liked that very much, I must say: not the cause exactly, but the spassing. And it's interesting that it's so great to spass. The days when they weren't supposed to do it, they were really pissed off.

RK: Watching them, were you envious? Did you want to get in there?

LVT: Yes, I think it's a wonderful thing, something everyone should try. Every other day. And many people do.

RK: Just to refresh yourself.

LVT: Sure. Like a shower – an emotional shower.

RK: But watching *The Humiliated* documentary, one senses that the mood soured for you at certain points in the production. Like the day of the barbecue – was that an especially black day for you?

LVT: Oh . . . I'm sure, I'm sure. But I don't think it was special to this film. You feel like you've done some good things, and then all of a sudden nothing works. And then I had some personal problems on this film. (*Sighs, profoundly.*) Do we have to talk about this? It's not important.

RK: No, sure . . . At Cannes, though, your actors testified to being very inspired by the making of the film.

LVT: Well, the good thing about it, which I think you can see in some of the films, is that it's very liberating for the actors. They are much more important in these films.

RK: Early on in *The Humiliated*, we see you shooting a scene that didn't end up in the released film, where the idiots go to visit Queen Margarethe. And it looks like trouble.

LVT: Oh, yes, that was the first day of shooting. And that was terrible, terrible . . . I couldn't see it while I was out there. But when I saw the rushes, it was . . . (*Shakes his head.*) But we had a long discussion the next day – I don't think it's in the documentary – about why it didn't work. Because it was very 'acted'. But of course, it was the first day. Still, it was strange, because we'd made a lot of tests before, a lot of spassing, all of which worked extremely well. But then, of course, when there's a camera . . .

RK: Well, that's what you tell Bodil Jorgenson: 'You've got to stop thinking you have to deliver.'

LVT: As soon as you forget that, you're on your way.

RK: You also tell the actors, 'If anyone has problems, it's Stoffer.' Why was that so?

LVT: (*After a mighty pause.*) I'm trying to remember. It's a long time ago, and I'm working on another film. (*Claps his hands to his face and rubs, as if stricken; but emerges smiling.*) It's all painful, it's all painful. And crazy.

RK: But you had happy days too, didn't you? Shooting the scene in the woods, you say in your journal that you had this great feeling, the work was reminding you of brilliant things that you loved in Tarkovsky and Truffaut and Widerberg . . .

LVT: And why is not in the film, this feeling, this brilliance? (*Laughs.*) Is that your question?

RK: No, but I wonder if you find it hard not to have the filter of other people's movies in your head when you're shooting?

LVT: I find that easier and easier because I don't see many films; certainly not the modern films. I see maybe three films a year. And not in a cinema either, only on video.

RK: Do they not interest you, modern films?

LVT: Well, I will say that it's not been so interesting lately that I've taken trouble to seek things out.

RK: There's a bit in *The Humiliated* where the camera roams around the detritus of the house, stuff the actors have strewn around. And we

see a VHS of Tinto Brass's *Caligula*. Was that brought in for research purposes, for the gang-bang scene?

LVT: No, I think one of the actors brought it in – and I have a suspicion who it might be. *Caligula*! I think Denmark's the only country where it was shown without any censorship at all. It's a fantastic film – you've seen it?

RK: Strange to relate, it was screened on Channel Four last week in what purported to be a 'Director's Cut'.

LVT: And what did that mean?

RK: Well, it ran at around two and a half hours, which is supposedly longer than any previous edition . . .

LVT: Or longer than any previous two and a half hours . . . No, but it's fantastic. One minute you have Peter O'Toole saying something, and then suddenly you cut to people just– (*Slaps his palm with his fist.*)

RK: Banging away.

LVT: Right, or fist-fucking, whatever. Amazing. But I think they tried to make a very different kind of film in the beginning. Then the producers came in and said no.

RK: Gore Vidal had written the script, and then all of a sudden he'd very definitely not written the script. But the acting in *Caligula* feels fairly 'liberated' too, given that none of them seem to understand what kind of film they're in.

LVT: (*Laughs.*) No, they have no idea.

RK: We went to see *The Idiots* at a film club in London the other week, and there was a very lively debate afterwards about the film and the Rules. One guy was arguing that the flashing back and forth between the interviews was a clear case of 'temporal alienation'.

LVT: That's very clever. But how dare they. (*Laughs.*) Why let them debate? Just throw them out of the cinema afterwards! 'Stop! We don't want any criticism. A lively debate, perhaps, but no criticism.' That was not exactly what the Rule meant from mine and Thomas's side. It had more to do with the idea that you can't pretend the film is set in Calcutta if that's not where you're shooting – that way of pretending to be somewhere else. But, yes, of course you can read the Rule that other way. So all I can say is, 'Do it better', you know?

RK: Of course, in the scene with Paprika Steen, there's a bit where we see the second cameraman in shot. Did you put that in there deliberately, or was there an alternative take you could have used?

LVT: I was shooting on that scene, I operated the camera you don't see. And my idea was to just take the best shots, no matter what. So you see a lot of mikes. (*Grasps up at our boom.*) And you see cameras. And that's fine with me. You know, I'm very sure you could easily make a film where you see a lot of cameras all the time, and the audience wouldn't mind.

RK: Your sticking to the non-separation of sound and image feels very dogmatic. It makes for some wonderfully chaotic moments, like the scene in the showers at the swimming baths.

LVT: Maybe. But we just – followed the Rules, you know? (*Makes a mock salute, affects a Germanic rasp.*) 'We followed orders. I am not responsible . . .'

RK: The film had a difficult time at Cannes in 1998, didn't it? A lot of critics didn't seem to know what they'd seen.

LVT: Or maybe they knew too well. (*Chuckles.*)

RK: But then it won the critics' prize, the FIPRESCI award, at the London Film Festival later that same year.

LVT: Oh, yes! Fantastic. What critics you have! Says more about them than about the film . . .

RK: In recent weeks, the video release has been banned in the Republic of Ireland.

LVT: Oh, yes. Now, that's fantastic. That's kind of like winning a prize. But it's very strange, isn't it, for the Irish to act like that? Because in Italy and Poland it's not been so bad, and they're very Catholic countries.

RK: Maybe none so much as the Irish. *The Idiots* is still 'on the shelf' in terms of an American release. Does that bother you?

LVT: And yet they bought it . . . No, I don't care so much. It's probably for the best. (*Laughs.*) And it's good to have a film on the shelf.

RK: You were quoted as saying that you'd come to dislike the work you did before *The Idiots*. Was that just a provocation? Don't you still find good things in a film like *Europa*?

LVT: I think there are good things in *The Idiots*, things I like very much. I haven't seen *Europa* for a long time. But I'm sure there are some interesting techniques there, tracking shots, cranes, whatever. Took long enough to do, anyway. (*Laughs.*) 'No, no, the camera – this is not good!' 'Why?' 'Can't you see? Just here? (*Mimes the pointing out of an infinitesimal error to a DP.*) Do it again!'

RK: Would you ever want to go back to working like that?
LVT: I can't imagine. It was a strange obsession. But maybe, you know ... (*Saul calls a tape change. We stand at ease. Trier stretches.*) I had dinner with Polanski the other night, you know.

RK: Really? How is he?
LVT: Short. (*The room erupts in laughter.*) Which was interesting. Normally I find I'm very short – so I try to talk to people on the stairs and so on. But of course he's one of my heroes, Polanski, from back then. Those early Polish films ...

RK: And he was the Jury President at Cannes in 1991, when *Europa* got a couple of prizes, and there was some controversy?
LVT: Oh, yes, I accidentally called him a midget in my speech, as I remember. But, as I told him, I was just quoting *Chinatown* – where he plays a midget, of course.

RK: Right. We were wondering about the logo of the Dogme95 website, this eye set in a dog's arse. Who came up with that?
LVT: Oh, I had nothing to do with it. I'm not so fond of the website as it is. I think we'll change it a little bit. At the moment it looks too commercial, like a PR tool for the films. It shouldn't be. It should be more – political. (*Smiles, raises one fist, then another.*) I used to be a communist. Was it this hand, or this?

RK: Well, your press cuttings have you down as the son of very leftist parents who rebelled against that upbringing.
LVT: Yes, but once you've rebelled back and forth more than a couple of times, then you're no longer very sure where you are. Right? Left? Then it's also difficult to figure out in which direction you should rebel next time. Confusing ...

RK: Your partnership with Peter Aalbæk, that's been ten years in the works so far?
LVT: Oh, yes. And it's still not good. (*Laughs.*) But we're working on it.

RK: He claims that when you first hooked up, you were both in something of a trough, yours artistic, his financial?

LVT: Oh, that's a lie. I've never felt that way. He has, though. All his life. But then he's a producer, it's part of his image.

RK: Well, he also claimed to be organizing Zentropa as a system of communistic cells, in tune with his old Left convictions.

LVT: Yes, well, it's become a little difficult for him. But I'm sure he's trying.

RK: So is that the plan for Zentropa, or for Dogme? Are you trying to build some kind of socialist co-operative?

LVT: (*Looks askance.*) We're trying to make money. But, if at the same time we can do the other . . . (*Laughs.*) We do have a new project that's very promising, or at least interesting, called armybase.com. We are making something like a film school on the Internet. Because I think that film schools in the form we have them today are kind of old-fashioned. Why should you go there? Mainly what they do is tell you how difficult it is to make a film, which is a lie, of course. So the main idea is that we build up a library of information that you can seek out on this website. If you're interested in a certain matter, then you search for it and find different angles, and we'll try to have some good people to have dialogues with. We'll put up master-classes and the like; I'll one, with Thomas. Also, my intention – at the moment it's difficult, just for copyright reasons – but with the films I do from now on, all the material will go on the Net, every take.

RK: What do you hope to offer by that?

LVT: Well, in terms of the directors I'm interested in, I know I would be very interested to see the material that they cut out of their films. And how did the first version look? So it would be interesting to make a place that contains a lot of first-hand material, all the things that you never see. Because that, I think, is what you can learn from. Film has become very much like magic tricks – you're not supposed to know how it's done, which is also very old-fashioned, especially if you think about the new techniques, the new cameras, and how everybody can produce their own films, which I think is fantastic. So it's about time there was a real debate. Nobody has really talked about film form or film content, not for many, many years, and the arrival of these new techniques makes it a very good time to have that discussion.

RK: So, with your rushes available in this way, students will be able to download them and do a re-cut of your film.
LVT: Sure, that's the idea. And of course that makes a lot of problems for the vanity of directors, and actors. But still I think it will be interesting.

RK: We notice you drive this golf cart around Film City; and Peter Aalbæk rides this big old motorbike.
LVT: Yes, it's a provocation of some sort, I think.

RK: How do you respond to it?
LVT: I pretend not to notice.

RK: Maybe you should just rock up in a tank one day, and roll right over that bike of his.
LVT: A tank would be good. Or a Spitfire, perhaps. You know, my generation has a lot of people who have never served in the military. And of course we are all obsessed with war. (*Chuckles.*) Have any of you been in the military?

RK: No. I daresay we never will.
LVT: Sissies. No, none of us. So that's why we're so crazy about all this stuff.

RK: Like Steven Spielberg and his World War Two crush. What would you say are the odds on Spielberg making a Dogme film? Thomas told us they'd had a perfectly agreeable conversation.
LVT: Well, Thomas actually gave him a little certificate so he could write in the name of his Dogme film. But if he does, we will never know. Because he's not supposed to be credited, right? So maybe it has been done already . . .

RK: You invited a lot of US directors to take part in Dogme.
LVT: Yeah. I never heard from anybody.

RK: Did that disappoint you? That none of them had the nerve?
LVT: No, I think it's a little strange, actually. Because it would be so easy. And it wouldn't take them long. Also, you can always say afterwards that it was only because of those stupid Dogme Rules that the film was terrible . . . But then I'm very glad that some people in Argentina, I think, have suddenly done a whole lot of Dogme films – ten, I think. One of them in just two days. Just like, 'Let's go', you know? And if that is the

only thing that comes out of these Rules, then I think it's fantastic – that people in countries like Estonia or wherever can suddenly make films, you know? Because they look at Dogme and think, 'If *that's* a film, then we can make films too.' Instead of just thinking, 'Oh, if it doesn't look like *Star Wars*, then we can't make a film.'

RK: Well, I'd have thought that as long as it doesn't look like *Star Wars*, then you're on the right track.

LVT: Oh, I see, and *then* you can make a film. (*Laughs.*) Well, OK. But then I haven't seen *Star Wars*.

RK: Me neither. I'm just running on prejudice here.

LVT: Right, like me. So we're agreed on *Star Wars*.

SM: Have you been involved personally in all these stories and rumours about Dogme that keep appearing in the press and the trade papers?

LVT: No, the only thing I've been involved with is I suddenly had a conflict with Mr Aalbæk about some colour regulations with *The Idiots*. It turned out that somebody put a lot of filters on the film. That was . . . stupid, stupid. (*Shakes his head.*) But now we've taken them away, and actually it looks much better. I think that the idea of putting a lot of filters on a scene is very old-fashioned. For many years now, every technical invention that's come along in film has had only the one purpose, and that is to smooth things out. So you make a film, and then you go to the lab and you put the same old filter on, so it's the same kind of bluish light in all the scenes – because otherwise 'it won't look real'. But what is real? If you look at something from one angle, it's one colour. You look at it in another, and it's another colour. But if you have experience in the medium, even just as a viewer, then you know you're still in the same room. But all these rules about the axis and so on, which I don't use any more – they're still hanging around from silent films. And of course, since then people have been trained, are still being trained, to watch films like that. So of course, there has to be a new film language. And I think it can be much more abstract. I think that within the brain of the spectator, there is a will to find the 'story-line', if you want to call it that, or the logic between the things that are happening. Just like if your brain wants to find a hidden figure in an abstract picture, it will. I'm sure that this will is what we're working with, so we should dare much more. And it'll be much more rewarding if film-makers loosen up.

146

RK: Then again, I've heard tales of punters walking out of *The Blair Witch Project*, asking for their money back, because it looked amateurish to their eye. Isn't there still a problem convincing enough people that they should buy tickets for what may look to them like an inferior product?

LVT: I do think that will change very much with these DV cameras. In a few years, everyone will be able to achieve high quality. Then this argument of 'Why pay money to see it in a cinema?' will cease to be the point. It will be about what the film contains, somehow. That will be what you pay for.

RK: Anthony Dod Mantle has shot three of the first six Dogme films, which seems rather significant.

LVT: Especially since he died, it seems, in *Breaking the Waves*. He was doing research on the film, so I used his name on a tombstone. And the minister reads over his grave: 'Anthony Dod Mantle, you're a sinner and you're going to hell.' In this new film he's suddenly turned up as a judge, 'The Honourable Anthony Dod Mantle'. And now he's burning in hell . . . he deserves it. (*Smiles.*)

RK: The change in the certification system has been described as a move from Catholicism to Protestantism. Is that fair?

LVT: Absolutely. It's a way for the priests to rid themselves of responsibility, right?

RK: And were you beginning to dread the prospect of having to watch many, many more submissions for Dogme certification?

LVT: Oh, yes, what a terrible idea. Especially with all this hand-held camera. (*Laughs.*) No, but the role of being a priest or a teacher is a terrible one, you know. So this way is much better. And really you can't control this Dogme. It's something that has to be . . . in the heart. Or wherever.

RK: And did Harmony Korine's film force you to this conclusion?

LVT: We were very sure of the problems with the old method. Of course, as long as somebody else is judging, then you are tempted to break the Rules without breaking them, right? And, of course, all the most interesting directors will go off in their own direction, because that's why they are interesting. But that means that they will tend to go to the limits of the Rules, even break some of them, while being smart about it. You can make visual effects that don't break the Rules and yet are against the idea behind the Rules. Or, anyway, that's how I feel. But then how I feel is not important any more . . . (*Sighs.*) Harmony was dogmatic in his own way. Now, Baden-Powell would have made a wonderful Dogme film, I'm sure. Just by making fire with two little sticks . . .

RK: But a terrifying film, I'd imagine. Much worse than *The Blair Witch Project*.

LVT: Yeah. (*Chuckles.*) Full of little boys running around naked in the woods, looking for Baden-Powell. 'Argh! I've seen him, I've seen him!'

RK: Do you fear that the likely deluge of Dogme films we're about to see will mean an accompanying slump in quality? Especially after the first entries were so well-received.

LVT: Yes, but I'm not afraid of that. You know Albert Speer had this theory of 'the value of the ruins'? He had studied the ruins of architecture in Italy and Greece and so on. And he built his own buildings very precisely, so that they would be nice ruins. He would use softer stones here and there, and he figured out how they would look when they were reduced to ruins. Very good, when you think how Germany looked after the war. (*Chuckles.*) But I found this an interesting idea. I would like the Dogme Rules to be 'found' in a thousand years' time, and looked at. And that would be a Dogme film I'd like to see.

RK: Right. Where the archaeologists hold the papyrus up to the light and say, 'What kind of a man made this?'

LVT: 'What was this madness?' (*Laughs.*) Yes. But, you know, it's been very difficult for people to take them seriously, these Rules. And that's where I'm very 'dogmatic', as they say. It's not interesting if you don't take it seriously – because then why do a Dogme film? It is a little game, right? So you should play by the rules. I mean, why play football if you don't want to put the ball in the back of the net? Of course, we have all put in some comments on the website about what we have done and where we've – failed.

RK: The famous Confessions.

LVT: Yeah, but now there'll also be interviews with each of us where we go into these things in more detail.

RK: And you also do these Reprimands to each other?

LVT: Oh, yes. (*Wags an admonitory finger.*) Then we also have this collective masturbation afterwards. It's kind of a ritual.

RK: Just for a spot of relief? To get it all out?

LVT: Yes, we try to get it out – on Søren Kragh-Jacobsen. (*Mimes the shielding of oneself from a torrent of ejaculate.*) That's been one of the nice things about this Dogme Brotherhood.

SM: While we're on this kind of subject, we went to see *Pink Prison* last night.

LVT: Ah! I haven't seen it. Was it fantastic?

RK: Well, not 'fantastic', no.

LVT: But was it pink?

RK: Not even that, to be honest. But we did run into the famous Porno-Lasse in the foyer. He helped you out on the gang-bang scene in *The Idiots*, right?

LVT: Oh, yes. It's hard for the professionals, you know. The erection Stoffer has in the changing rooms when they go swimming – that is his own. But at one point he couldn't manage it, which was a pity. But it's also kind of difficult for these porno guys to come in, because they don't feel at home. It's a different kind of set-up.

RK: Yes, I suppose it's not what they're used to. Nobody standing around with a fluffer.

LVT: No. (*Smiles.*) 'We are having wood.' Isn't that the expression?

RK: Right. But then I guess everybody has off days.

LVT: Yes. Except us when we're looking at Søren Kragh, of course . . .

'Well, that all got very intellectual at the end,' murmurs an amused Saul. Trier, meanwhile, groans with relief and sinks back into the sofa. But Jack leaps in to enquire if he's actually read Baden-Powell's *Scouting for Boys*, with its copious section concerning techniques for the avoidance of masturbation (consultations with the scout leader, cold showers, etc.). No, as it happens. As we pack up, Trier asks if I'm from London, and I explain that I spent my formative years in Northern Ireland, which is why I feign to speak with authority about why *The Idiots* is having difficulties in Eire. 'And are you a Catholic?' he asks. Certainly not, I insist, and enquire after his own alleged Catholicism. He's not saying. 'But you know, don't you, that everybody in this country is Protestant?' he remarks. 'Sure,' say I. 'I recognize the vibe around the place.' 'Right, like this,' he grins, and mimes a tremendous yawn. Thereafter he drives off in his cart. I weigh up the exchanges. He was very tired; and his tendency to straight-faced leg-pulling renders the idea of a 'conversation' somewhat nugatory. Evidently at one point he suspected I was hoping to pursue the 'personal problems' he encountered on *The Idiots*. In fact, I was only interested in the inevitable difficulties of managing a troupe of players. But then very likely he's had his fill of such difficulties, and the analysis thereof.

17 'That's sport, right?':
Søren Kragh-Jacobsen & *Mifune*

Back to the elegant environs of Nimbus, and I'm pleased to remake the acquaintance of Søren Kragh-Jacobsen, duly returned from Italy and, yes, very satisfied by *Mifune*'s multiple nominations in the European Academy Awards. He's concerned, though, about how the film is playing in London. We agree that the UK poster art – a headless chicken, no less – is pretty ballsy, but commercially worse than useless.

RICHARD KELLY: Let's start with the recent developments. What do you recall as the spark for the Millennium project?
SØREN KRAGH-JACOBSEN: It started at a Christmas dinner in Lars's home, after a good dinner, *foie gras*, a lot of drinks. I'm not sure if Lars came up with it; but he's used to being the mastermind, right? We got to talking about inventing something new. Then I received a paper suggesting involving all four Danish TV channels: even the stupid one, so to speak.

RK: And which one would that be?
SKJ: Three, and Three-Plus, because they just broadcast American movies and game shows. But I worked in television for ten years, from 1971 to 1983, and I know how competitive the channels are with each other, so it was clear that if you could get them all to work together and take up a whole evening of prime time, that would be a great goal, right? Then came this idea that the audience could edit their own film by going from one channel to another. And then there'd be a fifth channel with the screen split between four. And then, just to make fools of us as well, a sixth channel which will just broadcast the four Dogme Brothers sitting in front of some screens, *sweating*.

RK: It's certainly a test for the Brotherhood, too, working together for the first time. Can you foresee any tensions?
SKJ: Mostly we're friends, though of course we're competitors as well. But on this, I don't think we're going to be individually credited, like 'Søren did number Three'. I think Kristian was very clever when he said, 'I'm not into this if we're up there under our names, "Directed by".' So it's directed by 'The Dogme Brothers'. And that gives you a bit more air. Of course, people can go to Channel Six and see which director is working with which actor. But then we're also swapping actors in the middle, so you can't quite follow who's doing what, and when.

RK: Now that's fiendishly clever. So, will you have to stay sober on New Year's Eve 1999?

SKJ: I'm sure I will. I love to drink, it's wonderful. And actually, over years of working in this business, I've found that I've relied very much on people who have alcohol problems. For the last ten years, I've never drunk while I'm shooting a film. But I tell you, at quarter to one I will start, and by quarter to two you will see me *pissed*. (*Laughs.*)

RK: So can you describe the long, strange professional trip that brought you into the Dogme fold?

SKJ: I think I'm the only one of the Brothers with a working background. I trained as an electrician in the Copenhagen shipyard from the age of nineteen. But I always wanted to do films – my brother and I bought a 16-mm camera when I was sixteen. And in 1969 I went to FAMU, the Czech Film School in Prague. I wanted to be a documentarian. But I was thrown out in 1971. It was very Dogme – we never touched a camera or film.

RK: You just argued passionately?

SKJ: It was like going to university. Then you worked as an assistant director for your third or fourth year. But I'd always played music, rock music, since I was thirteen or fourteen. I have pictures of my first performance, singing in Town Hall Square – I think I was doing a Cliff Richard number . . .

RK: Oh, God!

SKJ: Terrible, isn't it? Even before I went to Prague I was a professional musician, working in nightclubs, playing 'Strangers in the Night' in a tuxedo. And I wrote songs. So I made my first record in 1973, and another in 1976. The last was in 1981. Then I wrote a couple of records for other artists . . .

RK: Well, we've gathered from our travels that your music is still very popular, very well recognized.

SKJ: Oh, I wrote a few that have been quite popular. I always compare music to film-making, though. It's like, if you're the band leader, you write a number, you go into the recording studio with the band, you conduct that number, and it either swings or it don't swing. Same with film – you go out with a crew, it swings or it don't swing. That's why I always compare the Dogme Movement to the 'Unplugged' wave in the early 1990s. I mean, why in hell did Eric Clapton suddenly decide to play unplugged? Because he was surrounded by new techniques in the studios. And so much is done to the voice now, it can be pitched up or broadened out or sampled or whatever. And suddenly these guys wanted to hear how good they really are, which is why they made these acoustic records, some of which are lovely, I think. That's very much akin to what we're trying to do with film here.

RK: So, in a sense, *Mifune* is your comeback album?
SKJ: My unplugged film, yes.

RK: How did you kick-start your film-directing career?
SKJ: I'd started in documentaries, and for a time I was actually rather scared of working with actors – quite a shy guy back then, you see. But I got going in the Youth and Children Department of Danmarks Radio, and made some short fiction films there. And at that point in the mid-1970s, there was another wave in Danish film, which we tend to forget about. Young directors protested against the older generation by making youth films, with young actors, aimed at the biggest section of the paying audience, namely the fifteen-to-eighteen-year-old age group. I came in at the end of that wave myself. I did my first feature in 1977, called *Do You Want to See My Beautiful Belly-Button?* It tells exactly the same story as 'Mona', which Hans who wrote the script might deny, but he knew the song very well. Anyhow, I was hooked straight away by the family atmosphere of film-making. So then I made another one, and then it was about time to quit TV once and for all. And I've since made seven or eight features.

RK: *Island on Bird Street* (1996) was a high-profile production, it went to Berlin and so forth. But I understand that was the point where you began to feel some discomfort with the whole nature of the film-making apparatus?
SKJ: I think I had the feeling even before. By the late 1980s in Denmark, it had become very customary for technicians in the film business to own their own equipment. And the more they could hire themselves out, the more they earned. They started coming up with techniques we hadn't seen before, and of course we could see the advantages of technology in making a more beautiful image, blah-blah. But you began to see more and more critics writing 'Here is another very good-looking, very boring Danish film.' The technicians were kings, you know? And very often I felt as if they were stepping on my domain, stepping over

my job. Of course, you have an authority as a director, but at the same time you're never completely sure that they're not right. So suddenly you had more flags for the light, and more advanced microphones, more cranes, more tracks. And very often I'd find myself standing there, having spent so long rehearsing my actors, motivating them, creating that very secure platform in front of the camera – because that's what it's all about. And then I'd hear, 'It looks lovely. But just give us one more hour with the lights.'

RK: Pretty galling . . .
SKJ: Right. Now, for *Island on Bird Street*, I used an English crew, and the English crews tend to be a little older on average than the Danish ones, where it's all people in their twenties wearing baseball hats. And the pace was different: we used half as much light, and older techniques, and I enjoyed that. But by now I was just fed up with international co-productions. We were working on a budget of three million pounds and being asked to make it look like ten or fifteen million. And I had a little boy in the lead role, so I'd stood up in London with my hand on a Bible, swearing that he would only work for so many hours a day. And then the money wasn't there when it should have been, and the crane was taken away. And the subject matter was dark, and it was very cold, and everybody got sick . . . In short, I was totally prepared when Lars invited me into the Brotherhood.

RK: It was time to hit the road to Lolland.
SKJ: Absolutely. And it was no accident that I wanted the *Mifune* company to live in camping wagons in the countryside, because that's what I'd done on my very first feature, *Do You Want to See My Beautiful Belly-Button?* And it was no coincidence, either, that they were both love stories. On the first one, we were a company of thirteen, we shot it in five and a half weeks. We had a gaffer who handled such lights as we had, we did a lot of it hand-held. And I wrote the score myself. Even though it was twenty-two years ago, my first feature was a fantastic time for me, and I wanted to make a replay, right?

RK: You wanted to get that old feeling back.
SKJ: Yes. And I did.

RK: How did you conceive the story of *Mifune*?
SKJ: I wrote a page of A4, saying what the story was, what I wanted to do. What can you say about this classic kind of love story? You place

two big-city people out in the countryside, and you make a story about how you can't run away from your past, how you have to clean up behind you. Basically, I wanted to do a summer film, I wanted to be surrounded by beautiful women all summer, and I wanted to have fun, for myself. Lars and I often talked about this. I said, 'Besides these Rules, this Manifesto, what is this all about?' And he said, 'Of course, it's to give you and me our joyful film-making back.' And I thought, 'Good. I'm going to make a film that I would take my wife to see on Saturday evening. And it won't have a French ending: not especially melancholic. I want to leave a happy audience.' Which I certainly hadn't done on *Island on Bird Street*.

RK: Was the title always *Mifune*?

SKJ: Yes. But I didn't title it until I'd found the house, so I could write to the location as well as the faces. The day I saw the place, I came back to the city and I read that Toshiro Mifune had died. Now, Mifune was a man who'd been entertaining me for years; he's someone who makes me feel that we're really one people on this earth. The first time I saw a Kurosawa film, I was amazed by how well Mifune communicated himself to the audience. He looked different, spoke another language; but he was funny, moving, handsome. And everybody understands him. Now, the crucial scene in *The Seven Samurai* is where Mifune's character has to admit that he's a peasant boy; and they start to respect him in a new way, and he grows because of that, because he doesn't have to lie any more. I said to myself, 'Kresten has the same destiny as Mifune in *The Seven Samurai*. He is a peasant boy who went to town to become a modern-day samurai. Now he's coming back to defend his village.' It's the same story.

RK: There is that fable quality to the piece. At the same time, like all the Dogme films, it's showing us another side of Denmark, in this case Lolland. But I don't suppose the film purports to be an accurate depiction of the Danish town-and-country divide?

SKJ: No, no. It's imagined, out of my head. I want the audience to believe one hundred per cent in the truth of the story, but it's a construction. Exclusive call-girls are not like that. Yuppies are not that stupid. You can't use a mobile phone in the country. In fact, things really ground to a halt out there in the 1960s and 1970s because of a big depression. It looks a bit like my childhood in the country. And it certainly is two-thirds sky, one-third land out there – it's very flat, which

I like. But there'd never been a feature film made there, which was a great advantage, because people are so fed up seeing film crews in this country. We have series being made all over Copenhagen, eight hundred commercials made a year. So you bump into a crew wherever you go. But not in Lolland.

RK: Where did you find your leads? I'm wondering if the bits of comedic business were preordained by the script, or did you find out what the actors were good at first?

SKJ: Oh, I'd talked to them before I wrote the script. I wrote the story for those three faces, one hundred per cent. I needed a romantic male lead; and Anders Berthelsen was already a television star in this country. Jesper Asholt I'd seen in a fourth-year production at the Danish Film School, and he had a look, as if he came from the countryside. I'd met Iben while I was out in Japan with *Island on Bird Street*. She was heavily pregnant, and playing a very small part in this film *Portland*, as a battered wife. She's very funny, very hectic – certainly beautiful, sexy. And she has a lot of secrets, a lot of layers. So I said to myself, 'She's a star', and I wrote that part especially for her. Then she'd say, 'Oh, I would never do that' – she's very smart, analytical that way. She would suggest dialogue, and I would think, 'Yes! Great! She's a woman!' And I'd go back and make changes.

RK: Anders Berthelsen is great at the physical humour, the *Mifune* imitations. An English journalist told me you informed him that 'doing Japanese' is a stock thing Danes do when they're drunk.

SKJ: I don't know about all Danes. But all this? (*Strikes a combat pose, makes a war-cry.*) Everybody does that. I know some of your countrymen who are pretty good at it too. And you don't (*grins*) even have to be drunk . . .

RK: Presumably working Dogme-style enlivened the relationship between yourself and your actors.

SKJ: Sure. There is a great advantage in the non-separation of sound and image. Normally, Danish actors are not a hundred per cent when they're behind the camera. If they're not 'on', they're never very good. But this way, they knew they had to give one hundred per cent, all the time. So I could move the camera around three hundred and sixty degrees and still find really good acting, which was new to me. Also, it happened to suit my temperament very much – this speed you work

157

at, this energy that arises in a production form like this. The actors arrive in the morning, and they have to take care of their own clothes, their costume and make-up. And they like to look good, so they're made to feel more involved. But secondly and most importantly – they work eight hours a day, and we do eight to ten scenes a day. They are warm like running engines. And so they give the piece an energy that I really believe you can see up onscreen. They were tired and happy every night. Of course, I took them as far away from Copenhagen as possible, so they couldn't slope away and drink beer in the evenings. And I was living with them, too.

RK: So you were in a position to enforce the house rules?
SKJ: Yeah – Daddy was there, to make sure they were home by ten. (*Laughs.*)

RK: In terms of technique, were there moments in making *Mifune* when it felt brand new? Anthony told us that at one point you were running around in an all-white outfit acting as a human reflector. That must have felt a bit novel?
SKJ: We were shooting Iben in a hotel bathroom, and this bathrobe was hanging up. So I asked Anthony, 'Can you see her face?' 'No.' 'OK, just a second. I think it's very *cold* in here.' And I put on this huge white thing . . . (*Laughs.*)

RK: Of course, you were the first Brother to shoot using a film camera with 16-mm film in it, rather than a DVC the size of a fist.
SKJ: I don't have anything against doing a feature film on video with three cameras. I did so much multi-camera work for television in the 1970s. But it was hard for me to think of shooting video in the countryside. And I said, 'This non-separation of image and sound – what's the problem if you have three cameras? It's too easy.' The challenge must be that you have one camera on your shoulder, you shoot film – I mean, that's sport, right? It's alive, organic – it looks a bit like Polish film, 1969. I wanted to go back there. (*Smiles.*) And I didn't care at all that all the love scenes indoors were red. I said, 'Come on! Love is red!' At the same time – Anthony got very tired in his back, carrying the camera eight hours a day; it was very tough for him. Several times I went out to pee at one in the morning – because I'm over fifty, right? And Tony would be standing out there already, and I'd ask him if he could manage. Now, Lars always says, 'Come on, that's what we did on *Breaking the*

Waves.' I say, 'You didn't work eight hours a day on that. You were putting up lights three or four hours, then you shot four hours.'

RK: Well – that was him told, I expect.

SKJ: Of course, several times I've run into a person who says, 'But it doesn't look like a Dogme film.' But Dogme is not a style, it's a set of rules. I asked Tony many times to stop moving, because I don't believe intensity and energy are in the restless camera. I think they are between actors. I decided I'd do it my way, and take whatever the critics would say afterwards. My story is more conventional, and even more conventional-looking as a film. But I was quite happy in Paris when the press asked me, 'Isn't this like an American movie?' I said, 'Yes, very much as Truffaut did with *Jules et Jim*, don't you think?'

RK: The music in the film is great. We're told there's a special resonance to the Kim Larsen song that Rud listens to?

SKJ: Right. And I happen to know Kim, so I got it very cheap. People were saying to me, 'Let's use one of yours! They're free!' I said, 'No way.' I did it once, in my first movie. Never again. It would have spoiled the film for me.

RK: It's also a wonderful musical moment when Rud has his friends over for the evening, and they're being royally patronized until one of them breaks out with this stupendous flamenco guitar.

SKJ: Sure. Of course, the point of that whole scene is that actually you don't always know who is the idiot. I've known Christian Sievert for many years and he's an excellent flamenco player, he's travelled in Spain and competed with some of the finest players there. And the great thing I found about flamenco is that you can edit very easily within this music. When Valdis saw the rushes, she said, 'You're crazy. You have sixteen different shots here with flamenco music under them. I can't cut this.' I said, 'Take the sound out and do whatever you like,' and she did. Of course, we had to be guided somewhat by the guitar-playing so as to come in at the right points.

RK: *Mifune* has some familiar Dogme faces, like Paprika Steen, which gives a kind of repertory feel to it.

SKJ: Right. Then there's Anders Hove, wearing the same costume he wore for *The Idiots*, I might add. I'd worked with him before, and I'd seen him in *The Idiots*, of course, and I was a bit disappointed (*winks*) that he was in there . . .

RK: This might sound a little offbeat, but I really notice the presence of mobile phones in all three Danish Dogme films.

SKJ: Were there mobiles in *The Idiots*? Yes! Of course there were. You're right, the films are full of them.

RK: It rather reminds me of how in the theatre, a telephone is just about the most useful prop you can have on a stage, in terms of relaying necessary information or introducing a plot point and so forth. So I'm wondering if mobile phones play the same role in Dogme films, if they're a handy way to beat the limitations?

SKJ: Well, at the start of writing, I had many more parallel stories with Copenhagen. But I couldn't afford to shoot more than four days in the city. I had 240 hours – six weeks, no overtime, eight hours, five days a week. So, of course it was easier just to use a mobile phone. And it provided the symbolism of Kresten being stuck out there without a signal. Also I needed Liva to have that line of communication to her friends. Maybe that's the weakest part of the film, I don't know. But I don't think you'll see many films from this day forth that don't have a few mobiles in them. I think they're here to stay . . .

RK: This change in the certification process: OK with you?

SKJ: It's the only right way to do it. For a long time I said, 'Why should we be over-gods in this process?' I mean, we didn't expect anything when we sat down back in 1995. We wanted to do four films in another way. We wanted a brotherhood. It was a form of protest against several things. But when it suddenly became a wave . . . I mean, why take our Rules? I think they work, but that's another matter. I find it shows something of a lack of imagination if people don't make new rules. I could give 'em a few suggestions . . .

RK: With Kristian finishing his film, and the Brothers having made a Dogme film apiece, has this chapter of the story run its course?

SKJ: Well, I just got home from Italy yesterday, and I was in France the week before that. And it's become a ritual now: the distributors meet you at the airport and the first thing they tell you is, 'People are getting a bit tired of Dogme.' 'OK, why am I here?' That reaction is especially true in France, I think. But hey, people get tired, and that's the nature of man, I think. You love it for nine months and then you start to talk shit about it, and that's just the way things are.

RK: Of course, it's no surprise that film industry people get a little

tired of Dogme, as long as you're going around the world and winning all these Festivals. A little envy there perhaps?
SKJ: Maybe. But of course they're tired of hearing about 'The Danish wave', blah-blah-blah . . .'

RK: So maybe they should go and make some waves of their own?
SKJ: Well, as I said, if we inspired anything in others then I'd hope it was a little self-confidence. I admire British film-makers, but why do they always have to go to Hollywood? They should make some very cheap films. I'm sure they've already started – I'm sure there are twenty low-price video productions waiting for their blow-ups right now . . .

RK: Can you see yourself making another Dogme film?
SKJ: If I reach a point within the next ten years where I really feel I lack spontaneity – I would do another one. Maybe I wouldn't call it 'Dogme'. But I would certainly make a film under limitations again, or a very fast shoot-from-the-hip movie. On *Island on Bird Street*, I wasted so much energy talking to producers, saying, 'This is not how things should be. Why pay me a fortune if you know everything better than I do?' Right now, I'm working on a very small story, very low-low budget. I definitely think that's what you need if you want to have one hundred per cent control. So, yes, I'll do it again.

The clapper-board is wheeled out, and I position it solidly across Søren's face. 'Very strange name, right?' he murmurs. 'I wish my name was Rock Hunter.' The room breaks up. 'Really. At the start of every interview, all over the world, I'm asked, "Please, before we go on, how do I pronounce your name?"' But he seems pleased when we confess that 'Mona' is never off our in-car CD player. Paula raises the potentially ticklish question of whether we might use the song in our film. But Søren doesn't linger for a second over the prepared release form, and has the demeanour of a man who knew more civilized times, before the remorseless ascent of entertainment law.

18 Paprika Steen:
The Deneuve of Dogme95

Nicolai has used his influence again. We head for the elegant upstairs dining room of the café, and on the glass partition is a sign, 'Reserved 7 p.m.–10 p.m.: Dogme'. So we're legitimate at last: the official interlopers. As we pile in with the gear, I wonder what the clientele make of us. Are we the coolest guys here? Or just another bunch of Dogme idiots? These thoughts are left hanging as Paprika Steen breezes in. Immediately, and with a winning absence of self-consciousness, she makes a fretful examination of her complexion in the mirrors on the wall, and laments the cycle of pore-clogging brought on by heavy stage make-up. She also complains of a sore throat – at the same time, there's a grain to her voice, suggestive of the love of tobacco, and sure enough, she's soon rummaging in her handbag for fags and matches.

Paprika is rehearsing Shakespeare at the Royal National Theatre, and my heart soars in the expectation that I can discourse knowledgeably on whichever text it happens to be. But, a thousand curses – it's *Love's Labour's Lost*, which might as well be in Danish for all my acquaintance with it. Compounding my failure, Jack nimbly steps in and strikes up a useful rapport with her on aspects of the play. He has, it turns out, just seen a cut of Kenneth Branagh's musical version starring Alicia Silverstone. 'I'm so impressed you know it,' trills Paprika. Jack shrugs this off winsomely, and I skulk in a corner for a while. The show is in the grip of Last Week Nerves, everybody wondering if they've really *got* anything here? Paprika is especially perplexed by certain passages involving Latin. I advise her that the trick in playing the boring bits of Shakespeare is to do them very, very fast; and she blinks patiently, perhaps waiting for me to follow that shaft of wit with something a little less asinine.

RICHARD KELLY: Paprika, you do seem to be indispensable to these Dogme movies. How do you feel about the association?
PAPRIKA STEEN: It's really just a coincidence that became a bit of a game. I think Lars saw me in some of Thomas's rushes for *Festen*, so he gave me a little part in *The Idiots*. Then Søren said, 'You were in the first two. You must be in mine.'

RK: Kristian Levring told us he was very upset that he hadn't been able to offer you a part in *The King is Alive*.
PS: He actually asked me to work behind the camera, before he even

knew what film he was going to do. And I would have loved to. But then, movie schedules always get changed, and you're always being hired three years in advance. So in the end I wasn't available. But, yeah, I felt like I should have been down there with them, in the desert. I don't know what I could have done – maybe just walked by and asked for a glass of water. (*Laughs.*) But somehow I don't think it would have been worth the air fare.

RK: What's your background, your training, as an actress?
PS: My mother was an actress, and my family is very musical, so I grew up in that kind of environment. There are three big drama schools in Denmark, all with five hundred applicants a year. And they take maybe seven people. So you just audition and hope; and it took me four years to get in . . . But I moved away from Copenhagen and my family, and I lived in a small city for four years. And I became extremely narcissistic, as you have to. I think Orson Welles said his worst nightmare was going to a restaurant at two in the morning and being seated next to a bunch of drama students singing show tunes. And I was exactly like that! But you have to do that, you have to be embarrassing.

RK: Did you feel you had good training?
PS: The school was like a leftover from the 1970s, when political theatre was really strong here, and when I arrived, it was a big mess. But the great thing for me was the voice-coaching, every day. I learned why I spoke the way I spoke. I'd had problems when I was younger. I was always shouting, and I lost my voice and had to have operations. But at the school, somebody took care of me and said, 'Don't do that!'

RK: How much film experience did you have before *Festen*?
PS: I'd only done a couple of movies. One was a children's comedy called *Hannibal and Jerry*. Originally, I started out with my own theatre group, and we wrote and acted and directed ourselves, so that gave me experience in improvising. Plus I did some television: a drama series, a sitcom, a Saturday night satire show. And I liked doing TV: shooting on videotape, in long stretches.

RK: So, did the Dogme95 Manifesto capture your imagination when you first heard of it?
PS: Sure, I was interested. I liked this idea of getting rid of everything. But then, I'm not technically grounded, so I couldn't imagine what

Dogme would mean until I was in it. Because once you start to work like that, it's a very physical experience.

RK: How did Thomas cast you in *Festen*?
PS: Well, he just transferred the entire cast from his previous film, *The Greatest Heroes*. And I'd had a small part in that, which I'd begged him for, because I knew him from when he was at film school, and I was in drama school. I called him and said, 'I want to be in your feature!' 'But it's about two guys . . .' 'I want to be in it!' So he wrote me a part. Then, when he cast *Festen*, as he's said in interviews, he just wanted to spend his summer with actors he knew, with his best friends. And they're all in there.

RK: What was your fix on the character of Helene?
PS: My favourite actress is Gena Rowlands, and I always wanted to be in a remake of *Gloria* – which Sharon Stone has done now, so I guess that's not going to happen. But I wanted to play a character like her: tough, a little neurotic. And a bit of a faded beauty – jaded, from too many parties. And my friend Thomas went and wrote me a part just like that! I figured Helene was like the eternal student – unsettled, all over the place. Every time she changed her university course, she had to change her ways: maybe she started out in medicine because she wanted to marry a doctor, but that didn't work out, so . . . But then I know a lot of women like that – in their early thirties, and still not sure of what they want to do. So she was easy to find.

RK: How were the vibes on location as you worked?
PS: It was safe, secure. I mean, I don't want to sound like Thomas is a guru or something, but we all trusted him. So it was a relaxed atmosphere: 'Let's try this', 'Let's do it again.' We were staying there too; if we had to shoot five days in a row then we slept there overnight. But then, you know, we had no grand ambitions for the film, we had no idea it would be so big. If we'd known that we would end up on the red carpet at Cannes, we'd have been much more strung-out.

RK: How did you find the experience of working to that roving little video camera?
PS: Oh, you get used to it very quickly. But then, I'm really near-sighted, and I don't wear glasses in the movie. And these cameras were so small, and we were shooting in huge rooms with lots of people. So I found I'd be peering about me, trying to get my bearings, thinking,

'Where is the camera? There? Or there?' I know that in the editing they had to lose so many shots where I just look straight in the camera. You can see I'm thinking, 'Oh! There it is!', and then I start acting. Thomas told us that the camera would follow us, and we shouldn't follow the camera. But my instinct was always to want to know where the camera was, where I should be directing my energy.

RK: A very hard habit to break, one would assume.

PS: There is this underlying idea to Dogme that's almost spiritual: 'Can't we just forget about being self-conscious?' But that's like trying to do an interview where you are 'totally yourself'. (*Smiles.*) I think some of the actors in *The Idiots* truly forgot the camera – insofar as you can ever do that. But there's a residual ten per cent awareness that's always there for actors. Otherwise they're lying, or they have a problem and should see a doctor.

RK: The camera catches a lovely 'true' moment of you, engaged in that banal pre-dinner kind of chit-chat, with a glass of champagne in your hand, looking as if you need to be rescued.

PS: Yes, it's that thing of, 'Oh here's my old deaf grandfather who tells the same joke every time. And I have to listen, and smile politely at the right moment. Yeah, yeah . . .' And meantime your eye is roving all round the room.

RK: Several Danes we've talked to say that *Festen* captures something specifically Danish in its evocation of that familial atmosphere. Do you agree?

PS: Oh, I think so; especially this business of people not reacting: 'It cannot be true that this is happening. He's over-reacting.' It's very Danish, to make this kind of denial. 'Can it be as bad as you say? Oh, no, I think not. Pass me the sugar, please.' Whereas the typical English attitude would just be blasé – 'Oh, really? As bad as that? And may I have the sugar, please?' I'm actually half-American. But we are connected with Germany in this way: we do have this rustic culture, we're peasantry. We eat our meat and potatoes, we go to bed early because we like to sleep. And we can't deal with conflict. Also there is this very Scandinavian tendency to silence. I mean, you won't notice it in me. (*Laughs.*) But it's in the nature of Danes to be dark, somehow. Heavy. Because it's cold outside. *Festen* has that feeling. As we get into the night scenes, there's a melancholy weighing upon things, a sadness there. But we laugh, just to make noise – to ward off the silence.

RK: So it was brave of Thomas to write a script like this, about this awful, black crime of incestuous rape.

PS: Sure. But *Festen* is not explicit. It's really about the repression of emotions in this family. I don't think of *Festen* as 'a film about incest', even though that's what the press have chosen to focus on. It's just the element that kick-starts the drama. But it's necessary because if you're making a drama about parents and children, and all the things that can or can't be said, and you want the audience to understand these deep emotions – you can't just take an ordinary problem. It can't just be a son coming home to say he doesn't want to take over his father's business. Or even a son coming home to say, 'Father, I'm a homosexual.' That wouldn't be enough. You have to create a huge conflict. And incest, everybody hates. Nobody will make excuses for it, like, 'Oh, but he has an alcohol problem.' I mean, this is just Bad.

RK: The horrible racism directed at Helene's boyfriend by Michael: does that address something within Danish society?

PS: We have a real problem here with this right wing that's coming up, alienating everyone from each other. The situation with immigration is getting worse. Every foreigner or immigrant here is having to face this attitude of 'We're paying a lot of money for you.' You've seen this with Margaret Thatcher. And these people don't know what they're talking about. But then the terrible, racist song Michael sings is a children's song that was around when I was a kid. But in the 1960s, the attitude was, 'It's OK, we can sing this, we're not racist. If we say the n-word it's not meant in a bad way because we all like everybody here.' We are against 'political correctness' in Denmark; so, if a minority group says, 'We would rather you didn't call us by such names', Danes won't say, 'Of course.' They'll say, 'Why? I don't have a problem with you, so why can't I say what I want?' I think maybe in American society, or in England, this problem has been discussed more. But we're just not there yet.

RK: Your character in *The Idiots* is called 'High-class Lady'. Do you suppose that's how Lars von Trier sees you?

PS: No, but I think he maybe feels I'm a little too dominating, too much in control of things. There's a scene in *The Humiliated*, the only one I'm in, where I say, 'Can we please get back to work?', and he shouts, 'I'm the director!' I get this feeling that I provoke him because I'm always on top of things. And it irritates him, so he gives me a part where I have to lose it.

RK: So he always tries to bring you down a peg or two?
PS: To humiliate me, yes. He can't win, not really. But then neither can I, because he has all the footage, and he can cut me out if he wants. I have a very small part in *Dancer in the Dark*, which he'll probably cut, as 'Woman in Factory'. See? I never get to have names! I had three lines and I was meant to do an American accent, so I studied everything very carefully. Then I arrive on set and he says, 'OK, let's just improvise this scene.' He's like that. When he directs, he'll very freely say, 'This is really bad, get out of the frame, I want Catherine Deneuve instead.' But that's OK with me, I'm not offended. If I'm bad, I'm bad.

RK: So when he first asked you to be in *The Idiots* for a day's shooting, you didn't hesitate?
PS: It was half a day's shooting, actually. From eight in the morning until two.

RK: Obviously, a very extraordinary atmosphere had been generated in the production. Did you feel that when you arrived?
PS: It was like coming to a party at 2 a.m., at the tail-end, after everyone's already done their stuff, settled their scores. You're like, 'Wow, what fun you must have had! What great food, what drink! Any leftovers? OK, just give me a drink and I'll find someone to go sit in a corner with.'

RK: Altogether a different piece from *Festen*?
PS: Of course. And the acting is very different. He takes a lot more chances, Lars, with his actors: he makes them go further out there, where it's really embarrassing – and that can be 'bad'-embarrassing. Bad acting. I went there too, but they edited it out, thankfully! But I had this truly embarrassing moment when I first meet 'the idiots'. I knew a lot of the cast, some of them are best friends of mine. Two of them were late that morning, so the day started with an argument, Lars saying, 'You've got to be here on time!' But they were laughing, looking forward to it, because I hadn't seen them 'spassing' before, and they knew I'd be really embarrassed. Then they started on me. 'Zeyn? Zeyn? What are you saying?' (*Reprises her character's excruciating exchanges with Jeppe.*) And I'm thinking, 'Oh, my God, what are they

all doing? This is really bad.' Two years on, I can look at that scene and know that's *exactly* what I'm thinking. I can see the fear in my eyes. And the reason I know I'm nervous is that I'm twisting my earlobe as I'm speaking. It's a tic that I have; I do it on stage too when I'm shy or embarrassed. I'm doing it constantly in that scene, and that's Paprika, not the character. So now you know my secret . . .

RK: Presumably Lars stage-managed the scene for just that effect.
PS: I don't know if he knew I would be so mortified . . .

RK: But doubtless he was very glad you were.
PS: Oh, sure. And anyway, what did I know? Because it turned out fantastic. We just improvised the scene about thirteen times, and then he cut it all into shape.

RK: How did you find the experience of Cannes in 1998?
PS: Too much. I mean, I really wanted to go. I was doing a play here in Copenhagen, but I got permission to head down there for two days, and I had a great experience. But after forty-eight hours I had an anxiety attack.

RK: What brought it on? The red-carpet treatment?
PS: Right. After the screening, everybody stood and applauded, and we're ushered out into this limousine. And I just cracked up: 'I can't take it any more! I'm not "Hollywood", I'm not used to having "assistants".' In Denmark we're accustomed to doing everything ourselves. Even agents are quite a new thing here. So it's a strange kind of pressure. I can't imagine what it must be like if you're really somebody, if you're Johnny Depp.

RK: But you were somebody: the female lead in *Festen*.
PS: Oh, no, I was still nobody. When the photographers were snapping away, they were shouting, 'Who's Paprika?' and I had to put my hand up and let them know that it's a girl's name.

RK: What did you make of the critical response to the film?
PS: We had this international press conference. And usually I'm quite happy to chat away to the press, say something stupid they can use – I don't mind. So there we are in this big *Salon de Presse* with all these international journalists, and I'm asked, 'So what's the difference between Lars and Thomas as directors?' And I start off, 'Oh, well, Thomas is a very classical director, and Lars is more–' Then suddenly

I realize it's basically the whole world I'm talking to. And I think, 'What am I saying? Am I saying Lars is not classical? Will he be offended? And Thomas is right beside me!' I just collapsed, I got totally self-conscious and said, 'Er, maybe somebody else should take over.' And I've never had that experience before. It was terrible. For the rest of the conference I sat there shaking, and smiling, the way a dog does when it's frightened. So – kind of a mixed experience . . .

RK: Did you get any tougher questions that that? Was there any reaction to the film that you found discouraging?
PS: Not in that situation. But when we were doing other interviews, there was an Austrian guy who kept asking me whether we had a Nazi problem in Denmark. I couldn't understand why, until I realized it was because of the moment where Helene calls Michael a 'Nazi', because he's so racist. The Austrian press seemed really upset with that, it meant a lot to them. So we got into a big discussion about Germany and the war. I just thought I was there to talk about *Festen*, so that was a surprise. And just to be polite I heard myself saying a lot of things I didn't know anything about.

RK: Suddenly you're the cultural spokesperson for Denmark.
PS: Yes. (*Laughs.*) And you can really say the wrong stuff . . .

RK: So, please, can you tell us now – what is the difference between Lars and Thomas?
PS: Oh, my God! Well, Thomas is my personal friend. So obviously I feel closer to him when we're working, I feel secure that way. And, like friends do, I can hit him and say, 'Don't talk like that!' or whatever.

RK: But you couldn't hit Lars von Trier?
PS: Oh, no . . . I would always die to work with Lars, and I'm flattered to have done that, even just for five minutes. But he's still 'Lars Von Trier'. He's still something of an icon to me – the way I would feel if I were working for Martin Scorsese, let's say. Also, Lars is a distant person, you know? He keeps a distance. And that's fine for me, and it's not wrong to do that. But then – I've worked with him for precisely one and a half days, so who am I to say anything?

RK: Søren Kragh-Jacobsen, meanwhile, is from a different school altogether, right?

PS: Oh, Søren is my generation's biggest idol, from when we were kids and teenagers. He made teenage movies and teenage records and we were all like, 'Oh, Søren Kragh-Jacobsen is the greatest in the world.'

RK: Did you buy his records?
PS: Not really. Everybody else did. I was more of a disco queen. But I bought one, a soundtrack to one of his movies I was really into: *Do You Want to See My Beautiful Belly-Button?*

RK: How did Søren sell the role in *Mifune* to you?
PS: He said, in the way he does (*imitates a grainy male voice*), 'I gotta talk to you after this. You gotta be in my movie, I can't make it without you.' The way he explained it, I thought she was going to be a lesbian, with some deep, dark secret. But I'm onscreen for maybe two minutes. It's a very small part, like a comment on the action.

RK: It's the 'tart with a heart', basically.
PS: Isn't it? And in the next movie I did the same. And I've had other offers like that. Suddenly I'm typecast! I used to always be the ugly intelligent one on the side. Now I'm the stupid naïve blonde. Which is funny, but easy. I'd still rather be Gena Rowlands, you know? But really, I can't say I've 'worked with Søren', like, 'Oh, those hard days!'

RK: You just had a few pleasant days together one summer.
PS: Sure, out in the countryside. A lot of laughs. Though we also had to beat up poor Anders, us girls. And this is Dogme, right? You can't hold back. So we really had to do it. We had to hold him down and stuff things in his mouth. And he was really choking. Not nice. Anders is just the nicest person in the world, a real Romeo. It was terrible for me when I had to do that. (*She's smiling, though; hands pressed demurely across her chest.*) I hated it. No fun.

RK: But he's a young guy, he can take it. I understand that when Thomas Bo Larsen had to beat hell out of Henning Moritzen in *Festen*, Moritzen was given a code word he could use?
PS: To say, 'That's enough.' Yes. Thomas was so respectful about that; I think he felt worse than Henning. Henning is seventy years old, and it was shot on a cold summer's night. He had stomach aches for two days before and after. Not so nice either.

RK: In the last week we've become great fans of Søren's 'Mona' song. Do you know it?

PS: Of course. It's a classic in Denmark: it's *the* song of the 1970s. Do you understand what the lyrics mean in English?

RK: Nope. But they sound lovely.

PS: It's all about a nervous boy trying to get this girl. He's saying, 'I can feel the wine in my blood–'

RK: I know how that feels.

PS: 'My voice is breaking, my hair is all wrong, I'm wearing all the wrong clothes, I'm shy. Oh, Mona, Mona, Mona . . .'

RK: I think I can understand that, too. Thanks, Paprika. I think we're done.

PS: OK. But please do take out the parts where I really can't speak English, so maybe I can get an international career. (*Laughs.*)

Afterwards we grab a couple of elementary shots of Paprika behind the clapper-board, but then she has an idea and asks for one more take. This time, as I crack the clapstick, she emits a startled yelp. We are unashamedly her fans.

19 'The fine thing we found':
Bodil Jorgenson & life among *The Idiots*

It's the final morning of our visit, and so with some wistfulness we set up downstairs with Bodil Jorgenson, alias 'Karen' of *The Idiots*. She's unmistakably an actress: a finely-tuned soul. By the same token, she's very funny too, full of deft little mimicries.

RICHARD KELLY: How did you get your start in acting, Bodil?
BODIL JORGENSON: I came late. And for a long time I only flirted with the idea, because I come from a little town in Jutland, where they hadn't really heard of acting. My parents were both teachers, and my brother and sister went to teacher training college, so I was looking for any excuse to avoid it myself! Then, after I finished school, I spent a year at Cambridge University in England, and I got to know people doing drama, and I got involved in street theatre. But I kept it a secret from friends and family: only the tourists knew. (*Smiles.*) Then I came back to Denmark to do a degree, but I also began studying with an actor in Jutland, still in secret. Then finally I was accepted in drama school here in Copenhagen, and at last I was able to announce that I wanted to be an actress! I graduated in 1990 when I was twenty-nine.

RK: How much experience in acting to cameras had you picked up before *The Idiots* came along?
BJ: Very little. There wasn't much film at the drama school. But in my fourth year, I was in a television piece, four monologues delivered straight to camera. It was a very provocative text – very sexual. Of course it was seen in Jutland, and my parents were shocked. All their friends were saying (*shakes head gravely*), 'She should have become a teacher.' But that was good preparation for *The Idiots*, because the same thing happened when that came out.

RK: What did you like about *The Idiots*, when you first read it?
BJ: The tragedy of the story, the sadness and the blackness of it. For a film to end this way, with a woman 'spassing' and spitting out cake in front of her family – I mean, if that can be a release for her, then you know things are really black! Also, I liked the idea that these young people could 'spass' from here to eternity, and it wouldn't do them a bit of good. It's their invention, and yet they don't know how to use it. But Karen does, and for her it's revelatory. She couldn't explain it in words, as I'm doing now, but she knows what it's for.

RK: It answers a deeper need in her?

BJ: Yes. So it's a good progression from *Breaking the Waves*, I find. You know Lars thinks of his last three films as a trilogy? They are sisters, the three women. Now Lars says he wants to make a film with Emily Watson and Björk and me . . .

RK: How much about Karen did Lars explain to you in person?

BJ: Nothing. Sometimes Lars likes to talk, other times he doesn't want to say shit. And it's really terrible. (*Smiles.*) He's a tyrant in that way. Each day you work with him, you can see he's decided whether or not he'll talk to you. But I like that too, because it's a kind of freedom he gives you. Sometimes he wants to be very psychological, and I don't believe in that. I can't just dig back into my life and discover why I am the way I am. I can't remember exactly where it all went wrong. (*Laughs.*) But Lars did a lot of that. Of course, we had this long session, myself and Anne-Louise who played Susanne.

RK: And techniques of psychotherapy were used to get Anne-Louise's performance out of her. But then you used a moment of emotional recall, didn't you, in order to cry?

BJ: Yes, Lars describes it in his diary. He got so angry because he couldn't work out what I was thinking of. It was just an old hymn from my childhood: a beautiful, sad hymn that we would sing at funerals, about the light of life, and the sun going down. I knew it by heart, so I only had to think about it. For me, it was also the story of Karen – the funeral she never went to, the funeral of her own child. I imagined that maybe she'd wanted to sing this hymn at the funeral, but she wasn't allowed. So she couldn't take it at home any more.

RK: She has to go AWOL.

BJ: Yes. And she's lucky enough to bump into these wonderful idiots.

RK: How did you set about the challenge of the 'spassing'?

BJ: We had one whole fortnight where we just rehearsed, and worked on the line between 'spasser' mode and the natural mode. So we ran around in Lars's garden, and we explored different types of phobias, and it was fantastic to watch each other working in this way. Of course, Karen was always a little outside the group. I had my one chance to do the 'spasser' mode in the window scene. But she was more like a little bird with no wings.

RK: Unlike, for example, Stoffer. But in *The Humiliated*, we see Lars saying, 'If anybody really has problems here, it's Stoffer.'

BJ: It's true. Because he's so much in control . . .

RK: And then so much not in control.

BJ: True. I mean, why do they have to tie him up in the attic? We all wondered about that scene.

RK: You're not sure whether Stoffer is acting, or whether he's genuinely deranged?

BJ: Yes. But it was part of the game, part of the ambiguity of the film, about what is play and what is serious.

RK: Towards the end, when Karen says her fond farewells to all 'the idiots', she doesn't mention Stoffer. He doesn't get a little tribute. Did you wonder about that?

BJ: Not so much. Because Karen knows he is the intellectual. It's not that he doesn't have feelings; but they have had their conversation, about why they do what they do; and she doesn't feel there's anything more to be said to him.

RK: Being in the midst of such a bizarre project, you must have looked to Lars for a lot of leadership.

BJ: True. I think Lars knew what he wanted to achieve, every day. But he also wanted to become a member of the group. He welcomed us, naked as the day he was born. And that, I think, was a big step. In fact, I was the only one who didn't drop one stitch of clothing for the film.

RK: Was that a relief?

BJ: That was . . . ah! (*Clenches a fist in triumph.*) According to the script, during the gang-bang scene, Karen was meant to masturbate – in fact, she was being forced to masturbate. But I talked Lars out of it! (*Laughs.*) I didn't think it was right for the character. But then, one day we went swimming in the sea because we were so tired out by all of it. And even then I went into the water with all my clothes on.

RK: Was Lars angry that you wouldn't comply?

BJ: Oh, I think it's just that he now has a certain idea of me – that I'm never going to take my clothes off. But he can say that. I also kept a diary during the filming of *The Idiots*. But I keep it close to me.

RK: You don't publish it for the world?
BJ: Exactly.

RK: *The Humiliated* captures this rather glum day where you all have a barbecue and talk on into the night.
BJ: We were right in the middle of the film, and the filming: right at the point where things start tipping downhill, getting darker, after they invite the real idiots to their house.

RK: Lars's mood gets noticeably darker through the day, and he says in his diary that he was jealous of you all, like a child at a party who's not learned how to join in.
BJ: Exactly. Everyone knows that feeling. And I felt very sympathetic towards him. But, you know, as a director he can never be part of us. But he took up the camera, and I think that helped him. Because he saw it all.

RK: Whatever the strife, it feels like a film where the process was as rewarding as the result. There's a lovely moment where Katrine weeps and says, 'I don't think we can find again the fine things we found here.' Did you find the challenge rewarding?
BJ: Oh, yes. Really, the toughest part came when we said, 'We've got to get this working now, we have to get this scene on camera.' And you couldn't think about what you looked like. You couldn't imagine what your 'status' was, like you could in the exercises you'd do at drama school. You couldn't be 'good' – I think Jens really had trouble with this. You just had to let go, and be there. And we very seldom got there. Also, Lars was right beside us, operating this small camera. And you can't cheat on him – really, you *can't*. You can cry, sure, but if it's not right, then it won't do.

RK: So presumably it got to the stage where you knew yourself whether the moment was truthful, before Lars told you?
BJ: Exactly. And as an actor, it's what you're yearning for in your work: where there are no limits, and it just comes out. But it was also something that I wanted to give; I wasn't doing it for Lars. And this was the fine thing we found making this movie, I think.

RK: Karen is a bit of an enigma to the audience, until that last scene that makes you reassess the whole film. How did you prepare yourself for such a crucial scene?
BJ: The apartment where we shot was on the outskirts of Copenhagen,

177

and I hadn't seen it before we played the scene. I only knew the layout, because I'd been shown a drawing for where we would be sitting and so on. Then we get there, after six weeks in this big empty house, and suddenly I'm ringing the bell of this tiny apartment. And when I went in, I couldn't breathe.

RK: It felt claustrophobic?
BJ: Very much. And I didn't know all of the other actors. I didn't know the woman playing my mother. But the actor playing my husband I knew; and I knew that he can be such an angry man. Then when he hit me, he really hit me! The next time we had to do it, I put the plate up in front of my face because I was so afraid of him. And the plate cut my eyebrow, and Lars shouted, 'Dogme blood!' So they filmed this trickle of blood down the side of my face. You don't see too much of it, but they got it. And then I had to go to hospital . . .

RK: Did you feel that was going too far, even for Dogme?
BJ: No, strangely enough. I mean, you always know in yourself whether it's right or wrong.

RK: Did Lars employ any other strategies for that scene?
BJ: Oh, yes. He had placed a photo of a baby on a sideboard in the room, and he told me to pick it up and look at it. And that was very, very sad for me.

RK: Did you all see the finished film together as a cast and crew?
BJ: Yes, in a little cinema. And it was really shocking to see. So provocative. You can't stop thinking about it. And I'm still not sure I know what it's about. A lot of people really don't like it. My mother hates it, this film.

RK: What do you think makes it so hateful to her?
BJ: I think the idea that social life could become so . . . so disabled, so painful.

RK: Did you get to Cannes for the big première?
BJ: I couldn't go to the red-carpet screening, because I was playing for forty people at the Royal Theatre in Copenhagen. And I think half of them were asleep. (*Rolls her eyes.*) Terrible. But then I went down the next day for the press conference. So I got to be a star for one day, being guided around by these security people, taken to strange apartments and picnics. It's crazy there in Cannes – people screaming

constantly, just because everybody else is screaming. I got a terrible headache . . .

RK: So how does it feel now to be part of the Danish New Wave?
BJ: Well, the eyes of the world are on Danish film right now. We also still make a lot of shit. (*Smiles.*) But I've just made a film which takes place at the end of the last century, and it's made on video. And it's very interesting that you can take these cameras anywhere, with a bunch of actors, and a good story.

RK: Do you think video is appropriate for all projects?
BJ: Well, these things are developing while we're asleep, aren't they? But then I did a film last spring with the old heavy equipment, and what really struck me was that we would do one or two takes, and no one was ever really satisfied. Very often it was the actors saying, 'I know I can do better.' But it was too expensive, and the day is too short, and there are lenses to be changed and so on. So I'd go home feeling we didn't really have the material we needed. But on *The Idiots*, we had so many hours to play with. You could go deeper and deeper into the mood of the scene, or in and out of a mood within the same take. It makes me think of Bergman's very deep psychological dramas, where he tried to film the innermost psyche. I think you can go very far in that direction with these cameras. Whereas with the big cameras it's just 'Cut' and 'Thank you'. Making movies the old way is so tough; you have to be so good. I can understand why actors get neuroses and make demands, like 'I want my trailer!'

RK: Has *The Idiots* experience stayed with you in other ways? Like the 'spassing', for instance?
BJ: I just did a stage play with Anne-Grethe Bjarup Riis, who plays Katrine. And we were doing it all the time. Even on stage we did it sometimes. Also at the Royal Theatre I work a lot with Nikolaj Lie Kaas, who played Jeppe. And he'll pull the same faces he pulls in the film. Sometimes you just feel it's the right time to do it – in Cannes, for instance. I was sitting with a bunch of film people from New York and Tokyo. It was like a Woody Allen film – better, even. I think the director of the Museum of Modern Art was beside me. And his wife was amazing – she knew everything about any subject you could mention. But everyone was talking, and I had such a headache, I felt sick. And I began to rock in my chair, and my head was lolling a bit . . .

RK: You were slipping into 'spass'?

BJ: Yes. They were taking my arm and saying, 'Are you OK?' I had to go back to the hotel. And I suppose if they had seen the film then they might not have found it so funny.

RK: Or maybe it would be doubly funny. Do you think Dogme95 will survive in Denmark?

BJ: Well, now Lars decides that it's dead. He'll say, 'I don't want to talk about this Dogme thing any more. It's finished.' It's not, of course. But I think Lars is the one who got closest to the essence of Dogme. I mean, I like the other films very much, but I think they could also have been made in the ordinary way. Whereas with *The Idiots*, from the first idea that Lars had, right down to the final film, it was Dogme all the way.

RK: Perhaps there will be others to pick up the baton?

BJ: Yes. You know, Lars asked Kurosawa to make a Dogme film. But then he died. And it's true that people have been here before: Godard, for instance. Such wonderful films he made – *Une Femme est une Femme, Vivre Sa Vie*. But Godard liked *The Idiots* very much, you know? Lars got a fax from him. I'm not sure whether Lars completely understood what Godard wrote – you know what Godard is like these days, if you've seen his latest films. But the fax was very positive . . .

20 Ewen Bremner's leap of faith

Minerva Pictures, London w1: Monday, 13 December 1999

We're waiting for an audience with Ewen Bremner, the young Scottish actor who left indelible marks on Mike Leigh's *Naked* and Danny Boyle's *Trainspotting*, before taking the eponymous lead in Harmony Korine's Dogme adventure. Saul and he are acquainted, so we're all reasonably at ease. I leaf the trades, and mull over a brief write-up of the first Korean Dogme picture, *Interview*, a first feature from thirty-five-year-old South Korean director Daniel H. Byun. Byun is shooting in Paris, where he once studied at the FEMIS film school. The piece is budgeted at $2 million, shot on DV and 35 mm (now that's sport!), and is built around a story-within-a-story, of a director interviewing people about the intimate details of their lives. Byun claims he 'absolutely agrees with the Dogme spirit', whatever that is. But I suspect further consideration, as Mr Bremner arrives.

RICHARD KELLY: So, Ewen, how did you first make the acquaintance of Harmony Korine?

EWEN BREMNER: We have mutual friends, who thought we might hit it off if we got together. And we did, we got on good. He knew a bit of what I'd done; then I saw *Gummo*, and I was completely excited by it.

RK: What made it for you?

EB: Its originality; and its bravery, and abandon. It's showing you very ordinary people, and a very ordinary place; whereas what you usually see in films are people trying to be ordinary. I think Harmony's very interested in the idea that what's ordinary in real life is extraordinary on film, and in *Gummo* he makes you aware of that.

RK: How did Harmony strike you in the flesh?

EB: He's . . . a very unconventionally oriented gentleman. (*Smiles.*) But he's got a great intellect. And, in the purest sense of the word, he's very 'punk' – he has a lot of integrity. Because he has no regard for how things are supposed to be. He makes his own rules and lives by them, which I really admire.

RK: So you seized the chance to work with him on *Julien*?

EB: I'd say it was a bigger leap of faith for him to cast me in a movie like *Julien* than it was for me to trust Harmony Korine. At the same time, it's kind of hard work trusting Harmony Korine, because he's in a volatile state of being a lot of the time. Not violent or anything; but not exactly the most consistent individual. But I did trust him, and I understood his ambitions for the film. I mean, *Julien* was made as 'a Dogme film', but for me it's also 'a Harmony Korine movie'. And Harmony Korine doesn't make movies like anybody else, so I knew it would present demands I wasn't used to. But still it was the most incredible opportunity I could have wished for. I felt privileged. The fact that it was 'a Dogme film' too was like icing on the cake.

RK: It was already going to be a Dogme film when you signed up?

EB: Yeah, the Brethren had already approached Harmony and said, 'Come and join us in the new wave and make the first American Dogme film.' And I think Harmony had a lot of sympathy with the ambition of Dogme. But he also knew it would be a big imposition, because he works very instinctively, to the exclusion of almost everything else, whereas Dogme demands discipline, it creates problems you have to solve. So Harmony had to focus his attention, in an ingenious way, to carry the film through under the Vow of Chastity. But it was good for him too.

RK: What did you make of the Vow of Chastity yourself?

EB: I thought it was very generous, in that it aspires to give the audience a gift that's brand new. Also it's aspiring to tell the truth, or *a* truth – not just a lie, a confection. You're meant to use what you've got, and not lie about it, which is an admirable ambition. And whether it's intentional or not, Dogme has made people realize that it's possible to make films themselves, using technology that's available in Dixon's on the high street. I think if you take it too seriously, like (*mimics apoplectic anxiety*) 'This must be hand-held! It must!', then it becomes like organized religion, and it's not healthy. But Dogme's aspirations are wonderful. And I doff my cap to them. (*Smiles.*)

RK: What kind of script did Harmony present you with?

EB: There was a disclaimer on the front saying something like, 'This represents a screenplay with an unconventional structure. The scenes are not in any particular order.' But they were, really. And the finished film bears a very faithful relation to the script. The scene might just say something like, 'A hard wind blows. Blackness. Silence.' Or: 'Younger brother is throwing rocks at a swan on a lake.' Others were much more detailed, with snippets of dialogue. But generally it read like a big long poem that was very beautiful. And you got the idea of the characters and their situation. Then, the week before we started shooting, Harmony asked me and Chloe to go away and write forty scenes each. So I had to write ten scenes with my sister, ten for myself, five with my father, five with my brother, and so on. Then we sat down together and went through them, and that threw up new ideas that Harmony would take away and write as scenes.

RK: Julien himself is based on Harmony's Uncle Eddie?

EB: Yeah. He's diagnosed as a paranoid schizophrenic, and he's a long-term state patient in a psychiatric hospital in Queens. But Julien is based on Eddie when he was a young man, in his early twenties, at the real onset of his condition. I was able to spend time with him, and that was crucial. He's a man in his mid-forties, and yet he's like a child in some ways. He's retained this childlike good nature that is so enthusiastic about anything and everything: about life, about love, his family, drugs, music – he loves it. I'd say his nature is very beautiful. But it's quite a punishing environment he's living in. Another invaluable experience I had was to do some voluntary work in a psychiatric hospital for six weeks, as a classroom assistant to people suffering from similar psychological conditions. They very kindly took me in, because they're not very keen on actors ordinarily. So it was a real privilege. And they all knew I was an actor. I wasn't going in there pretending to be Julien, or spying, you know?

RK: Julien also works with blind people. Did you arm yourself with any special research for those scenes?
EB: I had a bit of exposure in my childhood because my father taught blind children at a school in Edinburgh. I don't know if that set me in good stead for playing Julien, but it certainly didn't do me any harm. Of the kids they got in for the film, some were thoroughly blind, some were partly visually impaired. But they were very vibrant individuals, and I think that comes over in the film, which is excellent and refreshing. Life for these people is very ordinary, whereas usually when they're depicted in movies, it's so far off the mark – either you get the invalid tapping the white cane, or the spooky, mysterious seer character. But these kids were athletes and champion wrestlers.

RK: Not to mention the 'black albino straight from Alabama'.
EB: He's a stand-up comic in real life, that guy. He's a rapper and he's got his own Web business together. Really accomplished people, you know?

RK: So all in all, you immersed yourself in the role?
EB: Well, there were a few months between my being cast and the start of shooting, because we were waiting for Anthony to finish shooting another film. But I got over to New York as soon as I knew Harmony wanted me. Then the most difficult part for me was becoming American: a real ordeal, actually – fucking gruelling. Because I don't consider myself gifted with accents. And the dialogue's improvised, so I don't have 'lines' that I can use to practise the accent. I'm meant to be this character Julien in any situation, at any time. Plus, Harmony's so unpredictable, he doesn't like to rehearse anything; and most of the time he only likes to shoot one take. And then, because it's a Dogme film, I don't have recourse to go back and dub it later and polish up my dodgy accent. So I had to be as proficient as I possibly could. That was the worst part.

RK: Anthony suggested that you were in character for most of the shoot, that he only met Ewen Bremner at the wrap party.

EB: I know what he's saying. I mean, I didn't go to work as Julien. But I was living a bit disengaged. I did try to avoid Anthony, because he's a Brit, and I was trying so, so hard to be American. But also Harmony wanted me to be completely unrecognizable, even to him. He didn't want to acknowledge me as his friend Ewen. So I had this curly black perm, almost like jeri-curls, and gold fronts on my teeth. And he didn't want me to be wearing my own clothes when we met, only what Julien would wear.

RK: How did you and your fellow actors shape up as family? Could you accept Werner Herzog as 'Julien's father', rather than as Werner Herzog the legendary film-maker?

EB: It's no different from working with a famous actor. I'd seen a couple of his films, and I respect him totally, but I wouldn't worship him. Initially, we were a bit concerned about getting that family bond working, but it fell into place fairly naturally. The casting was right, Harmony's instinct served him well.

RK: A lot of improvisation involved: did you feel that Harmony was on top of the demands posed by working that way?

EB: Every director I've worked with works differently, they forge their own way. I've worked with Mike Leigh, and he has a completely different approach to improvisation than Harmony, or any other director: a method that he's developed throughout his life. I wouldn't say there's any method to how Harmony works with improvisation. As a result, a lot of the discipline that's required to work in that way I really had to be responsible for myself, and be as disciplined in myself as I could muster – to be ready to respond to the scene, and to Harmony.

RK: Did you find the technical set-up of Dogme made for more freedom than you're used to?

EB: The actors get into a more sensitive relationship with the technical crew. When you're making a feature film with film cameras, you've got to be so precise; not like this cowboy set-up you've got here. (*Grins.*) You're asked to walk very naturally, but still hit a mark an inch wide that's twenty yards away. With a Dogme film, you're able to devote more of your attention to your character, and responding to the scene. And a good operator who's got a strong sensitivity to performers, like

Anthony, is in their element on a Dogme film. So much was impro-vised, Anthony wouldn't know exactly what was going to happen in the scene. And, you know, usually when actors improvise, there are a few little gems that work, but generally it's a bit of a drag to watch. You're like (*nodding off*), 'Get on with it.' But it was as if Anthony was magnetically attracted to what was interesting in a scene. We shot long takes, and I'd always be thinking, 'God, there was so much dodgy stuff in there.' Then I'd watch his playbacks, and be stunned by what he managed to capture, how pertinent and concise it was. He'd really fol-lowed the energy of the scene from person to person. I don't mean to go on about Anthony – top bloke, though.

RK: He does seem to be one of the geniuses behind these films; he's got the gift.
EB: Oh, he does. I mean, we had a lot of operators, Harmony shot stuff too. And he had a lot of camera ideas himself. Every scene was shot with a different approach, almost like a film in itself. There wasn't an overall aesthetic. He was considered, though, in his choices. It wasn't ever this rambling thing of (*mimics a doped drawl*), 'Yeah, let's throw some cameras around.' He wouldn't shoot a scene until he'd cracked it in his head, how it should be attacked. I mean, there are scenes shot on Polaroid cameras. You wouldn't necessarily know, to watch it, because it looks like moving pictures. Whoever would have thought of that? When you're confronted with it, you just think, 'Fuck. Wow.' It might not suit every actor. But I feel relatively adaptable myself.

RK: Take a scene like the one where Julien is in a little room fanta-sizing a dialogue with his friend Hitler. How does a scene like that get built? How do you tackle it?
EB: I think the script said, 'Julien is in his bedroom firing a gun at a picture of Hitler on his wall.' That was about as much information as was related to me. But, you see, sometimes they left me alone with a camera. There were occasions when the crew weren't even in the room with me. (*Laughs.*) It would just be me getting on with it. But it sharp-ens your wits, that responsibility. I was going into situations with a spy-camera where nobody knew I was acting in a film. And you don't get a second take, right? The scene has to succeed as a piece of life, it has to seem like a real encounter.

RK: The scene on the bus, Julien cradling Pearl's dead baby, looks to

be the apotheosis of that. There you really seem to be acting without guy-ropes.

EB: People didn't know they were being filmed. We had about eight or nine covert camera operators on the bus. Anthony was sitting there looking at a book, but he had a little camera in the palm of his hand, and a little monitor wired up inside a hole that he cut in the book. So he's watching. And there's a camera in a bag, and one in a hat, one on someone's glasses. We're presenting real people with a real dilemma: a kid gets on a bus with a dead baby wrapped up in a dirty old towel. It was a real liberty we were taking. And for an actor it's a moral dilemma to get into a situation like that. It's a terrible thing to do. People didn't know how to react. *I* wouldn't know. In fact, the stuff they left in the finished film is the mildest stuff we got in terms of people's reactions. We did two runs because we didn't feel we had it after the first, but the reactions we got the second time – some of them were just heartbreaking. And some of them were really frightening. Grown men just weeping. A big man with a gun, asking the driver to stop the bus. People getting off the bus because they wanted to fucking kill me. We're lucky to be alive, really. And when it got too dangerous, I got a signal and I was yanked off the bus. Also there was a van full of PAs coming up behind, running to catch people as they came off the bus at each stop, asking, 'Look, you've just been in a film. Will you sign a release form?'

RK: Presumably some of them were angry to have had their emotions manipulated in that way?

EB: I think, generally, people were relieved. Because they had believed it was a dead baby.

RK: Are we to accept Julien's insistence that the baby is 'his'?

EB: I don't know. I believe him. But I think the audience can take it or leave it.

RK: Since you were Julien, though, obviously you had to choose, one way or another?

EB: Oh, I did. But then Julien believes a lot of stuff that you or I might not believe. (*Chuckles.*)

RK: Were you relieved to leave the character behind?

EB: Oh, yes, I really was. I always like getting back to my own little world. I forced myself to be American for the duration of the shoot, and even prior, which is a contrived thing to have to do. How you talk is so much a result of who you are, where you come from, what you're trying to be. So, altering it that seriously isn't great for your mental health, I don't think. A great relief, too, to shave off the curly perm. Horrible . . .

RK: Did you go to the Venice Festival for the screening?
EB: Yes. But it was kind of obliterated for me by my own expectations of the film, because I hadn't seen it yet. It had been such an intense experience for me, and my life here is so different, that every day, after finishing, I found myself wondering, 'God, what's it going to be like?' I couldn't rest until I'd seen it. And then I was pretty depressed when I saw it, because it was five months of my life, boiled down into ninety minutes. So I was thinking, 'Where's the rest of it?'

RK: What have you thought of the critical responses you've had?
EB: A lot of Americans seem to be taking it quite technically: like, 'OK, this is a Dogme95 film, I know all about Dogme95. Oh! But doesn't that bit flout the Dogme?' And if they knew what Dogme was, they'd know they're generally talking out of their arse.

RK: But there's a danger with Dogme, isn't there, that people will haggle over this conspicuous set of Rules, and so ignore whatever the soul of the piece is, which the Rules were meant to draw out?
EB: Some people only watch the film through a certain frame – fine. That's up to them. In my opinion, it's a waste of time. But the film exists in its own right. All the Dogme films stand or fall on their own merits. On an artistic level, everybody's taking the film very seriously, which is good. A lot of people *hate* the film. The big American publications, *The New York Times, Hollywood Reporter*, have treated it as a groundbreaking film. But they'll also say that it's not for their delicate readership, who might not be ready for it. So the review will say, 'Important film, incredible achievement, very new, very uncompromising, must be seen.' Then, a bit further on, in the same article – 'But you will not like it. And nobody will go see it. It's too disturbing.' Still, the British and European press I've spoken to seem to like the film. Very generally, I'd say older people haven't responded so well to it as younger people. But I think it has a very modern language. What Harmony's doing is twisting the language of cinema into new shapes, and it's quite alienating for people who have grown up with certain cinematic conventions. In my opinion, Harmony is the premier artist of our time just now. I can't help thinking that, it's

what I believe. And I don't expect him to be recognized as such in his time either.

Afterwards, Ewen's amusement at our 'cowboy set-up' is palpable. As I crack the clapstick before his face, he cheerfully shouts, 'Cheap!' Packing up, we chat about this ticklish business of *Julien*'s budget. As Ewen tells it, when he and Harmony toured the Festivals, Harmony was continually being asked to quote a figure. His stock reply was 'eighty million'. That's the spirit.

21 Downtime#2:
Dogmatic post-production, and prize-winning
Hollywood whoredom

I'm strapped aboard a Virgin jet, sipping Courvoisier from a plastic tumbler, feeling a lot like the character in *Viz* comic known as 'Spawny Get'. After a shiftless start, my new year kicked off on 4 January with an e-mail from Eliza Mellor at Minerva: 'I had a call today from the Independent Film Channel, asking if you were interested in going to Los Angeles for a presentation that they are giving to the TV Critics' Association to promote their original productions. It would be on 20 January in the afternoon, 1–2 p.m. They would pay your fare etc.' Well, I call that equitable; and a break would be nice. As a crew we remain on call to fly to New York at the drop of a hat; but Harmony Korine, our last man standing, has as yet evinced no willingness to make a contribution to the documentary. Elsewhere, and 35,000 feet beneath me, Saul is confined to cutting quarters in Soho, and sinking ever deeper into his uncomfortable director's swivel-chair. 'It's all painful' has become his daily refrain. Having experienced the Dogmatic joys of a tiny crew, a hand-held camera, and a brute disregard for lighting levels, now we must face the harsh and inevitable correlative of shooting DV: about 100 hours of rushes. At least Saul is in the safe hands of editrix Justine Wright, to whom he refers as 'Valdis', *en hommage* to Ms Oskarsdottir.

But inevitably, the shine has come off somewhat. Before Christmas, we had what was due to be a funny day out at a studio in East London's Mile End. The job was a 'proper' 16-mm shoot for the explanatory opening of the doc: Saul's baby, this – a forties *noir*-style murder scene that we repeatedly break down and rerun, each time introducing a fresh proscription from the Vow of Chastity, until finally it's just me and another bloke in jeans, shrugging at each other. Saul had shrewdly enlisted one of his most gifted mates, the young Irish DP Seamus McGarvey. And after our games with DV, it was kind of fun to play with the professional train set. And yet, as the day wore on, I appreciated anew why the Dogme Brothers got bored with the big lamps, the miles of track, the unwieldy Chapman dolly. Saul grew almost Trier-esque in his desire for detail; hence I smoked sixty cigarettes in a range of moody ways, and slumped to my death repeatedly on the freezing concrete floor. Stuart Milligan, an American actor looking a lot like James Cagney, only meaner, had the pleasure of blowing me away. A week or so later, we sat through seventy minutes of rough-cut. 'It's never as good as the rushes,' I counselled myself, 'and never as bad as the rough-cut.'

Well, my room's fine. Fact is, I'm in what is essentially a cottage, nicer than anywhere I've ever paid rent for; fitted with dining-room, bookshelves, two televisions, three sofas, and a big white bathroom just like the ones in the movies. The opulence is disconcerting. I suddenly wish I were married – my wife would be really impressed by me right now. As it is, I feel surreal and lonely. Who am I fooling by my presence here? Still, the people of Bravo/IFC are terribly nice, not least my new pal Elektra Gray. At the presentation itself, I burble away at a dais before forty or so journalists. My text is a considered refutation of the theory of Dogme95 as a big fat Danish marketing stunt. After all, say I, I didn't see McDonald's selling any Dogme95 'happy meals' last summer; just the usual crap about a phantom menace and what have you. A few chuckles for this; yet somehow I imagine these hacks are thinking that Dogme's got a lot to learn from Lucasfilm, and that whoever's presently responsible for its marketing should be sacked (already).

I have two comrades in this session: an occasional network news journalist called Jay Schadler, and the great Errol Morris. And inevitably their stuff is fascinating. For his Bravo show, *Tale Lights*, Jay is hitchhiking around the States with a DVC and a 'lipstick camera' (as the tiddlers are known), interviewing anyone who'll pick him up. He wants to show us 'an authentic America', one that's still full of people worth talking to. Errol's new show is called *First Person*, a series of interviews with ordinary people about their extraordinary lives. He's constructed a rig of twenty DVCs of various sizes to train simultaneously on the subject; and he enthuses about the possibility of delivering 'an unmediated experience' to the viewer. We chat afterwards, and he claims to be partly inspired by David Hockney's collage portraits made from innumerable Polaroids. At last I head back to my cottage, dreaming of dinner and drinks. Paula calls to say that Harmony's agreed to an interview, and they're off – now! So, one more mildly dispiriting irony at my expense: I come out to a junket to promote an unfinished film, and the junket prevents me from finishing it. Of course, mercifully, Saul can fill the breach.

It's Golden Globes Weekend, and my buddy Bill ('Irish') Higgins of

Variety is taking me round town on his ticket. So! To a party for the eminent Mike Medavoy, hosted by Ron Burkle, multi-millionaire boss of the Food-4-Less chain. His estate once belonged to Harold Lloyd and, once through the gates, we ascend the steep, scented driveway for about half an hour. Inside is an embarrassment of art riches: two garish Hockneys, a lugubrious Modigliani, a fiery Chagall, one of Degas's dancers. I'm told there's even a Renoir in the men's room. In the atrium, several starry nominees stand and sway, making patient conversation, very possibly sick of the sight of each other even at this early stage in the 'awards season'. Penelope Cruz is the belle of the ball, chaperoned by a solicitous Almodóvar. I'm more interested in the presence of Chloe Sevigny, nominated for *Boys Don't Cry*. But, incredibly, I'm not enough of a journalist to approach her and explain my project, even though she is surely the one person in the room who knows what Dogme95 might mean.

Around 11.30 p.m., the President of the United States drops by. He was in town, after all, having spent the afternoon playing golf with Jack Nicholson. Now he's here to press a little flesh; possibly doing a favour for his 'friend' Al Gore, or possibly more concerned for his own future employment. As he works the hallway en route to the inner sanctum, I chuckle to myself: there are stars, and then there are stars. But as he passes my end of an impromptu line-up, it doesn't occur to me to take his hand, not least because I'm nursing a drink; and I earn a Clintonian grimace. Ten minutes later, almost the entire party is back down at the gates, tapping their feet for the valets. Jon Bon Jovi (for it is he) stands, grinning, watching the stream back down the driveway: 'OK, we've seen the President, so we can all go home, right?'

North Gardner Street, Hollywood: Sunday, 23 January 2000

Bill's at the Globes ceremony, plying his trade. I sit in his apartment and follow the early results on the Web by way of his frighteningly fast cable modem. The surprise Best Actress is Kristian Levring's lead, Janet McTeer, in *Tumbleweeds*. But by the time Alan Ball and Sam Mendes have won their respective categories for *American Beauty*, suspense has crashed. It's time to go put my suit on, and prepare to do some parties. No point dilly-dallying, for this is an early town. I pitch up at Trader Vic's for the Dreamworks do, just as *American Beauty* claims Best Drama and lots of dressy young people start getting very happy. Luscious food is laid out: reefs of teriyaki beef, trays of sushi, piles of shrimp on ice. I collect my gratis quadruple Wild Turkey and stake out a dimly lit nook where I can wait for Bill in peace: the least conspicuous spot in the place. Moments later, a happy, handsome, diminutive fellow settles into the booth beside mine. I notice, first, that he has a Golden Globe in his hand, and second, that he's Tom Cruise. Behind him is a lofty blonde in a red dress, who slinks her way into the booth on my right. Unmistakably: it's Claudia Schiffer. Suddenly a wild pack of TV cameramen muscle in, and I'm now in the *most* conspicuous spot in the place. I see Sam Mendes accepting Spielberg's handshake, and he seems pleased: mischievous, even. Clearly, Hollywood is still receptive to certain discerning Europeans. Almodóvar, too, seems hugely popular. And wasn't *Festen* up for Best Foreign Film just a year ago?

Back at the apartment, I leaf the official Globes brochure, wherein numerous big directors are canvassed for their opinions under that nerve-straining rubric, 'The Future of Cinema'. Most are obsessed by digital technology: the available tools, the low costs, the chances for more film-making. The cutest contribution is that of Kevin Smith, who fondly imagines that new kinds of guerrilla film-makers – little kids, old-age pensioners – will be empowered. Steven Soderbergh is more wary, suggesting that quality doesn't rise exponentially with quantity. Neil Jordan fears for the loss of celluloid, that it will 'seem one day as beautiful and strange to us as Renaissance frescoes'. Rightly, Agnieska Holland is on a downer about the as-yet firmly locked system of distribution, exhibition, and marketing. And Alan Parker sounds peeved about the limited windows for foreign-language cinema in the US.

Naturally, no such survey is complete without Scorsese. And after a few wistful lines about the 'wild films' of the 1970s, he bucks up: 'Even now, there are people like Lars von Trier, a wonderful film-maker. He got furious, threw everything up in the air, and said, "Look, let's start from nowhere now. Let's go to video. No lighting. Let's recreate the language of cinema." I think it's very healthy when young people come in, throwing everything away. At least for a while . . .' This is something like a blessing from the Pope. What, I wonder, does Scorsese think of Harmony Korine? And Korine of Scorsese, for that matter? But it's not my place to put those questions – at least, not this week.

22 'What the explosion would look like':
Harmony Korine & *Julien Donkey-Boy*

Harmony Korine has been rooting around his production offices for a can of soda. Now he steps into the room and pulls the door behind him. 'We got a lot of fuckers spying round here,' he says in mock-conspiratorial *sotto voce*, and then casts an eye over the Minerva set-up. Paula is back on boom duties, and Braden King has taken over the second-camera chore from Jack. 'I like my name that big,' Harmony remarks of the clapper-board; and for perhaps the last blessed time, Saul explains the ripping conceit of a caption-free documentary, and our lazy approximation of a half-attempt at abiding by Dogme Rules. 'So, you broke a few,' remarks Harmony, chewing contemplatively on the butt of his cigarette. 'That's good . . .' The misconceptions over his own chastity, he hints, are taxing his patience.

SAUL METZSTEIN: So the idea of doing a film under the Vow of Chastity was suggested to you by Thomas Vinterberg?
HARMONY KORINE: Right. I had read the Manifesto right after they put it out. I liked it, it seemed fitting. And it didn't seem to me like shooting *Julien* under that guise would be a real departure from how I was going to shoot it anyway.

BRADEN KING: I was surprised when I heard that *Julien* would be a Dogme movie; surprised that it held any interest for you, in a way. Because I'd have guessed you'd have hated it.
HK: I think a lot of people thought that. I think it was for that very reason that I was attracted to it; that kind of traitor's desire. At the same time, just the concept of the group – this union, this brotherhood – is what's shocking, or foreign. But the actual Dogme rhetoric itself is very appealing, I find. I just liked the idea of giving myself to this holy endeavour.

SM: Once you decided to do it Dogme, did your script change?
HK: Not at all. I had kind of lost faith, and I still have very little faith, in a formal screenplay structure. It's just really boring to me. I don't like the idea of imposing these dead words or abstract notions on something that's alive, on the actors. In a way, I added a Rule to the Manifesto just for myself: I wouldn't allow any kind of a plot to seep through. I don't like plot-oriented movies. I like things that kind of evolve, or just begin and end – like life does. So I basically wrote a list

of scenes and images that were almost like looking at photographs. Common things, almost random ideas. Somebody eats a hamburger. Or climbs a tree. Or wrestles a garbage can. We would take those, and then whatever happened in filming would happen, and then in the editing I would make it into some kind of 'drama'.

SM: Though presumably the scenes with Julien and the dead baby were always intended to be the end?

HK: Oh, yeah. And there were things that I knew had to be seen at the beginning, to support the character throughout the film. But I was less interested in making a movie, like 'This is a film', than I was in making some kind of artefact that documented some kind of action. It was important to me just to present the images rather than offer one over-all viewpoint, because I wasn't trying to say any one thing. I just wanted to make something to watch.

SM: Why did you pick Anthony Dod Mantle as your DP?

HK: I was in pre-production, we were going to start within a month, and I was planning to work with the cinematographer we had on *Gummo* and *Kids*, Jean-Yves Escoffier. But then he got another movie, and I couldn't wait. And I had liked how *Festen* was shot, so I contacted Anthony. I identified with what he was doing visually, what he was trying to communicate. I noticed he had a really exceptional understanding of camera movement and foreground, and of working in the absence of lighting. It wasn't a desire to make uniformity, of using the same people for all Dogme films. Though that idea is appealing as well . . .

SM: You used the same editor too? Valdis Oskarsdottir?

HK: Sure. She wears mittens. And I liked her fingers.

SM: Why did you cast Ewen Bremner?

HK: I just liked the way he walks, really. He's very bow-legged; he can shoot an arrow with his knees. But we had to cut that scene.

SM: Werner Herzog has made films that have the same feeling as yours of mixing documentary and drama. Is his presence in the film a sort of hommage?

HK: Not really a conscious *hommage*, because I don't really like *hommages*. I dislike any kind of reverence. But Werner's always been a hero of mine, one of my favourite film-makers, since I was a kid. For me, he's the best of the German 'new wave', because he never seemed like he was in fashion, or that he had an agenda. I was friends with Werner anyway; after I made *Gummo* he contacted me. So it was more from knowing him personally, and knowing that he wanted to act, and that he was suited to the character of this maniacal German father. I guess we have a similar belief in this idea that there's a fallacy of truth in cinema, and that realism or *cinéma vérité* fall short. I've never believed in an ultimate truth in films, I think it's impossible to be completely honest because there's always a point of view involved in film-making. But in terms of truth in its purest form, there's something much more important, something that almost hovers above, and that documentary fails to achieve. I think it can only be achieved through a kind of manipulation, of making things seem as real as possible, but lying about them. So what you have hovering above is like a poetic truth.

SM: How seriously then do you subscribe to the idea that Dogme is more truthful cinema?

HK: I *have* to subscribe to that point of view, really. But I think if you follow these ten Rules, without question, they force some kind of issue of truth, or reflection of truth, from the actors, from the characters and the story – which ultimately you have to reckon is something more truthful than had you not worked that way. That's not to say that this way is the most truthful way to make a film. It's to say that you have to reckon with some kind of semblance of honesty.

SM: How seriously did you attempt to engineer Chloe Sevigny's pregnancy for the film?

HK: God . . . That's definitely a very serious matter. I'm very serious in anything dealing with potency.

SM: But you ended up absolutely against the Rules?

HK: Well, that was one of my Confessions. The try was definitely part of the Dogme. But my failure in it was . . . I wouldn't call it 'a sin' because I tried. It was just me shooting blanks.

SM: How many cameras did you use?

HK: About twenty in the end. Originally I'd had this idea of blanketing a huge wall with small camcorders, each one just a little bit skewed from the next in its point of view. So you'd have a set of views, maybe One through Fifty, all trained on the same subject. And I was interested in the idea of having to edit that footage, because you could approach it almost in a mathematical way. You could say, without looking, 'Camera Fourteen to Camera Sixty-five to Camera Thirty-three.' It would be completely random. So I'd originally wanted to do that. But I just didn't. (*Laughs.*)

SM: Lars von Trier is doing something similar, though.
HK: Yeah, I heard he's using a hundred cameras.

SM: Why all the hidden cameras, the spy-cameras?
HK: The reason I was attracted to video wasn't really to do with the aesthetics of that image. It was more about the immediacy of video, and I liked the idea of changing the psychology behind not just the director–actor relationship but the whole film-making process. Some of my favourite scenes in *Gummo* were the ones where there was no crew around. I'd go and whisper something to the actors between takes. It was like a 'mistakeist' art form. Or some kind of chemical reaction; like putting chemicals into a bottle and shaking them up, and documenting them, seeing what the explosion would look like. I wanted to remove myself. So I imagined what it would be like having two actors at a table, in conversation, each one wearing a teeny spy-camera on their shoulder. I would give them some direction, and then I would leave the house for a few hours, and let them go through their scene. And what I'd get would be these two matching one-shots that I could cut between. And that way, there would be no cinematographer, no sound-recordist, no director. So I was interested in the idea of making a movie without anyone, including myself, except for the actors, and seeing what would happen.

SM: Presumably that idea reached its peak in the bus scene.
HK: Yeah, that was pretty scary – one of the scarier scenes in the movie. I had wanted to use a real dead baby, a cadaver. And I didn't want to hire actors for the bus, I wanted to see what would happen if people on a bus saw this little infant corpse, and this boy crying over his dead nephew, or whatever it is. Just the reaction to that. So it was hard to deal with the lawyers, because they were scared that somebody on the bus would have a heart attack, or maybe shoot Ewen. We had to do it outside New York. And I was too nervous to get on the bus, to be honest with you.

SM: So where were you?
HK: I was in the van, reading.

SM: Did you have a video relay?

HK: No, I didn't really want to see what would happen.

SM: And what kind of things did happen?

HK: Oh, just your basic reactions. What you would expect, for that kind of thing. I think people are used to it on the bus these days.

SM: Did you find yourself with a very high shooting ratio?

HK: I'd really wanted to just shoot and shoot and shoot without really thinking of the consequences; not only of shooting too much film. But if you're shooting 35 mm, you can only shoot maybe four minutes at a time, and I wanted to be able to shoot two-hour takes if needs be. Anyway, we ended up with almost 100 hours of footage.

SM: So were you forced to be very compressed in the editing?

HK: Well, the first cut was about six hours long – which I wanted to put out, in that form. I wanted people to take a tent to the movie theatre, and sleep over. I'm not one of those people who takes the stance that editing is where the film is really made. But the film comes together there, and you want to make the strongest film you can make. Or – maybe you want to make the weakest film, I don't know. Sometimes my favourite parts are considered the weakest, the bits cut out are the ones I find most interesting.

SM: Ewen said he was a bit shocked at first by the final length.

HK: At how short it is? Well, that's the thing. I would love to make a movie that's three months long. Before he died, Andy Warhol was talking about wanting to make a biblical epic. He was going to photograph each page of the Bible, estimate how long it took to read, and then project the Bible. So, ultimately, he'd make the greatest biblical epic ever. I'd love to make a movie where the viewer spends three or four months in the theatre, but I don't think anyone has that commitment any more. I mean, I do. I would – I'd try to live there. But I don't think there are many people who have that kind of zest.

SM: Can you describe your encounter with the Dogme police after you'd finished the film?

HK: The final act, the receiving of the Dogme stamp: what happens is that when you're finished with the movie, you fly to Denmark, and you present the Brothers with your film. I confessed my sins against the Vow of Chastity beforehand. Which weren't very many. And then they watch it and go over it with a fine-tooth comb, scene by scene. Or at least they try. And then they tell you if you've done it properly or not. And if you have, everybody goes out to eat, and drink a lot.

SM: Thomas told us he found *Julien* a rather aesthetic film.
HK: I don't see what kind of movie isn't aesthetic. I mean, either the aesthetics are appealing or they're not. But there was no conscientious decision to make 'an aesthetic film'.

SM: He also admitted that Rule is impossible. He said with *Festen* that they didn't pre-plan how anything would be shot.
HK: Neither did we. Our approach was always to watch the actors do it first, without imposing any kind of direction on them; and then to think about the best way the scene should evolve. And then, lastly, to think about the best way to film the scene – whether to do the whole scene in Polaroids, or to film it from half a mile away with really long lenses, or with spy-cameras, or at different speeds. The question being, 'What would complement the action, the drama?' I mean, it would be very silly to say, 'OK, I'm going to shoot a scene in black-and-white now', without thinking of what the scene is. Sometimes you realize that the scene is just an action that only needs documentation, some *cinéma vérité*, without any help from the camera.

SM: Did the Brotherhood ask you to make any changes to the film, as was put to Jean-Marc Barr?
HK: Oh, yes, I heard about that. No, they didn't ask.

SM: What would you have said if they had?
HK: Well, if it was something valid that I felt could be changed, then I'd have acquiesced. But the whole idea is that you make a film under these Rules not wanting to cheat. There's really no reason to make a film this way if you have this notion of leniency. So, for me and everybody else involved, it was about putting these Rules on a wall and saying, 'We can do anything we want within the confines of the Vow of Chastity.' There were some things that we did that weren't traditional Dogme, such as voice-over, which we had to do manually. The actor would speak into the camera while we were on location for the scene, or we would pre-record on a micro-cassette recorder and then play it into the camera as we shot. And there's superimposition of images, but they were done in-camera, not in post-production.

SM: What surprised me when I went to speak to the Danish Dogme guys is that I thought they'd be much more heavily ironic.

HK: Well, the thing is that there's no irony to this, and there shouldn't be. A lot of people think it's a kind of joke, or there's some kind of levity involved. But I know that I wouldn't be interested in Dogme if there was any irony attached to the Vow of Chastity. It's a very serious thing.

SM: But you must believe there's some marketing attached to it?

HK: Oh, I don't know about that. (*Smiles, holds up his hands.*)

SM: Haven't people accused you of jumping on the Dogme bandwagon, or them of jumping on yours?

HK: No, no. That's a horrible accusation . . .

SM: How would you respond to it?

HK: Well, I would say that it didn't really help the box-office sales. That accusation has no bearing. I mean, in America the idea of doing a Dogme film for the money, it's like . . . if anything, it would hinder you.

SM: Whereas in the UK, people only seem to discuss Dogme in terms of budgets.

HK: Which is a disgusting thing as well. I mean, I'd like to make a movie like *Titanic* according to the Vow of Chastity. The economics of it were never a factor, at least not in my thinking. And I don't even think making a Dogme film is necessarily all that cheaper than doing it regular. It probably would have cost me less money to do *Julien* in a different way than this.

SM: Ewen Bremner told us he thought there was a problem with the reception of *Julien* in that people were seeing it as a Dogme film first and foremost, rather than looking at it for what it is.

HK: It's not something I'm really concerned about. For me at least, the Vow of Chastity was something very personal: more for the director, but also for the actors and crew; and very technically oriented, about how you make the films. There was ideology involved. There was a religious element to it, you were asked to follow the Vow of Chastity blindly, much like the Ten Commandments. But all of a sudden it seemed like you had this minority of cinephiles or supposed 'experts' interested in the Dogme95 idea. I wasn't making a film like *The Idiots*, or like *Festen*. I was concerned with making things I hadn't seen before, and having to do them in this different way. A lot of people misinterpreted that as sinning or breaking the Rules, which was a really boring argument to me. Ultimately you want people to watch the film for what it is, not with this kind of mathematical analysis, and without any real knowledge of what was done.

SM: But you could argue that all film-makers privately make rules for themselves before they start a film; and the Dogme Brotherhood just happened to publish theirs.

HK: I don't know that all film-makers do. I think most don't even consider it, or even care. But the good thing about the Dogme Rules is that they were written obtusely enough that they weren't so restricting that I couldn't do what I wanted. I just had to go about it in another way, do things more manually a lot of the time.

SM: Would you concede that at a certain point, if you spend so much effort trying to bypass the Rules, then why bother?

HK: Oh, it was never about bypassing. That would be a heathen thing to do. (*Laughs.*) And I feel very much ingratiated with my fellow brethren.

SM: The Manifesto draws parallels with the French new wave, and makes certain criticisms of it. How seriously do you take that?

HK: In my opinion, with the exception of Godard, the French new wave failed – because in a lot of ways they became what they hated. There was this élitist bourgeois romanticism. That's not to say I don't love a lot of the movies that came from that time. They're some of my favourite films.

SM: What do you think will be the legacy of Dogme?

HK: Oh. (*Chuckles.*) I just hope it can breathe under water.

SM: Can you see more invention in people using these Rules?

HK: I definitely hope so. And I hope it becomes more and more militant. But I think it probably won't. In a weird way, I don't think Dogme is extreme enough. So I'd say, 'Step up to the plate. And be extremely militant.'

SM: Dogme is much discussed in the context of European cinema, but how do you feel it's perceived in America?

HK: From what I've noticed, people don't really care. This idea of a 'movement' or 'wave' has very little bearing or effect. When I was in Europe with the film, it seemed much more prevalent: people knew about Dogme and were concerned about it. Here, of the people who saw *Julien*, I'd guess maybe ten per cent of them had heard of Dogme. And out of that group, maybe one per cent knew anything about it beyond the name.

SM: And probably they were the bastards that wrote about it.
HK: Right. It's always the one per cent. (*Raises a fist.*)

SM: Is that kind of film-making much harder here than in Europe?
HK: No. I don't think it has much to do with the geography. I think it has more to do with an individual acceptance of the Rules, and an individual desire to do a film in abidance by them.

SM: Do you think Hollywood has paid any attention to Dogme?
HK: No. I don't think it ever will. And I don't think it should. I don't think Hollywood should ever pay attention. I think it's good where it is (*smiles*), it's just great.

SM: But it gives you some focus: being un-Hollywood?
HK: No, I think I'm very Hollywood and commercial, I do. What's *Julien* grossed, about a hundred million? (*Laughs.*) It's like *Toy Story 2*.

SM: Would you make another Dogme film?
HK: Lars talks about religion, and the Vow of Chastity being almost like a church. And a church is a nice place to go if you feel you need to repent. I couldn't make all my films that way, and I don't think I need to. I'm sure the next movie I make will probably use a completely different method. And I'll go against a lot of what I have previously hailed in the Vow of Chastity. But it's nice to know the Vow exists, so that after I've sinned I can always repent.

BK: Can you talk about the ways in which you feel that beauty and perversity are intertwined?
HK: For me at least, you can never look at something and find it wholly beautiful, or wholly disturbing. When people accuse me of being interested in things that are 'grotesque', there are so many arguments in there that I don't understand. I mean, I'm attracted to girls with scars on their faces. I like girls with missing limbs. I always have. I'm sexually attracted to that. So a lot of times, what people consider to be grotesque, I'm really aroused by. But I also like the idea of making things a bit more confusing. I think what's gross about a lot of movies now is that things have become so simplistic and so one-way. They

exist on a very even plane. If you're making a film about life, based in some kind of truth, it's much more complex. And you can take something that's supposedly grotesque, an ugly image, and you can beautify it, shooting it in a certain way or adding some lovely music to it, making the image much more emotionally complex.

SM: Thomas said that, paradoxically, all their Danish Dogme films had been very personal films. Do you think *Julien* is any more personal than *Gummo*?

HK: No. It's maybe more *adamant*. It deals with fewer characters in a much more cloistered environment. But I really only know how to make one kind of movie, you know? I don't know what that movie is, exactly. But if I could describe them in words, then I wouldn't feel the need to make them, or project them. The reason I make movies is so that I can decipher these things on a personal level, learn things about myself.

The tape is running down. Paula has a last request: can Harmony offer a 'one-liner' on *Julien*? 'One-liner? You mean like Milton Berle?' he asks. 'I'll do a song-and-dance, if that's what you want?' 'No, just a description of the film will do.' A long pause. 'OK. It's about someone that hears voices. And gets really close to his sister, on a real personal level. And is drawn to the Third Reich.' A longer pause. 'Well, I'd go see it,' offers Paula.

As for me, of course, I'm watching all of this *post facto* on VHS. I like the idea of Harmony making *Titanic*: it reminds me of Godard's contention that Hollywood should be forced to work in 16 mm and 8 mm, and the 'underground' in 70 mm. And what now seems precious to me is that Korine and the Brotherhood recognized kindred spirits in each other, and so, symbolically, joined hands across the ocean, making a small but significant transatlantic *avant-garde*. Doesn't this at least offer the prospect of an international solidarity among young filmmakers, demanding the impossible, eager to assault the mainstream, rushing on to the street to tell their stories from down there?

23 Downtime#3:
Wonderful, wonderful high taxation

The NFT is putting a lid on its month-long season of recent Danish films by way of a torpid platform panel session, chaired by journalist Michael Soby, who's also the Danish cultural attaché to the UK. He's having a hard time stirring up the crack. But then, it is Sunday. And the audience (including a solid component of Danes) are patient in their desire to hear more tales of the Danish miracle. Ulrich Thomsen (looking a tad more grizzled than he did as poor Christian in *Festen*) observes that international success has bred a robust cultural confidence in Danish film. In his case, he beams, it means a lot more offers; and out comes a rambling anecdote of his work on the last James Bond film. Nevertheless, he still speaks fondly of the making of *Festen*; how 'laissez-faire' the process was. 'Are you saying the production was disorganized?' quips the man seated at his shoulder: Morten Kaufmann of Nimbus Film. For his part, Kaufmann pours a little wry scepticism on proceedings. He reports that Nimbus are repeatedly dealing now with directors who say, 'We want our lights and costumes. We don't want that Dogme shit.' So, after the clean-up operation, the backlash.

The most substantial contributions of the afternoon are from Henning Camre: former head of the Danish Film School, now Director of the Danish Film Institute; and unostentatiously assured of what his bodies have done for Dogme. He notes that the recent success of Danish films has fairly tickled the politicians, and so enabled the Institute to lobby for increased subsidy from 'a position of strength'. The Institute's main representation to Government was that they be given the chance to boost production output, keep Danish films visible in the marketplace, and so consolidate the rediscovered domestic audience. Clearly, the argument washed. The Government hiked up central funding from £20 million to £35 million, 'a radical increase', now making possible the Institute's backing of twenty-five features a year, and fifty to sixty documentaries. As Camre cheerfully puts it, 'This is a heavily subsidized culture. But for some strange reason, Danes have decided to pay their taxes. And they've learned that when you pay tax, you get wonderful things for free.'

Afterwards, I have a few pints with a fellow audience member: Carsten Jensen, who's presently a visiting Fellow at Birkbeck College, while his wife Birthe is teaching at the London School of Economics. And we're joined by the graceful Helle Iben Absalonsen, a Danish MA student at Birkbeck, who's contributed some research to the Minerva documentary. Both of them are amused by London's sudden hunger for bulletins from Cool Denmark. But in the course of our chat, they direct me to the work of Danish novelist Aksel Sandermose (oft likened to Strindberg, Conrad, and Jack London, o lucky man); most point-edly, to his 1933 novel, *En Flyktning Krysser Sitt Spor* (*A Refugee Crosses the Tracks*). The action is set in a fictional town called 'Jante', in which a prohibitive ten-point code governs social and moral norms of behav-iour. Both Carsten and Helle affirm that, among educated Danes, 'The Jante Law' is commonly invoked (and with no intent to flatter) when attempting to describe the Danish mentality. Back home, I'm able to drag those ten Jante rules off the Internet in less than a minute:

1. You shall not think you are special.

2. You shall not think you hold the same status as us.

3. You shall not think you are smarter than us.

4. Don't imagine you are better than us.

5. You shall not think you are more knowledgeable than us.

6. You shall not think you are more important than us.

7. You shall not think you are good at anything.

8. You shall not laugh at us.

9. You shall not think that anyone cares about you.

10. You shall not think you can teach us anything.

I find myself flashing back to how Peter Aalbæk summed up the Dan-ish complex: ('Whenever you stick your head up a little too high out of the bush then somebody comes along with a baseball bat and beats you back down again'). And, before he got on to penis sizes, didn't Thomas Vinterberg tell me: 'Everyone here is longing for something bigger; and when it's finally offered, we say "no"?' At the time, I smiled and nodded, little knowing that these off-the-cuff quips had such a long cultural lineage behind them. The Jante Law reaffirms this notion of a consensus culture, resistant to vaulting ambition and needless ostentation, desirous always of modesty and austerity, nurturing an egalitarianism which nevertheless might be seen to shade into smugness or unexamined conformity. And that's all OK with me.

Then again, how much thin gruel can a thrusting young cultural capitalist like Aalbæk force down, before he starts hankering after a larger piece of pie? The question suggests itself to me forcibly as I browse a glowing special report ('Denmark shines through Dogme haze: Danish film-making reaches new heights') from the 4 February edition of *Screen International*. Therein, the ever-ebullient Aalbæk is quoted by Jacob Neiiendam: 'We're a shitty little country, so we look to the world. We were forced to start thinking internationally about ten years ago, and we are starting to feel the results now. We are most successful when we are exotic, and now the foreign markets are more interesting than the local.' More fighting talk. One only wonders if those interesting foreign markets will display a sufficient interest in Zentropa products that lack the desirable exoticism of, say, Bjørk. Or Jennifer Jason Leigh, for that matter.

24 'Is this the promised end?':
Kristian Levring & *The King is Alive*

The Union Club, Soho, London W1: *Thursday, 9 March 2000*

Kristian's producer Patricia Kruijer has graciously set me up for a return engagement with the big man. Last Friday I saw a final cut of the film, and was riveted. As Kristian pledged, the piece has indeed 'darkened', and greatly to the good. On the page, it was a kind of savage sitcom, encased in a brilliant but vulnerable literary conceit. Projected, it has gravity and pathos; it maroons us in a world of limbo, of dreadful exigency. The playing is superbly nuanced. And it clips along, from the moment the tour bus shudders to a dry halt in the Namibian desert, hundreds of miles off track, victim of a broken compass.

As the scornful Charles (David Calder) is quick to observe, 'This is a serious situation.' Jack (Miles Anderson), a gnarled Aussie in a bush hat, issues some basic survival instructions, then strikes out alone for help. And so this mob of tenderfoots are left to fend off the desert on a diet of tinned carrots and duty-free booze. They set fires, collect rainwater, make desultory attempts at 'effective activity'. Kanana (Peter Kubheka), a wizened native, watches them from his shack. He's joined by Henry (David Bradley), an English scholar now reduced to the chore of script-reading, who nevertheless retains a gimlet eye for irony. 'Is man no more than this?' he chuckles harshly. 'It's old Lear again, isn't it?' So he sets about rewriting the play from memory, and convincing his fellows to attend 'rehearsals'.

A curious casting then takes place, not least for the key role of Cordelia. Henry is fond of the dark young Frenchwoman, Catherine (Romane Bohringer); yet she clings to a knowing hauteur, and rebuffs his 'paternal care'. Gina (Jennifer Jason Leigh) is helplessly gauche yet earnest, and Henry suffers her bottle-blonde head upon his shoulder. Tortuously the play struggles to its feet. But Henry's Lear, the alcoholic American Ashley (Brion James), has barely stammered out 'Nothing will come of nothing' before he succumbs to delirium tremens. And under the play's baleful influence, relationships splinter. Charles strikes an odious bargain with Gina, making his participation contingent upon her consenting to regular fucks. American shrew Liz (Janet McTeer) realizes her husband Ray (Bruce Davison) is hopelessly inert, and goads him by making brazen advances to the bus driver, Moses (Vusi Kunene). Charles's lumpish son Paul (Chris Walker) tries to fettle Moses on Ray's behalf, and his wife Amanda (Lia Williams), no more the Fool, realizes that her helpmate is a brute.

Worse, having observed the fondness between Henry and Gina, Catherine acquires the green eyes of Regan, and poisons Gina. Doubled up in agony, Gina is now at least at liberty to spit out her scorn for Charles. Demoralized Ray staggers out into the desert, in a suicidal echo of Kent. ('My master calls me, I must not say no.') A few miles out, he finds Jack's dry bones, and carries the news back to the hopeless band. Zombie-like, they make up a burial party; upon their return, Henry discovers Charles hanged from a rafter, and Gina cold as the grave. The ending is all fire, darkness, and blink editing, as Henry intones Lear's 'Howl' soliloquy over the dead body of Gina, and a gang of itinerant labourers, the unlikely rescuers of this decimated band, drifts into shot.

Patricia tells me she was watching me as I watched, wincing and arching my back against my seat as things got ever bleaker. I relate this to Kristian, who accepts it affably. 'I was at a screening we had a few days earlier,' he remarks, 'and I got this feeling of "Who the fuck is the guy who came up with this cynical shit?"'

RICHARD KELLY: You've got a brilliant ensemble performance piece here. And the editing feels absolutely to the bone.
KRISTIAN LEVRING: Well, the editing has been about distilling, extracting the essence, getting down to the powerful moments. One thing I tried to do as much as possible was to build scenes from the same takes. For instance, David Bradley and Jennifer Jason Leigh play a dialogue scene, sitting up on a hill. And what's in the film is one take. Two cameras, but one take – take two, in fact. And that was *the* take, you know? And I think you feel some kind of intensity in their relations, precisely because of that.

RK: So are you satisfied with the finished item?
KL: I think I am. It's easy to talk, and say that you want to do things differently; but then at some point you have to go out and do it. But I'm happy I have. And people seem to like the film, it provokes strong

reactions. But still, it's been said to me that it's not a very commercial piece. And it's like this kind of stuff isn't allowed any more – whereas in the 1960s and 1970s, that was why you went to the cinema: to have these kinds of experiences. Maybe film has lost its edge. If you go to the theatre, you demand some substance, some weight. In film it's unacceptable.

RK: Well, as Mogens Rukov says, 'There is this thing called the mainstream, and it just keeps streaming and streaming and streaming.' So you have to be clever to fight it.

KL: Sure. I'm aware I've got to get in the ring for this film. The real problem I have now is that I want to carry on in the same direction; and I can see that there's a fear of that in the business. I know it's a dark film, but I wouldn't say its *essence* is dark. In fact, towards the end of the shoot, some of the actors were afraid it was getting too sentimental. Nobody else has been of that opinion before or since. (*Smiles.*) But, to me, the film has a happy ending, at least for some of the characters.

RK: For Henry?

KL: Oh, yes. Because he's a very cynical man at the outset. He has lost a daughter, rejected his own life with his wife and his child; that's his Lear story. So, through the film, he's asking himself, 'Who is my daughter? Is it Gina? Or Catherine?' And when he finally cries for Gina, and does the 'Howl, howl' speech, something has changed profoundly in him. The cynicism in his heart is somehow . . . exorcised. There is a life for him.

RK: What about the couples?

KL: For me, there is a real possibility that Liz and Ray will stick together and find a way. Paul and Amanda won't; but then that's good for them. She has found a strength in herself. And by the time Paul shaves his head, he's becoming a different man.

RK: In the script I felt that Paul posed a bit of a problem, because he's an oaf and everybody knows it. But in the playing and the way the others react to him, he's human, and he has pathos.

KL: When you write a script, specifically an ensemble, every character has to be so sharply defined on the page that you very easily slip into cliché. But I didn't want Paul to be an unsympathetic figure, because in many ways he's the character who's closest to myself. (*Smiles.*) Take the scene where he sits by the fire with Moses – it ends awfully, they fight. But you can see an introspection in Paul, a realization that he is

211

dependent upon his wife. A seed has been planted in him.

RK: Right. There's something in the way Paul says to Moses, 'You can sit here and talk to me for a minute.' In the script, you sense Paul's just itching to bash the bloke. Onscreen, you feel he'd much rather have a conversation.

KL: Paul has this primitive mind-set: 'If you want to fuck our women, then you've got to fucking *fight*.' But in fact, he really needs Moses to be his shrink.

RK: As Liz puts it: 'White men don't like their wives fucking black men.' And, interestingly, your film follows *Festen* in making a dramatic issue of interracial congress. Is that just a coincidence?

KL: I think so. For me, Moses is the most difficult character in the piece. He's a given: because the bus needs a driver, and the driver must be native. Moses is the man who leads them out into the desert, right? (*Smiles.*) So I had to use the character. But you cannot portray him as an idiot – he's the one black man surrounded by whites: it would be misunderstood. At the same time, I couldn't go into the political correctness of making Moses somehow better than everyone else.

RK: As Catherine, you cast a younger actress than you planned to, but Romane Bohringer projects that intelligence superbly.

KL: She also projects that way young people have, of holding very strong opinions that they're nevertheless not completely sure of. So they try to be tough about things. Whereas Charles has had a longer journey through life, and he says things with such authority that you believe his conviction. But they are linked, Catherine and Charles, they are part of the same family.

RK: They both do dreadful things to Gina . . .

KL: Oh, yes. Charles is the baddy, of course. But the interesting thing about Charles is that everything he says is true. I heartily disagree with his cynicism. But the way he analyses the world is quite sharp. When he asks Amanda how she can manage to live with Paul, he's right. It must be horrible! It's just the fact he's saying it so bluntly to Amanda that's terrible.

RK: Like Gloucester in *Lear*, Charles has a bit of a blind spot, which is his absurd *amour propre*, his idea that he's still a fine figure of a man.

KL: But he also sees things very clearly. He is the first one to realize that they are really in the shit. But I think the big disappointment for

Charles is the decision to put on *Lear*. He would rather they had mounted a big golf tournament out there in the sand. (*Laughs.*) Which he would have won, of course.

RK: The play is rehearsed without a 'Regan'. But as Catherine and Gina start to vie with one another for Henry's favour, it's as though Catherine is Regan. Is that fair?

KL: Of course. We used the play as a touchstone in all sorts of ways, taking certain themes, swapping them around. But then English is not my language, and I had to prepare myself very rigorously for this. I had to read a lot. A lot of the actors have Shakespeare in their roots, and we were discussing subtle matters of language. There were things that were completely changed in the making. Take the scene where they're rehearsing Act One, Scene One; Liz is doing Goneril's lines very badly, and she says, 'I need to know something about who these people *are* . . .'

RK: Something of a director's in-joke, that line?

KL: Well, a director friend saw the film the other day and laughed at it, because it's the classic comment you get from actors, often quite rightly. But Henry shows them that you have to find this in the words. As written, he was going to say everyone's lines – Gloucester's, Kent's, Edmund's. But we were rehearsing the night before we needed to shoot and it didn't work, it was obvious. We needed another idea. So we worked on a later speech of Lear's: 'I disclaim all my parental care.' David Bradley did it wonderfully. It's not done at all as it should be in the play, where Lear is very hard and angry. Henry puts in far too many emotions, far too much of himself. But it's not about giving a great reading of Lear, it's about Henry finding himself in this text. He says the same to Amanda: 'Listen to what the Fool has to say to you, and then let it come out.' The answer is in the text.

RK: The text goes a little awry in places: presumably a deliberate way of showing that Henry hasn't quite succeeded in setting down *King Lear* entirely accurately from memory?

KL: Oh, absolutely. Very little of the text is exactly right. There are bits of *Hamlet* and *Macbeth* that creep in . . .

RK: Nevertheless, the film throws such an acute light on *Lear*. I really think it could be used as a tool for teaching the play, much like my friend Professor Colin MacCabe uses *My Own Private Idaho* and *Chimes at Midnight* to teach *Henry IV*.

213

KL: Well, thank you. There is an intellectual puzzle in there, but it's fun, as long as you're not just trying to flaunt your intellect. There's nothing more boring than intellectual films. There were a couple of scenes I cut out for just that reason: like what we called 'the casting scene', where Henry imagines who will play each role. It was a bit too show-off. Only people who knew the play could get the joke, and that's wrong.

RK: Certain other scenes have changed utterly. When Ray and Liz fret over what the play's about – in the script, it's almost throwaway. But onscreen it's become very pointed about their fraught, childless marriage. First, you have the humour of Liz's suburban American description of Lear: 'He's got two daughters. Or is it three? Anyway, he's got a couple of kids.'

KL: That was Janet's idea . . .

RK: Then there's that sharp exchange: 'You get to play the evil daughter?' 'That's right. I play the real bitch.' I didn't see those words on the page.

KL: No. We struggled a bit with that scene: we shot for two or three hours and it didn't work. So I called a little half-hour break, and we all sat and thought. I think the problem was that it was too much of a comic scene in the way we'd conceived it and first shot it. I realized it needed some kind of hardness to it. So you have Liz saying, 'You don't have to worry. Nobody falls in love. And everybody dies in the end.' Some people wanted me to take it out. They felt maybe Liz was picking on Ray too much. But, to me, Ray is the guilty party in that relationship. Liz is paying the price of Ray's passivity, and she's trying to push him.

RK: When you were shooting the bit where Jack declares that there are 'five rules' for surviving in the desert – as a Dogme director, you must have had a smile to yourself.

KL: Well, to me, Jack is a joke. To say there are five rules for survival – I mean, that's an idiot. But I realized that if it were played as a joke, it would damage the film, it wouldn't be convincing. So I made him serious. Basically, everything he says is right. But when he's asked why they shouldn't burn the bus tyres and he says, 'Never let off all your ammo at once' . . . I mean, that's complete bullshit. (*Laughs.*) Of course they should burn the tyres right away, why wait five days? Get those fires started!

RK: Well, you fooled me. It's a charged moment when Jack says it,

and Paul and Ray seem to take it very seriously.

KL: But Jack says a lot of things like that. Like when he tells Paul and Ray to dig their cesspits further apart. He does that because he's a bit offended they're laughing at Moses. But the reason he gives them, 'To stop the spread of infection' – I mean, what is that? Again, bullshit. (*Laughs.*)

RK: I guess that's why Ray laughs so loudly and maniacally when he finally stumbles upon Jack's skeleton in the desert.

KL: Yes, which is rather a theatrical idea. But I think it works, it's quite gruesome in its own way. You know how we made the image? After Jack had left, we went out there with his clothes, laid them out, filled them with stones and sand. You can still see our tracks in the sand. We left them out there untouched for six weeks, and the wind did the rest.

RK: OK then. Let's see if I can catch you out on any of these Rules. In the early scene where the group are drunk and dancing to disco music on the ghetto-blaster, you've got some nice hard sound-cuts in there, which reminded me of *The Idiots*. But the music also carries over cuts in places.

KL: We shot the scene with three cameras, so we always had the cut-away. But we shot it endless times, and it was a nightmare to edit. Nicholas spent two weeks on it. Ordinarily, if you're doing a scene like that, you put on the music and then turn it down just before you roll, and you ask all your actors to speak loudly, so you get this false impression. But here, if you listen to the song, it's completely cut into pieces. When it became too unmusical, it was too distracting, so we had to find the compromise on where to cut sound and picture.

RK: But there's a fine, nightmarish quality to the music going round and round, like a loop. And Jennifer Jason Leigh's dancing is quite stupendous.

KL: All in all, I think we gained more than we lost.

RK: Kanana has these gnomic savant voice-overs in which he comments on proceedings. Harmony Korine has had nothing but trouble about whether voice-overs constitute code violations. But it sounds as if you used the same ruse as he did.

KL: As you can probably hear from the quality of it, we used Henry's Dictaphone. Kanana recorded the lines, and we played them back while we shot those out-of-focus pictures. That's why there's no other sound there.

RK: You said to me last year that it's impossible not to make aesthetic choices; that one always has a preference.

KL: Oh, I'm working on my confession at the moment, and that is absolutely my biggest problem with Dogme. I really struggled with it intellectually. I took out all the obvious camera movement, camera describing, camera storytelling. But I was never sure what was right and what was wrong.

RK: There are some beautiful images in the film; as when Catherine is reciting Cordelia's lines in blue morning light. Or when Ray is wandering through the desert – shadows on the sand-dunes, picture-perfect. Presumably you saw those in the viewfinder and couldn't resist framing them properly?

KL: Well, if you take the blue scene: I said to my DP, Jens, 'We're not allowed any optical work, but you can work with the white balance on the camera as much as you like.' There are two white balances on these cameras, one for red and the other for blue. You have to set one of them, and Jens used the blue one to colour the image. Is that Dogme or not? I don't know. I think Lars would probably say you should use the same white balance all the way through. But it doesn't say anything in the Rules about that.

RK: It certainly doesn't. So you've got right on your side.

KL: Now, with Ray in the desert: it was a wonderful day, we shot with three cameras, and I operated one of them. We were lying in the sand, and I was seeing a picture: he's there, the sun is there, there's a shadow, there's a dune. Now I'm interested in photography; and of course, you frame. What's taste and what isn't? I've talked to Lars about this, because he shot a lot of *The Idiots* himself. So his taste makes every frame in the film.

RK: And yet, uniquely for a Lars von Trier film, there's nothing in *The Idiots* that makes you think, 'What a fabulous shot!'

KL: But that's just Lars's taste right now, not wanting to make shots like that. That's still an aesthetic viewpoint. It's too banal a lie to say that, just because you make something anti-aesthetic, it's divorced from aesthetics. So at one point I gave up and decided I'd frame.

RK: Right. So how did the New Year's Eve project go for you?

KL: I think . . . we could have done it better. I say 'we', including myself, so you know I'm not blaming the others. In my opinion, we made one big mistake. We made our own little films, instead of looking at the whole thing. And I don't think we gave the audience a chance. The idea that people can edit themselves: to get what that is, that's very hard.

RK: Well, presumably you can only learn by trying it.
KL: But everybody just got confused.

RK: Do you see a way now that you could have solved it?
KL: Yes, I think there was a way. It's basic storytelling. It's about, at the very beginning, presenting your story and your form in a very precise way. And I think that should have been done on each channel. From then on, you can move out, and then people can make their choices in an informed way. That was the biggest mistake, I honestly think.

RK: But Nimbus will still release it as a feature?
KL: I'm not sure what they're doing with it. But I think it's wrong to call it a 'feature'. It was more a documentation of that night. And, as that, I think it works wonderfully. I'm not sure it works as a normal story – people may be disappointed. But there are some interesting things in it, for sure. And you can probably see each director's taste fairly clearly.

RK: Since your film completes a quartet of films by the founding Brotherhood, is it fair to say that the most vital stage of the Dogme experiment is complete?
KL: I agree and I disagree. Now they're making a whole shit-load of Dogme films, and I'm sure some good will come of it. But, yes, you can say that, as a statement, it's probably completed.

RK: Well, waves have to break, movements tend to be about certain individuals in certain places at certain times. Pauline Kael wrote an essay about Godard in 1968 after *La Chinoise*, arguing that he'd taken cinema over a bridge, but burned the bridge behind him. So his imitators were doomed to fall in the water.
KL: Yes, that's a good example. But it's almost too difficult for us to say. I know I will use some of what I've learned in another film. And there are lines in the Manifesto that remain very, very interesting. '*To force the truth out of the characters and settings*' – I think Dogme has proven itself in that way . . .

217

25 The Author's Conclusion

Crouch End, London N4: Monday, 17 April 2000

Oh, mama: can this really be the end? It's all painful. But there's no point in stalling. So I will make avail of the magic numbers, and quickly say ten last things that I reckon to be forcibly true and pertinent in this strange case of Dogme95:

1 Hollywood shoves out more motion pictures than just about anywhere else (except, yes, India). But tune out the noise for a moment. Can anybody argue that they're really exceptionally good at it? Any better than the average, say? Hardly. And yet they flood the world with garbage, and virtually drown the few decent pictures they can muster. In its lust for overseas markets, its bullying conception of free trade, its refusal to be *proportionate* about things, Hollywood must be held responsible for the fact that most movies are boring and mediocre.

2 Dogme95 was driven by a genuine disgust at this prevailing odour, and a genuine desire to reset the rules of engagement. It was a game played in high seriousness, prankish, mock-solemn, and yet 'one hundred per cent idealistic'.

3 But Dogme95 itself was – is – four Danish films by four Danish directors. *Really*. The Brothers never said Dogme was *the* way, just their way; and for a limited period only.

4 Their Rules were full of holes, paradoxes, implausibles. Godard made very similar points a lot more sharply, with less fuss, and free of Trier's towering irony. But a useful point was reasserted: it's instructive and enjoyable to do hard things, *with difficulty*.

5 Trier was the prime mover, the 'mastermind'. But even this 'forced brotherhood' was able to function in concert and set a creditable example of how creative unions can be achieved. Godard had it right when he diagnosed the recurrent failure of mainstream directors to function in co-operatives: 'They don't want to produce films together

. . . The directors want to be on their own, and prefer to go to an unknown father – Fox etc.' Of course, you can say that Dogme95 has its own big daddy in television and state subsidy; but the films themselves were proudly unmarked by this patronage.

6 If one needed proof of the fact that Dogme challenged the mainstream, cop an ear to some of the reactions it provoked. Many claimed to hate the idea in the first place; most of the same were quick to crow over what they took to be its inevitable corruption. But Dogme95 has seemed to make certain industry types rather sickly over the wastage and flatulence of their film-making. These are the people who deride 'cheap films' and 'shakey-cam', arguing that Dogme is not a serious way of making films. The guilty flee, though none pursue.

7 Dogme95 created conditions for an international solidarity of *avant-garde* film; and fellow film-makers conjoined themselves to it, with clear and unwavering passion. Hurrah, then, for Harmony Korine. American independent cinema used to mean a lineage of Anger, Deren, Cassavetes, Shirley Clarke – name your own favourite. Post-Miramax, it seems to mean comedies and shoot-em-ups starring character actors who otherwise earn their keep for Jerry Bruckheimer. But Korine is someone who gives honour to the notion of independent US film, rather than vice versa.

8 The Brothers didn't cling to power, they divested themselves of thrones, powers and dominions as quickly as was possible. This is not how you go about making a profitable franchise.

9 As for this DV business: we must yet await a Dogme picture that can honestly uphold Rule#9. But digital video means more production, more communication, and more time spent sketching with the camera for directors, which as Kristian Levring points out, is good exercise; it can suggest different ideas. This is why Godard once advised that Michael Cimino spend a few years making hard-core porn, or shooting a documentary on Nicaragua, rather than labouring over some $45 million magnum opus.

10 In short, Dogmatists everywhere now seem to support every revolutionary movement against the existing cinematic order of things. They labour everywhere for the union and agreement of the radical, experimental and *avant-garde* film artists of all nations. They openly

declare that their films can be made only by the forcible overthrow of all existing conditions of production. So let Hollywood tremble at a Dogmatic revolution. Oppressed film-makers of the world have nothing to lose but their cranes. They have audiences to gain.

A last thought on this digital utopia: though production has been liberated by the little cameras, distribution and exhibition remain formulaic. 'Art-house Cinema' still means an assortment of inaccessible venues, fed by the cycle of festivals, subdued by the Prints & Advertising clout of the mainstream. The Internet proposes a solution to this, as it does for everything else right now. But all film-makers want a decent projection, if they're honest. Can anyone imagine Lars von Trier submitting a work on which he has truly laboured to the confines of a 'web-cast première'? To ask that question is to answer it. As I write, *Dancer in the Dark* is due to compete at Cannes next month, and the Palme d'Or must be a distinct possibility. (I've already heard the word 'masterpiece', twice.) *The King is Alive* is tipped for a spot in the 'Certain Regard' sidebar. And Jean-Marc Barr's *Too Much Flesh*? We await.

The Name of this Film is Dogme95 had its first FilmFour cable transmission on Sunday, 26 March, in the graveyard slot of 11.45 p.m., following the UK television première of *Festen*. As yet, I don't know of a single person who saw it; or rather, no one's told me that they saw it. Nevertheless, it was bought and paid for, and will now attempt to find its intended audience, as the Independent Film Channel prepares to air it in June. Last week I did a little telephone interview for *Brill's Content* magazine, which had received a preview tape. The reporter began with some considerate words about how enjoyably 'jokey' and 'ironic' was the film's take. Oh, no. That is not it at all. That is not what I meant *at all*.

As I look back across the months that have brought this twisted project into being, I still see about me so many signs of Dogme95's rude health. The Dogme Secretariat is finally geared to process applications for certificates; as of 9 March, the website made ominous note that there are nine international feature films presently awaiting certification. Whatever Peter Aalbæk's deliberations, the non-profit fee for the Secretariat's services has been set at five thousand kroner ($640), and more generously budgeted pictures are asked to voluntarily pay thrice that; though requests for a waiver will also be considered. All sorts of high-minded and/or foul-mouthed exchanges still happen daily on the bulletin board of www.dogme.dk. Judging by my postbag, there are feverish film students up and down this land currently penning graduation theses, and shooting graduation shorts, that seek to salute or demolish the Vow of Chastity. I myself am now looking to rent a little farmhouse in Lolland, and engage a personable housekeeper, so that I can devote myself exclusively to the joyous task of thinking and writing about the Dane, his culture, and his good, good society. Can anyone say truly where this bold enterprise will end?

Postscript

So Trier finally got his Palme d'Or. Luc Besson's jury voted the top prize to *Dancer in the Dark*, and Bjørk copped the female performance award, so reviving the Festival's irregular tendency to bestow this distinction on the biggest celebrity in attendance. Certainly, *Dancer in the Dark* was the event of the festival: its first morning screening caused crash-barrier crushes and angry altercations, as some holders of hard tickets were denied admission. In the cool of the evening, hours after the mêlée, it was clear that Trier had once again split the critical pack with this brazenly melodramatic, doggedly hand-held musical-tragedy.

My friend Louise Brealey of *Total Film* told me she felt rather sorry for anyone unmoved by it. But the hardest blow was landed the next day by Derek Elley of the daily *Variety*, who reckoned the film 'artistically bankrupt on almost every level'. He decried the resurgence of Trier's 'romantic fatalism', taxing him for 'gratuitously deconstructing the genre and lacking any feel for music and movement beyond the most obvious'. Your correspondent wasn't so offended, but saw *Dancer in the Dark* as dispiriting proof that Trier had resorted to his old bag of tricks: contriving once more (as David Thomson spotted early) to give virtuosity a bad name, and with little of his former panache.

Operating the camera himself, Trier manages at least to get some nice, 'real' moments from Jean-Marc Barr and Peter Stormare. (Maybe it was this virtue that prompted Matthew Sweet of the *Independent* to mislabel *Dancer* as 'a Dogme film'. Or maybe it was just the fleeting presence of Paprika Steen.) But the whole mixture is hopelessly self-defeating. The musical numbers provide no transport or uplift, unless you're a devotee of the odd sounds emitted when Bjørk opens her throat. With her impish child-woman persona fully intact, Bjørk gives nothing like a performance, as her character is made hostage to outrageous fortune and traipses towards the gallows. I confess, I still can't understand why Trier is so fond of torturing women in the hope of drawing tears from his audience. To these eyes, his most moving creation remains that bold self-portrait, Stoffer, in *The Idiots*.

What next for Trier? 'Something on a much smaller scale', according to the steadfast Vibeke Windelov. 'He and I are going to sit down some time after Cannes, choose his favourite actors, and then have him write a story for them,' she told *Screen International*. 'I plan to just put them all in a summerhouse in the north of Denmark in June next year...' Sounds like trouble to me. Other reported Trier wheezes include a big costume drama; the final chapter of his TV series *The Kingdom*; and an idea for a thrill-ride in Tivoli Gardens.

The King is Alive bowed in the 'Certain Regard' section of the Cannes selection, to generally favourable notices, though elements of Dogme-jaundice could be discerned therein. And Daniel H. Byun's *Interview* emerged in the Market, without a certificate but billed as 'Dogme#7', 'The First Asian DOGME film'. Incredibly, within the first five minutes, *Interview* manages to cram in several dolly shots, some moody lighting, inter-titles, a director's credit and a tinkling music-score. Rarely can a talent have set out so purposefully to fail an audition. Next!

Thomas Vinterberg dropped into Cannes to announce that his next feature will indeed be *It's All About Love*, scripted by Mogens Rukov and himself. Apparently it's all about two ex-lovers, one a world-famous ice-skater somewhat bored by her celebrity, who meet again in New York and set off across the USA to revive their relationship. 'I want to throw myself into a larger exploration of life,' Thomas told the press, 'and this is a big love story which, in all humbleness, embraces the whole world.' Birgitte Hald will produce, for Nimbus Film and Komrad Film, at a projected budget of $8–10 million, and shooting is due to start in March 2001.

Søren Kragh-Jacobsen, meanwhile, let it be known that he will start principal photography on *Skagerak* in summer 2001. He and Anders Thomas Jensen will co-author the script, and again, Birgitte Hald will produce, for a budget of around $4.5 million. It's the tale of a young Danish woman who comes to England and, short of funds, takes up an offer to become a surrogate mother. Iben Hjelje is signed up for the lead. 'I see it as Barbara Cartland goes *Trainspotting*,' Soren told reporters, with a grin.

And what Dogme-news from the trades? Marianne Slot's Liberator Films, the Paris-based arm of Zentropa, was said to be readying ten French-language Dogme shorts for shooting in late 2000. The idea is to gather them into a compendium for theatrical release, and screening on Zentropa's TVropa.com. Elsewhere, What Else, the Dutch label formed by Els Vandervorst and Peter Aalbæk, has four Dogme scripts in hand. 'We hope to get at least two of them in production next year, and sell them as a package,' Vandervorst told *Moving Pictures*. When I hear the word 'package' bruited about in Dogme-discussions, I see Thomas Vinterberg's grimace. Does this fresh flurry testify to Dogme's ongoing vitality, or merely the love of a lousy buck? Proof will be in the pudding. Meanwhile, there are rumours on www.dogme.dk of two more certified pictures: *Fuckland* (Argentina, dir. José Luis Marques) and *Babylon* (Sweden, dir. Vladamn Zdravkovic).

And finally – on 28 September, 2000, the Danes will vote decisively on whether to join the single European currency. Alongside the Swedes and the Brits, they are the last demurrers. Prime Minister Rasmussen has kicked off the 'Yes' campaign, arguing that non-participation will lead to crushing speculation against the krone by predators of the George Soros variety; whereas the Euro will encourage foreign investment and general economic stability. Maybe so. But what Rasmussen isn't saying is that the Euro compels its member states to apply swingeing 'austerity measures' to their budgets, not least in the region of welfare benefits. Rasmussen's is not the only social democratic European government caught in this deflationary vice; and it appears to be bleeding support.

Carsten Jensen smiled ruefully when he suggested to me that Denmark might be first in Europe to see the electoral revival of the right-wing. As it happened, Austria beat them to it, with the ascent of Jorg Haider's FPO. But the xenophobic tinge in Danish politics has acquired an edge in the current favour for the staunchly anti-EU Danish People's Party, which might yet form a future coalition government with the Conservatives. Fronted by housewife Pia Kjærsgaard, the DPP calls for slashing of both the tax burden and welfare spending; also for the prompt expulsion of criminal immigrants, stricter policing of the border with Germany, and 'a viable repatriation policy for refugees'.

On this score, right and left are holding an ugly auction over who can be nastiest. Immigrants, refugees and asylum-seekers are the prime scapegoats for fears about a drop in living standards. Yet their numbers already seem to be on the wane in Denmark, and the right isn't bothered to ask how the economy will cope with the coming shortfall of cheap and easily abused foreign labour. This racism is a pan-European problem. It's obvious why it occurs; less clear how to fight it. Movies have no answer, of course. But there's a lot of Denmark in Dogme95, and you can look at those films and see a little dark mirror of that society. In *Festen*, Michael's instinctive insult to an unfamiliar black face ('Hey Charlie Brown, you've come to the wrong place') marks the film unquestionably as a work of 'the here and now'. There, too, Dogme has proved its point.

Appendix 1: The Dogme95 Manifesto

Dogme95 . . . is a collective of film directors founded in Copenhagen in spring 1995.

Dogme95 has the expressed goal of countering 'certain tendencies' in the cinema today.

Dogme95 is a rescue action!

In 1960 enough was enough! The movie was dead and called for resurrection. The goal was correct but the means were not! The new wave proved to be a ripple that washed ashore and turned to muck.

Slogans of individualism and freedom created works for a while, but no changes. The wave was up for grabs, like the directors themselves. The wave was never stronger than the men behind it. The anti-bourgeois cinema itself became bourgeois, because the foundations upon which its theories were based was the bourgeois perception of art. The *auteur* concept was bourgeois romanticism from the very start and thereby . . . false!

To Dogme95 cinema is not individual!

Today a technological storm is raging, the result of which will be the ultimate democratization of the cinema. For the first time, anyone can make movies. But the more accessible the media becomes, the more important the avant-garde. It is no accident that the phrase 'avant-garde' has military connotations. Discipline is the answer . . . we must put our films into uniform, because the individual film will be decadent by definition!

Dogme95 counters the individual film by the principle of presenting an indisputable set of rules known as THE VOW OF CHASTITY.

In 1960 enough was enough! The movie had been cosmeticized to death, they said; yet since then the use of cosmetics has exploded.

The 'supreme' task of the decadent film-makers is to fool the audience. Is that what we are so proud of? Is that what the '100 years' have brought us? Illusions via which emotions can be communicated? . . . By the individual artist's free choice of trickery?

Predictability (dramaturgy) has become the golden calf around which we dance. Having the characters' inner lives justify the plot is too complicated, and not 'high art'. As never before, the superficial action and the superficial movie are receiving all the praise.

The result is barren. An illusion of pathos and an illusion of love.

To Dogme95 the movie is not illusion!

Today a technological storm is raging of which the result is the elevation of cosmetics to God. By using new technology anyone at any time can wash the last grains of truth away in the deadly embrace of sensation. The illusions are everything the movie can hide behind.

Dogme95 counters the film of illusion by the presentation of an indisputable set of rules known as THE VOW OF CHASTITY.

'I swear to submit to the following set of rules drawn up and confirmed by Dogme95:

1 Shooting must be done on location. Props and sets must not be brought in (if a particular prop is necessary for the story, a location must be chosen where this prop is to be found).

2 The sound must never be produced apart from the images, or vice versa. (Music must not be used unless it occurs where the scene is being shot.)

3 The camera must be hand-held. Any movement or immobility attainable in the hand is permitted. (The film must not take place where the camera is standing; shooting must take place where the film takes place.)

4 The film must be in colour. Special lighting is not acceptable. (If there is too little light for exposure the scene must be cut or a single lamp be attached to the camera.)

5 Optical work and filters are forbidden.

6 The film must not contain superficial action. (Murders, weapons, etc. must not occur.)

7 Temporal and geographical alienation are forbidden. (That is to say that the film takes place here and now.)

8 Genre movies are not acceptable.

9 The film format must be Academy 35 mm.

10 The director must not be credited.

Furthermore, I swear as a director to refrain from personal taste! I am no longer an artist. I swear to refrain from creating a "work", as I regard the instant as more important than the whole. My supreme goal is to force the truth out of my characters and settings. I swear to do so by all the means available and at the cost of any good taste and any aesthetic considerations.

Thus I make my VOW OF CHASTITY.'

Copenhagen, Monday, 13 March 1995

On behalf of Dogme95

Lars von Trier, Thomas Vinterberg

Appendix 2: 'I Promise to Try Harder'

Below are ten rules of composition that I drew up on 29 March 1999, having being commissioned to make this book. I'd been thinking about the 'gonzo' ethos that Hunter S. Thompson tried to instil in his *Fear and Loathing in Las Vegas* ('My idea was to buy a fat notebook and record the whole thing, as it happened, then send in the notebook for publication – without editing'). But then Thompson didn't manage it, so how the hell could I? I reproduce my rules here because there may be some small sport for the reader in flipping back through the volume and figuring out where each one was broken. Some proved pathetically vulnerable: rule 6 is broken on page 1, rule 9 on page 129. (In fact, rule 10 is broken on the cover.) But, as Lars von Trier has conceded, it all comes down to individual conscience: 'The important thing is that you can look yourself and other people in the face . . .'

1 The content of the book should be composed sequentially, using a single notebook or loose-leaf binder, as per the form of a journal. No subsequent re-ordering of content is permitted.

2 Interviewing of subjects must be done face to face. Reporting of meetings, location visits etc. must be written up in situ – no subsequent revisions are permitted.

3 The locations and physical circumstances in which writing and interviewing take place must be described at the outset of each chapter, journal entry, or strophe.

4 All recorded interviews must be transcribed verbatim. Extracts may be selected for publication, but no editing within the text of these extracts is permitted.

5 While writing and interviewing, the writer-interviewer must wear an amusing costume or item(s) of apparel, to remind him not to take life too seriously.

6 No discrete 'art-works' (books, films, pieces of music, paintings etc.) other than the films of Dogme95 should be referred to in the preparation of the text, or used as reference points within the text.

7 The book should not offer superficial 'gossip' (e.g. the private lives and recreational habits of interviewees should not be discussed, unless interviewees wish to have such discussions).

8 The standard forms of 'film journalism', common to magazines and newspapers, which focus on 'star' actors and plot synopses, are not permitted.

9 The format of the book should be 186 mm by 120 mm. It should not exceed 128 pages.

10 The 'author' should not be credited.